CHAMPIONS OF SILICON VALLEY

CHAMPIONS OF SILICON VALLEY

VISIONARY THINKING FROM TODAY'S
TECHNOLOGY PIONEERS

CHARLES G. SIGISMUND

JOHN WILEY & SONS, INC.
New York • Chichester • Weinheim • Brisbane • Singapore • Toronto

This publication is designed to provide accurate and authoritative information in regard to the subject matter covered. It is sold with the understanding that the publisher is not engaged in rendering legal, accounting, or other professional services. If legal advice or other expert assistance is required, the services of a competent professional person should be sought.

Library of Congress Cataloging-in-Publication Data:

Sigismund, Charles G.
    Champions of Silicon Valley : visionary thinking from today's technology pioneers / Charles G. Sigismund.
        p.   cm.
    Includes index.
    ISBN 0-471-35346-9 (cl. : alk. paper)
    1. High technology industries—Management. 2. Computer industry—Management.   3. Computer software industry—Management.
    4. Leadership.   I. Title.
    HD62.37.S56 2000
    620'.0068—dc21   99-39994

Printed in the United States of America.

10 9 8 7 6 5 4 3 2 1

To my children,
David and Katie,
who make a better world worth working for,
and to Barbara,
who simply makes the world better.

Acknowledgments

For the time they took from their busy schedules to meet with me and most of all for their willingness to think honestly and out loud with me, I am deeply grateful to all the individuals whose experiences with vision appear in this book. In addition, I want to thank Greg Steltenpohl, founder and former CEO and chairman of Odwalla, for the many conversations we had discussing his experiences with vision. I learned as much from him as anyone I've met, and only a focus on the technology companies of Silicon Valley kept his story from this book.

Contents

Introduction

This book is about vision all the way through its hard transformation from idea to reality. Taken straight from the minds
of the people who created or now champion them, this book
is about some of the most important and influential visions
in Silicon Valley, the ones behind the microprocessor, the
personal computer, the Internet, and biotechnology. But
even more, it is about the acts and practices that produced
these visions and how they were used to guide and inspire the
building of new companies—and new industries—or the
transformation of old ones. The *Champions of Silicon Valley*
examines the compelling visions that are alive today, rather
than those stuffed and mounted as now-popular "vision statements." As Yeats once said of a poem, a vision seems to be
made of a "mouthful of air." And yet it can change the world.

I have some experience with this myself. For over a
decade I worked on that grand, but ultimately failed, vision
of factory automation. And, I have a vision of a different and
better way of working: an economic system built on the
tremendous and still largely untapped power of knowledge.
I, like every individual with a vision, want to understand better what it will take to make that particular vision real.

Leaders and aspiring leaders don't have a ready source
that addresses what they need to know about conceiving and
implementing a vision, giving them real examples to learn
from. Most books on the subject are really about strategic
planning, and most advocate methods that are far more bureaucratic and analytic than supple and intuitive. Certainly
they don't show what I've seen work in Silicon Valley, where
there exist a multitude of successful methods for working
with vision, as varied and effective as the individuals and

1

organizations that work with them. I decided a better way to learn about vision would be to look at a number of specific visions and the methods used to execute them. So, I began investigating the success experienced by Silicon Valley companies and their leaders through field research and interviews. From that experience, I was able to develop lessons and general principles that may be of value to others in their own unique situations.

As I began to conduct the first interviews for this book, I made every effort to suspend any belief that vision is the exclusive product of visionaries—that vision is some gift or faculty that only rare individuals are blessed with or somehow develop. To see something you hadn't expected, you have to suspend your expectations. You have to begin by not knowing. I tried to do this and, as a result, lessons were revealed to me that I hadn't expected. I was able to understand the intuitive thinking and pragmatic art of vision much better. The term *visionaries* tends to hopelessly muddy the waters. It projects a heroic mythology into an already complex subject. And it prejudicially leads the viewer to thinking that vision is an isolated incidence of brilliance. Examined closely, vision is far more collective than individual, and far more a practical process than an inexplicable gift.

Silicon Valley is exploding with entrepreneurial, pioneering, and inventive companies and people. Managers and business professionals all over the world look to Silicon Valley for its leading ideas, technologies, and products, for the way it seems to define the best (and sometimes the worst) of the modern economy, and they try to emulate it in creating their own futures. Because I wanted to understand what it takes to make a vision real, I looked for Silicon Valley companies that have successfully led the way in new fields and created new business models. I learned, as the reader may be surprised to see, that there is an extraordinarily complex relationship between vision and the successes of Silicon Valley.

Most of the interviews for this book were conducted with current CEOs. I also included several people who had been CEOs during the formative stages of their companies, plus several venture capitalists, who play an important role in selecting and working with CEOs. In today's corporation, the CEO is given responsibility for making visions real. One of the points this investigation drove home for me is the extent to which a company's vision really does depend on the CEO. Chairmen don't generally have nearly as much impact on the vision—even if they founded the company. And if the CEO doesn't take vision seriously and work with it well, no one else can effectively make up for it. If a vision is going to inspire and guide a company, the CEO has to champion it and speak for it—even though he is often not the original creator.

■ WHAT IS VISION?

Vision was not a subject that appeared much in business discussions until around 1980. In the 1980s I worked several years for General Electric (GE), a company that had been well known and emulated for its structured and elaborate strategic planning system. Jack Welch, then fairly new as CEO, scrapped the old system and bureaucracy and let it be known that he wanted his executives to develop a sense of intuition for their businesses so they could respond faster and more appropriately to opportunities and challenges in their environment. He wanted a sense of vision rather than an elaborate plan. And although GE never quite got the hang of Silicon Valley's way of doing high-tech business, Welch's new approach did come closer than the old one to the way successful Silicon Valley businesses seem to operate.

Although vision is not strategic planning, it can productively guide and profit from a strategic planning process. But for many practitioners, vision is a more lively, concentrated, and powerful replacement for traditional strategic plans. It is something they carry around in their hearts and minds, not something filed away for periodic review. If everyone in an organization truly sees and is inspired by the same picture of where they're headed and the way they want to conduct themselves in getting there, they can largely know for themselves what they need to do; they don't need to be told. In a rapidly changing world, vision is a kind of anti-plan for accomplishing important, even transcendent goals.

The word *vision* necessarily tends to make us think of things we see, of light and images. Indeed, many images and pictures will be evoked in the chapters that follow. The people in this book constantly paint verbal pictures. These pictures serve to concentrate and condense thoughts—including visions—and to make them far more vivid and memorable. You will also see an emphasis on feeling and intuition. The seeing you do with vision requires more of your body and soul than just your eyes. But I also stress the oral—speaking and listening—medium for working with vision. Visions are best communicated and kept alive orally. Oral communication, rather than the fixed words of vision statements, matches the organic—living, breathing, changing, adapting—and the contextual nature of vision itself. Writing is a useful and often necessary exercise, but it can't take the place of face-to-face communication.

To stay as true as possible to their living quality, the visions presented here are taken from oral dialogues, from extended discussions I had from 1997 to 1999 with 11 men whose visions have not only lit up Silicon Valley but much of the modern world economy. Each chapter presents these different visions and the different ways each man approaches vision. Each chapter captures these leaders thinking out loud at specific moments in time. At earlier or later periods, their words and their thinking could very well be different, and their visions could be different. Real visions are alive and organic, changing over time, as are people's skills in creating, communicating, and executing them. The chapters are organized roughly to illustrate the process for vision that emerged from these interviews, what Federico Faggin called the "arc of vision" from creation to articulation and communication to execution.

The arc of vision shows the immense power of ideas. In "The Moral Philosopher and the Moral Life" William James said, "All the higher, more penetrating ideals are revolutionary. They present themselves far less in the guise of effects of past experience than in that of probable causes of future experience, factors to which the environment and the lesson it has so far taught us must learn to bend." The best visions are just the sort of ideals that James was talking about: They are not predictions of the future, but causes of a different and better future. How do they do that? How and why do people create visions in the first place? When you communicate yours, what's the best way to do that? Where does the tremendous energy come from that people with visions seem to radiate, and how can you make the best use of it? Since visions refer to things not yet real in the world, how do visionaries know what they're doing to make them real? And just what *does* it take to make a vision real? The stories of the visions that follow provide real world answers.

Chapter 1

Execution Is Everything: John Doerr, Kleiner Perkins Caufield & Byers

The writer Wallace Stegner spent a lifetime trying to correct the popular myth of the rugged individualist who settled the American West. He demonstrated how this arid land actually was—and could only be—settled by people who cooperated and worked together. As American CEOs have become celebrated heroes, the same correction is needed in the popular myth of the lone entrepreneur and visionary. Developing something new and sustainable in the harsh and unforgiving environment of business requires the collaborative effort of many people. The hard work of making visions real takes teamwork. John Doerr has seen this truth while observing and contributing to the visions of Silicon Valley for nearly 20 years.

Silicon Valley venture capitalists like Doerr are a unique and powerful force behind visions that have a chance to become real. They provide funds to start new companies and they help recruit and nurture the teams who run them. A venture capitalist's office is often the site of the earliest critical test for people with a vision, especially one based on new technology. If they communicate their vision effectively, they can get the funding they need faster and at a better price, and they'll have a useful ally to help open other doors. If they don't, they'll find it much harder to get started. One of the most prestigious and influential offices they could try for this test is John Doerr's. Doerr has backed Sun Microsystems, Compaq Computer, Intuit, Macromedia, Netscape, Amazon .com, and @Home, among other companies. But it isn't enough to convince Doerr of your vision. Before Doerr's firm, Kleiner Perkins Caufield & Byers (KPCB), will back a company, all the partners have to agree. Even funding a vision requires a collaborative effort.

One of the first questions I asked Doerr was whether he also had a vision in his own work as a venture capitalist. He said, "Yes. It's a team vision." At one time, KPCB had a yearly planning session when the partners formally reviewed their vision and developed plans to make it real. But because of the speed and extent of changes in the 1990s' business environment, they now hold these sessions twice a year. Vision matters at KPCB.

When I asked what KPCB's vision is, Doerr hesitated for a moment, not wanting to reveal *all* of the vision, even though it will have changed by the time this book is printed. Doerr sees his company's vision as part of its knowledge advantage in deciding how to deploy resources. Vision lies at the heart of their strategy. But Doerr didn't hesitate to describe the larger picture it's part of: KPCB sees a new economy being built on four pillars, the:

1. Microchip,
2. Personal computer,
3. Internet, and
4. Life sciences, especially genomics.

Each of these pillars has to do with knowledge: the knowledge to advance technology in these areas, and the knowledge each pillar supports. Success in the new economy will depend more than ever before on networks and relationships among people who can bring all this knowledge together.

JOHN DOERR ON THE NEW ECONOMY

In the new economy, you will use all kinds of services on a Net that we can't even imagine today. It will come very quickly. Just a little over four years ago, Jim Clark and I were hanging out at Cafe Verona in Palo Alto, strategizing—that's too glorified a word—making plans for Netscape. It was another era, before the first commercial browser. In fact, Netscape was then Mosaic Communications. If I fastforward to the future of the Internet I see something we call the Evernet. It's always on, it's high speed, it's ubiquitous—in your home, in your place of work. There will be many more platforms than HTML and the PC. Information appliances like the Palm Pilot will be handheld, wireless, connected, and always on. The TV-top computer will offer broadband video service and it will be connected and always on. Tomorrow's Evernet will shift more choices and power to consumers.

Consumers have more choice and power today because of the ground broken by Amazon.com and Healtheon. That will only increase. People will be taking charge of their health care and learning more. Taking charge of their kids' education. Demanding more from their service providers and institutions.

The Net will have a tremendous effect on all institutions, reinforcing some while disintermediating others. Take online retail. Trillions and trillions of dollars are spent by consumers on goods and services. No one forecasts online retail to be more than 15 percent of the retail economy by 2010; even though that's a small fraction, it's still a lot. More and more business is going online. And woe to the institution that doesn't think about and have strategies for tomorrow's Evernet. In 1998, there were more books sold than ever before—more through physical bookstores, more through online bookstores. The primary demand for books increased, even as online bookstores grew dramatically. People still like going in and browsing at their neighborhood bookstore. But

---

JOHN DOERR ON THE NEW ECONOMY
(Continued)

---

some of the big-chain impersonal bookstores are hurting the most.

Some channels are going to be displaced. People don't like going to drugstores, so that's a natural for online commerce. Some channels are going to be reinforced. Take shopping for a new home—you wouldn't buy one without visiting it with a realtor, but the web can help you make the right move by simplifying the experience.

We are building a new economy. We can do so because a long time ago the United States, as a people, made social choices to invest in public education, fund federal research, and encourage innovation with the patent system. Today we're reaping the benefits of more than a century's worth of public investment in education and research.

In Doerr's view, Silicon Valley's environment contributes greatly to KPCB's and other venture capitalists' ability to help create a new economy. Silicon Valley has three great research universities: Stanford, Berkeley, and UC San Francisco. Their first-rate research is conducted in a heady environment where entrepreneurs are willing to fail in their attempts to bring innovations to the market. And they aren't penalized for it, although each venture capitalist would prefer that someone else fund the failures. Doerr also is grateful that the market ruthlessly determines winners and losers. But within this environment, I wanted to know how KPCB goes about realizing its vision. The answer I heard sounds deceptively simple: It puts together and backs teams. "Great teams," Doerr would add. But how does KPCB do that? How much can it influence these teams? And how do effective teams operate?

■ TEAMS WITH VISION

At the heart of every great technology company is a superb technologist or visionary. Examples that Doerr cited were Bill Joy and Andy Bechtolsheim at Sun, and Jerry Yang at Yahoo!. Often the CEO is not the main visionary, although sometimes he is. Jeff Bezos at Amazon.com and Andy Grove and Gordon Moore at Intel are CEO visionaries.

Usually a great company has one or two visionaries, according to Doerr. The more the better, as long as they're all committed to the same strategy. Whoever the visionaries are, the CEO has to be superb at communicating their visions, then extending and filling them in with his or her team, and doing the work required to make them real. "Execution is what's hard," says Doerr. "The vision is real when delighted customers experience magic moments when they use your product or service."

Vision exists, energizes, and guides a company—or it doesn't—without a venture capitalist's involvement. At best, a venture capitalist can identify people with vision, honor them, and help build a team around them. Doerr says, "If the best way to predict the future is to invent it, maybe the second best way is to finance it." KPCB can tell when a team has a vision "by the light shining in their eyes," by their passion and the electricity among them. Doerr notes that this is not a world motivated just by money and electrons. Visionaries are driven to make a difference, and thereby give meaning to their lives. Having a vision for what you do all day is important.

Visionaries are driven to make a difference . . .

As important and reassuring as it may be to see vision shining in the eyes of a team, there are still limits to what that reveals to a venture capitalist or anyone else serving on the board of a company. According to Doerr, "It's nearly impossible for a board of directors to know what's really going on in a company. The proof for me came in 1988 and 1989. I took what was supposed to be a 90-day sabbatical, which turned into a full year. I left KPCB to manage a 4,000 person division of Sun Microsystems. We split the company into the server operation and the desktop operation. I was the general manager of the desktop group reporting to Bernie Lacroute who reported to Scott McNealy."

Included in the desktop group was a 386-based PC project to port the Sun operating system to an Intel processor and make a workstation-caliber machine. Unfortunately for Sun, the resulting computer wasn't compatible with the PC and all its software, so it didn't do well. Another of the group's efforts, Andy Bechtolsheim's SPARC Station, became a great success.

"As a board member, I thought I was pretty involved in Sun. I used the products, knew the founders, talked frequently to customers, and worked to get UNIX standardized. But once inside the organization, I discovered that the board didn't know everything about what was going on inside the company. Perhaps if you attended all the staff meetings you might really know, but ventures are a collaborative process, everyone can't possibly do everything."

Over time, a board's most direct influence on a company's vision is in hiring the CEO, giving him or her periodic feedback, and if necessary, firing them. Doerr has found that natural leaders emerge on boards of directors. You want the CEO to be the leader of the board, but not to dominate it. On behalf of the shareholders, you want the board to challenge the thinking and strategies of the CEO and the team. Strong CEOs want that. They want the perspective of outsiders. Call it vision, call it scar tissue, but great CEOs want the point of view of directors who are not competitors but who are knowledgeable about the business and new trends and opportunities. Not many CEOs want their boards to be a rubber stamp. According to Doerr, "the job is just too hard to do without that rare commodity in business: constructive critical feedback on your vision, your strategy, and your team's execution. It comes back to the same point: While vision matters, execution is everything."

Vision matters, but execution is everything.

The constructive critical feedback Doerr mentions requires intellectual honesty, something Art Rock also talks about. Like vision, this too is something the board can't create or instill. The CEO and team must establish intellectual honesty in their culture. Doerr has found that as a venture capitalist or a member of the board, your only influence is through the selection of the CEO and the inspection of their processes.

What happens if the board makes a bad choice in the CEO? According to Doerr, "The board is usually the last to know if the CEO is not doing the job. I've been fortunate to start with able entrepreneurs who've grown with their business—like Scott McNealy, Jeff Bezos, and Donna Dubinsky. Sometimes an entrepreneur will come to us and say they'd really like to get a world-class coach to take the company to the next level. Scott Cook, founder of Intuit, did that and we found Bill Campbell. Jim Clark asked who would be the best person to grow Netscape. We found Jim Barksdale. We do a lot of recruiting with founders and entrepreneurs to help them build their team."

■ BEST IDEAS WIN

Doerr has an idea of what it takes to make a vision real. He's worked for Intel and Sun. He's served on the boards of many companies. And he has visions of his own as well as those he shares with his partners. His approach to vision reflects what he's learned from this experience.

Doerr defines vision as what might be and what ought to be. His view is that strategy is how you make the "might be" real, understanding your own competence and the web of other players—competitors and partners—who can counter or contribute to your efforts. It requires an intellectually honest assessment of the environment and market needs. From that you can develop a plan. You should be disciplined and clear enough to write one page on your vision and one page on your strategy and each objective. Finally, the plan should be broken down so that each individual in the company has one page that describes the results they're responsible for. Then, on a regular basis, you have to review both the results and the objectives to see whether you accomplished what you signed up for and whether that's still relevant and what you should be doing next.

The process Doerr advocates underscores the emphasis he puts on execution. It's a process that any organization could use, whether it has a vision or not. I wanted to know what difference vision makes in this process. He said it's important for any organization to be "vision-ready." That means "it has to have a culture where the best idea wins." It has to be receptive to new ideas. It has to check its vision all the time, on its own and using outside advisers. There should be a creative phase in developing the agenda when there are no bad ideas, although that can't be done every day. KPCB, for example, goes through this several-day process twice a year. The key is to institutionalize a regular and habitual process, one that is not overly formal, where you're looking for great ideas. "Once you have a sense of what the next great thing might be, you've got to be nimble and quick. Act on it. And keep testing your vision."

Part of the process in developing and testing a vision is to assess the environment. Is there a large unmet market need? What do customers want? What does technology make possible? Then you write down the *objectives* that will realize the vision, the "whats" of the strategy. And then write down the *key results,* which is how you're going to get them done. According to Doerr, "It's very important to distinguish *what* you want to accomplish—like winning the Super Bowl—from *how* you want to win the Super Bowl." On a regular rhythm, it's important to define and communicate the key results so they're clear, measurable, shared, and linked across an organization. Because, as he says, Doerr hasn't seen anything of consequence done by a solitary individual; he believes that it takes teams and leaders. Some individuals are more visible than others, but doing anything that matters requires execution by teams. Doerr has found that more and more, single companies can't make anything significant happen. "It requires whole ecosystems. New companies and alliances are being formed faster than ever. All that is very exciting, and we have the virtually free communication of the web to thank for all this."

In Doerr's view, it comes back to this simple principle: Effective work can be reduced to a set of key results that can then be measured with some frequency. You've got to be disciplined and make those measurements, whether it's monthly or quarterly. "At the end of the allotted time period, you mark off the key results, but you also pay attention to the objective. And if either the key result or the objective is no longer relevant, you ditch it. Forget it. You fine tune the vision along the way. At the same time you're assessing whether you accomplished what you signed up to do, you question every one of the key results and ask if they're still important." Doerr first learned this approach from Gordon Moore and Andy Grove—who probably adopted the system from Hewlett-Packard and ruthlessly and rigorously applied it at Intel. Doerr notes that it was the first thing that Eric Schmidt installed at Novell when he became CEO and was charged with the task of turning around the company. "Eric had to infuse a new vision for the network directory-based services Novell could offer. He followed through with focused accountability to make it happen."

The key difference that vision seems to make is a willingness and effort to constantly test the relevance of both the results and the objectives they're matched with. According to Doerr, "The healthy companies I know challenge their ideas constantly. And they let the best ideas win, no matter where they come from. The CEO, with the values and style he or she establishes in the company, determines the value of ideas over other forces like office politics. The best ideas win if the CEO trains, educates, and supports that way of working. But you also have to commit. There can and should be healthy disagreement, but once a decision is made, you have to commit or get out of there. Many times there's more

---

Healthy companies challenge their ideas.

than one right answer. The most important thing is to pick one and get on with executing it instead of letting the best become the enemy of good or better. It comes back to leadership and the style and values of the CEO."

■ MANAGE TIME AND PRIORITIES

In addition to the planning and reviewing process he learned at Intel, Doerr has found another important tool that aids in executing vision. It is critical to be objective about where you're spending your time. Time is a crucial resource that Doerr believes in allocating carefully.

Doerr admits to having a couple of time buddies—his partners—with whom he reviews time allocation every month. "We set priorities and try to deliver high service levels, and make sure our time fits our priorities. I credit my partner Kevin Compton with helping us think clearly about this. There's a lot of coherence at KPCB because we've got the same priorities: Family first. Second is serving our partners. Third is the ventures, the entrepreneurs, and CEOs that we've invested in and backed. The fourth is new ideas, new projects."

Doerr estimates that about 20 percent of each month's time is devoted to reviewing new projects. KPCB receives over 3,000 plans each year. Each one is read, although not by every partner. They divide the projects by 10 and those 3,000 plans are reduced to 300 first meetings a year. Now they're down to 30 a year per partner, or two first meetings a month. If a project looks attractive, a second meeting will be held and more partners brought into the process. Any one partner can say no to a project, but it takes all partners to say yes for a project to be approved. "The message from the company is that we're backing this project all the way, we're not going to let it run out of money, we're going to work with the entrepreneurs and founders, however complete or incomplete the team is. That's the full service we deliver."

After the company agrees to back a venture, a partner may join the board of directors. Board seats aren't tenured positions. Every year Doerr and his partners consider whether or not to stay on a certain board. "As long as we're adding value and are wanted, we'll stay. We don't leave a board just because the company's gone public. We work hard to help build strong teams, strong boards, and durable companies."

Making sure you're clear about your priorities and that you actually spend your time in a way that matches those priorities reinforces the planning and review process Doerr learned at Intel. Both call for regular review, according to a rhythm that matches your work. "Every organization that's concerned with strategy has to be in a rhythm to review it regularly. Otherwise, the urgent will push out the truly important. Establish a rhythm, a healthy process for assessing whether you're going where you need to go."

> Every organization that's concerned
> with strategy has to review it regularly.

■ COMMUNITY SERVICE

The teamwork approach to vision that Doerr advocates is not limited to private business. It can also be applied to social change. Doerr and others are applying it to realize a vision for improved literacy. His eyes brighten when he talks about it.

"A priority for me and my partners is community service, primarily improving public education. We need to help every eight-year-old kid learn to read. Forty percent of eight-year-olds in America are unable to read at grade level. It's criminal. We've got to recommit—statewide and nationwide—to high standards in public education based on accountability, choice, and competition. Give teachers the time and incentive to be well prepared. Empower principals as leaders. Get parents involved, and make public education work."

To help make this vision real, Doerr and several other technology executives started the NewSchools Fund, a new venture fund backing "education entrepreneurs" with money and expertise. Its CEO is Kim Smith. "NewSchools is pushing for radical, scaleable changes in public education, both from within and outside the system. It aims to start up, speed up, and even help turn around failing public schools. We have already backed three entrepreneurial efforts—both nonprofit and for-profit."

NewSchools' goals are to improve education outcomes and create a nationwide network of education entrepreneurs. The idea for the fund sprang out of meetings among technology executives and political leaders. The meetings demonstrated the teamwork Doerr believes in: "Al Gore challenged us to find a way to re-invent the schools. Steve Case suggested a venture approach would be powerful. John Kernan from Lightspan insisted we needed more parental involvement and better connections between home and school. Netscape's Marc Andreessen proposed building an 'education dashboard,' and Marimba's Kim Polese led a group of companies to build and demonstrate a prototype. Then, in June 1999, a team from Jerry Yang's Yahoo! Lightspan turned on the Education Dashboard, a free portal service named *Lightspan Page One* on Yahoo!"

Another online venture that NewSchools helped fund and recruit expertise for is a schools guide called GreatSchools.net, led by Bill Jackson. Jackson is an education entrepreneur who persuaded every school superintendent in Silicon Valley that parents should know the goals, performance, programs, and needs of their schools. Like Zagat's guides, GreatSchools offers an editorial point of view. It reviews every school in Silicon Valley in a participatory way that enables schools to express what they need from the community. GreatSchools posts each school's test scores, needs, and long-term plans.

Doerr enthusiastically reports that "*Success for All* is another venture that we're excited about. It is already eight years old, but in 1998 it became independent of Johns Hopkins University where it started. *Success for All* was founded by entrepreneurs Bob Slavin and Nancy Madden. Their Reading Roots and Wings programs are used daily in a thousand schools across the country. The program is typically adopted by a diverse, urban or rural school, where the kids are reading well below their grade level."

Success for All's programs are only deployed if 80 percent of a school's teachers vote to adopt it. Once adopted, reading literally becomes the school's number one priority. For the first 90 minutes of the school day, every student spends intensive time on one task: reading. Instead of being grouped by grades students are grouped by reading ability. They read to each other, one-on-one. It's constant reading. Tests are given every eight weeks. Twenty minutes of homework is assigned every night, which has to be brought back to school signed by a parent. If the homework is not signed, the student works with a mentor and completes the assignment instead of going out to recess. If a parent doesn't help with the assignments for five days, community services get involved.

Success for All is a nonprofit venture. The first year costs a school of five hundred students $70,000. That pays for materials and two trained paraprofessionals. The second year costs $30,000, the third year $20,000. The program costs about $120,000 over three years to reach 500 kids. "Learning to read changes the lives of these kids forever. *Success for All* has been used in over one thousand of America's 80,000 schools—but we need it in 10,000 to 20,000 more."

The NewSchools Fund is to education entrepreneurs what the KPCB fund is to technology entrepreneurs. According to Doerr, NewSchools backs the best education ventures, discovering, sharing, and scaling the best entrepreneurial practices. "There's no question that throwing money and talent at a particular school will solve a problem, one-off. The problem we *should* address is the bottom third of America's 80,000 schools. It's the bottom third of our kids that are getting left behind."

Besides backing education entrepreneurs, Doerr and his partners are learning that public policy matters. Another group of technology executives founded the Technology Network in 1998. The president, Reed Hastings, a technology and educational entrepreneur, raised $4 million to change the California charter public school law. Basically, Hastings persuaded the California legislature to take all the limits off charter schools. That $4 million investment will help create one hundred new schools every year for a decade—competitive, innovative public schools of choice, which must be held accountable for improved educational outcomes. According to Doerr, "That's 1,000 new schools over a decade, serving 500,000 to 700,000 kids a year. That's more than a 1,000 to 1 return on investment. Our success there points the way to more private-public policy efforts."

The new economy offers unprecedented opportunity for those with vision.

In the end, the question is: How do all the vision, teamwork, execution, new ventures, and investment of time and money in education help each of us realize our full human potential? Doerr believes that "the new economy offers unprecedented opportunity for those with vision and a willingness to take risk. Education is the key to ensuring that everyone can benefit."

Conceptualize and Execute Gigantic Change: Don Valentine, Sequoia Capital Management

While studying religious prophets, the sociologist Max Weber became fascinated by what he called the "charisma" that enabled them to lead people to break with the established order and create something new. For Weber, charisma is an extraordinary transformational power seen in rare individuals and even some objects—a gift of their natural endowment. In the view of some, vision is a similar rare gift, an almost magical power held by the few people who truly deserve to be called visionaries. In business, these are people who establish whole new industries, whole new ways of meeting some human need or desire. To Don Valentine, vision is a gift we may be lucky to see in a few people per century.

Before he founded Sequoia Capital in 1972 and became one of Silicon Valley's most noted venture capitalists, Don Valentine helped found National Semiconductor, and before that he was a sales and marketing executive at Fairchild Semiconductor, the company whose alumni went on to create so much of Silicon Valley. Since 1972, Valentine has been a director of many of the Valley's pioneering high technology companies, including Atari, Apple, Oracle, Electronic Arts, and Cisco. In all this time and among all the business leaders he has worked with or seen, he says he knows of only two visionaries: Bob Noyce, who helped found Intel, and Steve Jobs, founder and twice leader of Apple.

Valentine is "less generous," by his own account, than many other people who also see vision as a human faculty given by grace rather than a skill or process that can be learned. Other people who still see vision as a special talent believe they see it in far more people, far more often. John Doerr acknowledges many people he has known as visionaries. Valentine sees vision from the outside, as unapproached and unapproachable by most mortals, including himself. Doerr and most of the others in this book see it more from the inside, as something they and others can both approach and use.

Valentine's view is a "great man" theory of business history: There are long flat periods of insignificant change, when suddenly a heroic individual comes along and virtually single-handedly changes everything. This is not a theory of history I share, but it is one I've encountered often in Silicon Valley and one that demands a place on any jury that judges the visions that have come out of there. In its own way, this approach to vision may encourage others to attempt revolutionary changes while warning them about just how difficult that is. A rather ironic warning, given the source: Don't expect ready help from venture capitalists like Valentine. Most of the time they're more interested in funding the much safer variations and evolutions of established visions.

■ VISIONARIES ARE UNIQUE

In Valentine's view, a visionary not only has to see a different possibility but has to make it real—not merely conceive

DON VALENTINE ON VISION AS A
RARE ATTRIBUTE

Vision is an exceptionally rare attribute. There are probably two words that are massively abused. One is unique; the other is vision. To me unique means a singular event, a singular person. Not the most unique person I met this hour, but maybe once in a lifetime. Vision is the same thing. There are almost no visionaries in Silicon Valley. There have been almost no visionaries in this country—in my opinion.

In technology, I would say Bob Noyce and Steve Jobs are visionaries. I'm not sure if it was Henry Ford or Alfred Sloan or somebody else in the automotive industry, but early in the twentieth century a person recognized that the time was right for a different form of transportation, and a whole new industry was created. Most presidents around here, most technical people, think of themselves as visionary. To me all they're doing is some minor nuance or evolution based on something that someone has already done countless times.

Bob Noyce's name is on the original patent for the integrated circuit. There is no Silicon Valley without the integrated circuit. There is no personal computer. There is no a lot of things without that first concept of an integrated circuit and the manifestation of the integrated circuit in the microprocessor. Think about all of the companies and all of the presidents that have used Bob Noyce's original concept. All they have done was apply known technology—constantly being enhanced by Intel—but known technology in a different application.

Now it might be perceived as uncharitable to suggest that the people who founded Adobe, as an example, weren't visionaries. They used the Apple Computer in a distinctive way. But all they did was implement a very narrow capability on a particular, then popular platform. I'm not charitable enough to call those people visionaries. They're implenters. It's the

---

DON VALENTINE ON VISION AS A
RARE ATTRIBUTE (Continued)

same as the difference between revolution and evolution. Ninety-nine percent of everything that's happened in Silicon Valley has been evolutionary.

Noyce was one of those figures who started an industry. Steve Jobs created an industry. He decided that minicomputers could be made in a way that was affordable. And they could be made for a price that allowed you to have one in your home. Phenomenal concept and implementation.

Visions start something new, something enormous. The initiation of the automotive industry, as a wholly new form of transportation replacing the horse, was one of the other visions in this century. Visions are about one or two or three gigantic events in a century. All the rest are wonderful but rather predictable, rather obvious.

Going from the then-existing form of home entertainment, radio, to something that had video was a visionary step. Going from black-and-white to color was really just pedestrian, evolutionary. And if David Sarnoff is the name that should be identified with the creation of television, I would certainly consider putting him in the same class as Bob Noyce.

---

or conceptualize, but execute. "A vision that doesn't happen is like that question I've never understood, 'Is there sound when a tree falls in the forest and nobody hears it?' I don't know how to deal with a vision that never happened."

An explorer who makes a discovery is not a visionary. Valentine observes, "People confuse great discoveries with vision and are inclined to consider the discoverers as visionaries. I would offer the example of Madame Curie, who found something by complete accident. I think a great many things are found by accident, not through conceptualization and execution. Noyce conceived, designed, implemented, and patented the integrated circuit." Then he formed the company that executed it. Noyce created something. The rational conceptualization, the recognition of the right timing, and the force of character to make it happen distinguish Noyce from a discoverer.

Valentine's insistence on intention and creation over discovery didn't seem to fit with what I'd heard of the microprocessor's history at Intel. One of the stories I'd heard (later amplified by Gordon Moore and Federico Faggin when I spoke with them) was that at first not many thought the microprocessor was good for more than a small calculator. Only after its memory business got in trouble did Intel eventually discover—more than intentionally conceive and create—the uses for which the microprocessor became famous. I asked Valentine about that.

He accepted the fact that there was some serendipity involved. He said, "I would interpret the events differently, but I would certainly defer to Gordon Moore if you can get him to talk with you." In Valentine's view, the creative effort occurred at Fairchild where the integrated circuit was created. The microprocessor was designed and recognized as a computational product. The question was where to employ it cost effectively. At that time, minicomputers were available from DEC for $200,000 to $250,000 with 8- or 16-bit instruction sets. The original microprocessor was a 4-bit product. So, would you put this computational capability in a $250,000 product world, or in the world of calculators, which cost $100 or $150? The technical capability of the product was more likely to satisfy the calculator world than the computer world.

But Intel had formed; it developed products and held many of the original patents on memory devices. Its patent position and memory capabilities were easier to sell, because it wasn't necessary to conceptualize a solution. According to Valentine, all start-ups, when they're guided correctly, take the easy way out and go where customer demand takes them. As a result of that, he observed, "The microprocessor's capability was somewhat subordinated, because customer recognition and demand for the product wasn't as significant as it was with the memory devices. Intel acted appropriately for a start-up. It leaned in the direction of what the customers wanted—memory and e-proms. Only after the microprocessor was implemented in an application did it begin to flower."

All start-ups, when they're guided correctly, take the easy way out and go where customer demand takes them.

Valentine's point that start-ups should take the easiest path they can find and follow customer demand seems to be at odds with his insistence that visions must be intentionally created and revolutionary. Following that logic, visions don't belong in start-ups, even though Noyce's Intel was a start-up, and so was Jobs' Apple—funded in part by Valentine. Many people think Silicon Valley venture capitalists and start-ups are doing all kinds of revolutionary things. In fact, as Valentine agreed, the kind of revolutionary change that can start an industry would typically have a hard time getting funded here in Silicon Valley.

Valentine added that part of the narrowness of either his definition or unwillingness to accept many people as visionaries is because of where he is. "I have always been in a place where I have a very good idea of what the future is. People in Iowa are mystified about what goes on here—mystified because they're not part of the fabric of the environment. If they were, they would not be so mystified." Valentine also believes he had the great advantage of having worked for Noyce. When the patent was granted on the microcircuit, Valentine, who was in charge of sales and marketing, asked, "What are we going to do with this?" He and Noyce spent a long time on a number of occasions talking about Noyce's vision of what would become of this product and how the world would be changed by it. "So I heard an unusual articulation of that vision, not available to everyone, which persuades me still that he was an unusual man who had an unusual recognition of having changed history. Unwritten history."

Valentine went on to say, "It isn't because I don't know all of these other people that I'm so uncharitable in my willingness to endow them with the term, *visionary*. I would go back to Steve Jobs to amplify my position." At the time Valentine financed Apple in 1977, minicomputers were selling for $200,000. Companies had been started that made electronic games, using 8-bit microprocessors, and microprocessors were becoming very common. Computers were an obvious application, but Jobs envisioned a computer in peoples' homes, several computers in peoples' homes. "Not imbedded computers that did things with a home's utilities, but computers people operated on their own, manually. Absolutely no one believed that in the early 1970s."

Having heard many stories about Apple's founders, I wondered why Valentine emphasized Steve Jobs' role so prominently without mentioning Steve Wozniak, his partner and the more technical of the two. In his opinion, Steve Jobs articulated the idea; Steve Wozniak was behind the detailed execution of a lot of the electronics of the idea. "But I believe it was infinitely more Steve Jobs' vision of the future that made the persuasive arguments, years in advance of what has happened."

At that time, in the mid-1970s, IBM was still the major computer company in the world. The second most powerful computer company in the world was DEC. The Japanese computer companies largely made clones of the IBM 360 system. The other major players were minicomputer companies like Data General and Prime. They all made machines that cost hundreds of thousands of dollars. The microprocessor had been around for a decade, "but they didn't get it. Not one computer company got it. None of the seven dwarfs who were being put out of business by IBM had the vision to recognize the opportunity. None of them said, 'Here's something we can do that IBM can't.' All the guys in Boston missed it. The whole bunch missed it. IBM missed it."

I wanted to know if Noyce missed it, too. "No. It was one of the things that he believed made sense. And it was why I think he and Jobs had chemistry. But other bright people running powerful companies didn't understand the future. Jobs understood the future. Jobs made the future happen. I don't think the demise of Apple should in any way diminish the justifiably deserved accolade: Jobs was the visionary for the personal computer business." [*Note:* I met with Valentine in the spring of 1998, when Apple's fortunes were so low it seemed the company might soon disappear.]

■ HOW VISIONARIES DO IT

If vision is a rare gift that few people possess, then explaining what vision is and where it comes from and how it works calls for biography—or a surrender to the mysteries of grace. Vision is about visionaries and their transformational powers. I asked Valentine what was different about Noyce and Jobs that enabled them to do what they did. From his perspective, his focus on technical matters and technical people, both Jobs and Noyce had a much better sense of the reality of technology. They could bend it to their will as Jobs did in the 1970s and the 1980s. "Through Jobs' leadership, he could make things happen that were very difficult to do. Things that were on the edge of technically achievable. And he made those achievements happen faster. These were different people." In Valentine's opinion, they had a vision that was grander, broader, and more global, with higher impact. And interestingly, they thought in terms of things that are done or used by consumers, by individuals, not so much by corporations.

"The ultimate market is selling one to everybody. Henry Ford's vision of one car in every garage, two cars in every garage—everybody would have one." The personal computer has become the latter twentieth century embodiment of the Ford concept. The largest markets in the world occur when individuals want to own fairly expensive things. In the early 1950s, a television was that kind of an expenditure for a family. "Maybe the family spent $700 to buy a whole new form of entertainment that was crude and small and imperfect to watch; programming was boring and not very extensive. But ultimately everybody would have one. Or two."

As I was listening to Valentine talk about Noyce and Jobs and considering the implications of confining vision to visionaries, it occurred to me that developing a shared vision in an organization must be impossible. "Shared vision" becomes a meaningless oxymoron.

When I asked him about that, Valentine said, "Shared vision is an important part of implementation. I don't think Noyce or Jobs had partners in the conceptualization phase. Both were very different but incredibly charismatic leaders. Noyce had more understated, historic, intellectual, and technical prowess. Jobs had much more aggressive, individual, presentational power. He was able to create great articulation, even when he was 20 years old, with no significant formal education."

To Valentine, shared vision is a different thing altogether from vision. It makes a much smaller impact and belongs on a different scale. Valentine believes that shared vision refers to evolutionary ideas and the evolutionary people who process them. They may do great things—but not revolutionary things. They move the ball forward. And sideways. Sometimes they create great companies, oftentimes great fortunes.

"I would be inclined to think of Bill Hewlett in that way— a very collegial manager. I don't think a great technologist, but a brilliant, collegial, evolutionary kind of thinker. And a builder of a great company." Valentine believes that Hewlett and Packard accomplished what they did, in significant part, through management style and only secondarily through technology. "I don't think HP has ever been especially good at anything. They have nice computers, but they were second. And they have nice instruments and they have nice printers. I think they implement extremely well."

In Valentine's view, a company like HP that instills collegial participation is largely built on great execution. It's almost never first. It takes market share from leaders, who are often vulnerable to being overtaken by a brilliantly managed company. "HP may be the best local example, over a 50-year period, that we've ever created."

When I wanted to know why Valentine thinks there aren't more visions and visionaries, he was inclined to accept the statistical answer—a rare confluence of genes that create brilliance, at the right time, in the right place. There might have been 10 other 20-year olds as brilliant as Jobs but they didn't know what he knew. Perhaps they were in Iowa, Florida, or Tennessee, and didn't have the opportunity to grasp what was happening. Jobs was, fortunately, in the right place. He had an important learning experience at Atari, where he was a "minor, junior engineer or senior technician level guy, but an exceptionally inquisitive and bright one."

Valentine went on to observe that luck and good parents help. But the visionary rises above whatever his or her background is and recognizes the trends of the time, sees the possibilities for change, and intuits how to move. "Very few people think in terms of moving the economy in a new direction, or creating an industry. Most people are barely able to think about creating a company. We talk to people all the time who have terribly crude ideas about how to create a company. None of them think about creating an industry. It's a rare individual who's able to conceptualize on that scale. Can you imagine the temerity of somebody who's 20 saying he's going to start a computer company and kill IBM? That requires arrogance, cockiness, and some other traits one might not like so well. Nonetheless, they are required to take on somebody and say, 'Look, you missed it. We are going to do this stuff and you guys are not even going to believe it!'"

Very few people think in terms of moving the economy in a new direction, or creating an industry.

Valentine referred to the dominant people in the PC business to emphize his point. "Compaq is a new name. None of the minicomputer manufacturers ever got into the business. That is not unique to computers of course. The buggy makers didn't make automobiles, somebody else did. Going back to HP, though, to give them credit: 22 years later they're becoming a consequential, maybe even seriously important supplier of PCs. This is to their great credit, because DEC could never figure it out. Data General's a disaster. Prime is gone. IBM is still losing market share. None of the Japanese ever got a grip on it except in portables." HP, however, in its careful, well-managed, patient style, is making its way up the ladder toward the top. Many companies, like Packard Bell, have rapidly gained then lost momentum. "HP was able to do what no one else could. Certainly it isn't vision. It's a corporate commitment and a plan and good execution and patience. They grind it out; they have the same product as Compaq or Dell. Nothing differentiates them except their ability to produce and execute. Not visionary people to me. Important people. Necessary people. But not people who create industries."

■ LIMITS OF CHANGE

The more I thought about Valentine's view that vision is revolutionary and creates whole new industries, the more I was struck by the doubt that venture capital would support such visionaries. Even though both Noyce and Jobs had started new companies with venture funding—and even though Valentine himself had backed Apple and Jobs. Why aren't there more visionaries creating new industries? The finance industry in general and venture capital in particular often work against the revolutionary changes Valentine talks about. They look for relatively safe investments in something they already know. Instead of making revolutionary change likelier or easier to happen, they make it harder.

"Venture capitalists are no better than the entrepreneurs. I don't think there's a better way to do it. The venture system in this country is the best in the world. But there are more innovators than creators in the world." To Valentine, an innovator is different from a creator. How do you develop more creators? They don't come from a predictable educational program. They don't necessarily come from a great environment, although Valentine does think it's better to be in Silicon Valley than it is to be in a lot of other places in the country. "The environment here is full of finance capability and interest in finding innovators or company founders or technologists. But there's not much interest in finding revolutionaries." That would require embracing enormous risks, such as having no way to easily identify the size of new markets. "Partly that's because people like me invest from a partnership format that lasts only eight or ten years, during which time we have to start them and finish them. It's very difficult to orchestrate a revolution within eight or ten years, so many of our self-imposed pressures derive from a timetable that doesn't especially encourage revolutionaries."

But revolutionaries are rare also. In part that's because we go through technology plateaus. In Valentine's view there are relatively long periods of time when not a lot happens, because the existing technology is being implemented and the playing field is fairly even. Suddenly, somebody will recognize something and make a change, which makes the playing field very uneven, and the momentum will start again at a very high speed, for either existing companies to catch up to the new trend or new companies to be created to capture the new trend. "We have these flat periods that happen often and are prolonged. You could say that until the Internet-investing frenzy started in 1994 or 1995, there was a flat plateau, not a lot was happening in the way of very differentiated technology."

The explosion of the Internet seems to pose a problem for a great-man model of history. There is no one name associated with its rise. So I was curious to know what Valentine thought had happened to make the Internet such a phenomenal attraction after existing so quietly for 20 years. "Nobody especially understood the usefulness of it. The rate of growth of users was insignificant. The implementation of e-mail, which is a primary application on the Internet now, really only started in 1994 or 1993." An enabling application is needed to cause momentum and Valentine thinks e-mail will be viewed historically as the enabling application that caused the rise of the Internet.

"In the early days of Apple, that was always the question: What does this *do*?" In 1978, the memory system was an audio cassette; it could take an hour to download a program. What does it do? The question was unanswerable, because it didn't do anything that could justify the effort. It was a computer. It could do all the things all computers always did, only much more cheaply. Then an answer emerged: If companies bought $250,000 products to do computer computations, individuals would buy them for $3,000 or $4,000. According to Valentine, the fact that nobody had the imagination or the software to do anything wasn't particularly well thought through, but the Apple did one thing—it allowed people to learn how computers worked. It was a self-educational tool. And nobody ever understood, in his opinion, that that was an important enough application. "Then the evolutionary guys stepped up. One, two, three. Guys like Adobe. The applications got the engine moving."

Valentine told me that Noyce required companies like Applied Material to create the process equipment Intel needed to make more elegant microprocessors. It was fairly evident to Noyce that in time, many things would have to happen so integrated circuits could be made more and more dense. It was hard to articulate which would come first, which would be the most important, but it was clear that microprocessors could not be made with the kinds of equipment existing then. What was needed was a whole industry: dozens of companies, employing thousands of people who would somehow invent and continue to evolve ways to make it happen.

Even accepting Valentine's assessment about what Noyce and Jobs did, there are still limits to how revolutionary they were. They did something new, but not so new that it wasn't understandable to the people around them. Even if they reached into a future that no one else quite saw with the same conviction, they didn't reach a hundred years into the future like some of the builders of Europe's great cathedrals. They both reached for something that they could implement within a relatively short time. Is that hands-reach timescale an important element in vision?

"A year is not a constant term. Noyce lived in digital years. Before that, Sarnoff, for example, lived in analog years." To

Incremental changes are happening faster.

Valentine, a digital year is equal to ten analog years. The time compression is important. "Whatever happened, prior to 1970 the standard was one year equals one year. In 1990, perhaps the standard was one year equals 10 years. In the year 2000, one year may be equal to 20 years. The rate of change is radically faster now. The changes aren't revolutionary—incremental changes are happening faster." Valentine offered retail trade and the Internet as an example: When people build malls, it takes years to establish a tenant base. There is usually a first round of tenants, then a second round of tenants; finally, the mall gets going. It takes years of shipping catalogs before a solid consumer base is established. Now, the opportunity to buy electronically is changing the timetables in retail so they're radically faster than before. "The necessary behavior modifications are implemented digitally and facilitated digitally, comfortably and rapidly. Things change now at a totally different rate. Twelve months is no longer a year. No one intended that. It's just the way things are."

Chapter

3

Recognizing New Patterns: Federico Faggin, Chairman of Synaptics

The microprocessor without doubt is one of Silicon Valley's most important products. Since Intel introduced it in 1971, the microprocessor has fueled the growth of semiconductor companies, computer companies, manufacturing equipment companies, software companies, networking companies— most of what Silicon Valley is known for. But its importance doesn't stop with business. Microprocessors are the brains inside countless everyday products we all use, from calculators to cars to talking greeting cards. When people talk about smart products, from smart buildings to smart bombs, in reality they often mean there's a microprocessor inside that can be programmed to perform tasks that thinking humans would otherwise have to do.

The man who led the Intel team in developing the microprocessor was Dr. Federico Faggin *[pronounced fa ZHEEN]*. Faggin is a physicist and inventor who was born in the Veneto region of Italy, near Venice, and received his doctorate in physics from the University of Padua. He has made the Silicon Valley his home since 1968.

In the United States, Faggin first worked at Fairchild Semiconductor, where he led the development of silicon gate technology, an important building block for integrated circuits including the microprocessor. In 1970, Faggin joined Intel where he led the team that invented and developed the microprocessor, the 4004. If silicon gates and microprocessors were all he ever helped invent, he would be a giant in the history of technology. But Faggin has done much more. While still at Intel, he led the development of more than 25 other integrated circuits, including the 8080 8-bit microprocessor. In 1974, he left Intel to cofound and become the CEO of Zilog, where he conceived and developed the architecture for the Z80, the most successful 8-bit family of microprocessors in the industry. In 1982, he moved on to cofound and become CEO of Cygnet Technologies, where he conceived the Communication CoSystem, an intelligent voice and data peripheral for the personal computer.

Then, in 1986, together with celebrated Caltech professor Carver Mead, Faggin founded Synaptics to perform research and develop commercially viable neural network applications. Neural networks are computational devices designed to process information and learn on their own, without having been programmed, similar to the way scientists think real brains work. In the future, neural nets may prove to be a more fundamental and world-changing invention than the microprocessor. As Faggin said in our discussions, "Neural networks have proved to be a better way of solving pattern recognition problems than traditional computer technologies. Pattern recognition is an extremely deep domain. All computing problems can be reduced to that." It also turns out that pattern recognition is at the heart of his approach to vision.

When I first met with Faggin in the early 1990s to discuss neural networks and their future, one of the application domains we talked about was pattern recognition, especially the recognition of handwriting. Standard artificial intelligence techniques had gotten nowhere with that task, but neural nets were making solid progress. He specifically mentioned some work done for American Express to read images on charge tickets, and work done for the postal service to read ZIP codes. We also talked about other, mostly industrial applications, such as optimizing the flow of work through a semiconductor fabrication line. These were all successful experiments, but none of them was yet making a large impact on the world. By 1998, Faggin could talk about applications that were finally affecting a much bigger audience.

If you have or have seen a laptop computer with a touch pad instead of a mouse or eraser head to control the cursor, then you have witnessed an application of Synaptics' neural network technology. These touch pads let you use the free motion of your palm or fingers to move your cursor where you want it. This is a practical application of neural nets' remarkable abilities to sense and process variations in touch.

If you were in China you could see these same touch pads used in a more complex way. They allow a user to input and process Chinese characters without requiring a huge, complicated keyboard or other cumbersome system to accommodate the thousands of different characters in the Chinese language. In 1998, Synaptics was setting up a major activity in China to bring this application to fruition. The neural net technology in the pad is used not only to sense the touch of a finger or palm or some kind of stylus, but to recognize Chinese characters. What happens is this: A small window with two sides opens on the computer screen. On one side are listed six characters thought to match the character being drawn, in the order of probability the neural net estimates for a match. The other side of the window is used for control. The center window is where the characters and the text appear, as with a standard word processor. The neural net system starts to offer choices after only three strokes. "On average, you have to write only half the strokes," said Faggin, "so the system is roughly twice as fast as writing by hand." There's still another benefit to this system: It provides access to characters that native writers don't fully remember, but are able to recognize when they see them. With so many thousands of characters in Chinese, this is a significant aid.

Faggin is a very rare man in any case, but he's even rarer in Silicon Valley. He is certainly very inventive, as are other scientists. What is rarer still is that he is a working, inventing scientist who also runs a company responsible for turning inventions into commercial products. He has experience across what he calls the whole "arc of vision," from conception to reality.

Most CEOs and chairmen do not come up with the basic product ideas their companies are founded on. They are, as Faggin says, "converts" to a vision that has already been created. Their job is to implement, to execute. They may have visions about other important matters, but not usually about the basic product. For example, "Andy Grove had almost no product vision, but he did have vision about organization, about how people could come together in new ways to get things done. He was always talking about that, long before he became CEO of Intel." Faggin's experience includes the vital task of making visions real, but it also goes back to the very beginning, before the visions were even ideas. He has deeper roots in vision than most CEOs.

Faggin's broad experience has left him with a number of attitudes about the whole discussion of vision. First, it is a very serious and real subject for him. As I came to understand in the conversations I had with him from the spring to the winter of 1998, vision is an art he practices. Second, perhaps because of that, he wants to be very careful in distinguishing just what vision is and what it is not. For example, he disparages "dreamers'" and "science fiction writers'" claims to vision. Vision doesn't count unless it's "on time" and it's made real. Period. That is why he likes being in the business world; he gets to work on the whole process, from vision to reality.

■ CARRYING THE FLAME

Imagine a stormy mountain peak, high in the Alps, with a small primitive hut near the top. Night is coming. In the twilight you can see a man carrying in his hand something that glows bright, like a living spark. The man is carrying this spark down the edge of the mountain to a small village that has no light at all. That is the Promethean image that represents Faggin's vision as well as the way he sees vision working.

Before the man could produce the spark, he labored on the invention with a small group at the very top of the mountain, right at the boundary between heaven and earth. They'd brought a few tools from their workshop hut. The man and his colleagues were focused on creating artificial light for the long dark mountain nights. Such a light would give their village more time to spend on the things that mattered most, including their own personal development and spiritual lives. The men huddled at their work, sometimes lifting their heads up and to the side, but with a stare that showed concentration, perhaps a brief interior dialogue between a thought and an intuitive feeling. And then, in one brief moment, you could see the man raise his arm and head and shout in triumph. He had a spark, trapped but alive in a small box.

The man didn't immediately rush out with the light he'd been seeking. First, he had to prove to himself and his colleagues he could produce it again. He repeated the pattern of actions that led to the spark. The pattern worked. Next, he and his colleagues discussed what they had done and why they thought it worked, what principles were involved. After they talked, they made some changes to improve and refine the device that made the spark and then tested it some more. Sure enough, they could produce the spark even in the wind, and it would spread to the fuel they offered it and burst into flame. The winds would buffet it some, changing its shape and direction, but the flame survived and turned the darkness into light.

Then, it was ready. Just at the edge of night, the man feels his way carefully down to the village, carrying his flame. He is convinced they'll be ready for it, that its use will spread from household to household as they see how beneficial it is. But he also knows it will take some time for the villagers to really see and understand what his spark machine can do. Lightning is the closest thing they've ever seen, and that is terrifying, dangerous, uncontrollable. They won't expect and therefore won't see at first that a human tool can make fire. But the timing is right, the winter of long nights is just beginning. Before very long, the entire village will glow as brightly as if lit up by a full moon.

■ MODEL OF VISION

To Federico Faggin, vision is, to begin with, "a new awareness of what's possible." But awareness alone isn't enough. The new possibility has to be expressed so other people understand it, get involved, and help make it real. This *process* from awareness to reality is vision. In actual practice, the process isn't so neat and logical, but it helps to think of it as comprising four major steps. Someone has to:

1. Have a vision;
2. Communicate it;
3. Create a market for it;
4. Then make the vision real.

Vision is, to begin with, a new awareness of what's possible.

All four steps are necessary, although the same person doesn't very often perform them all. In Silicon Valley and elsewhere, that just doesn't happen very often. In fact, very rarely does one person alone perform any one of the steps. Vision is much more a collective process than the action of a lone individual. "The story of the hero sells better, but it's wrong."

The story of the hero sells better, but it's wrong.

Because Faggin is an inventor, I especially wanted to know more about the first part of this process, what he calls "having a vision." Although he thinks this first step varies depending on whether the vision is about a product or a scientific discovery or something else, in general his theory is that it has five components:

1. A stimulating environment.
2. A person aware enough to be affected by this stimulus.
3. A work focus, a "point of accumulation," although it doesn't have to be specific. Generally, the focus is primarily on the problem to be solved and only

secondarily on the means for solving it. In the case of a product, you have to "conceptualize what this product ought to be in order to create the change you want to make in society."

4. A moment of inspiration when the focus and data from the environment come together and a new pattern emerges. This is the "Aha!" moment.

5. A conscious recognition of the new pattern, which includes a sense that, for example, a product based on this pattern can actually be made, together with a sense for how to make that happen. "It's as if the vision includes a blueprint for how to implement it."

It's as if the vision includes a
blueprint for how to implement it.

Faggin emphasized that these five elements are simply a deconstruction of a process not so neatly defined in real life. "It's just a way of talking. If you don't have the talent for this sort of thing, it won't make sense."

The difficulty in making sense out of vision, especially the first step of actually having a vision, is more than just a matter of talent, however. It's a matter of what vision itself is. "Vision belongs to that class of things that can't be fully comprehended by reason, just like dreams and intuition, things outside the well-explored dimensions of what it means to be human. It is not like a mathematical theorem." With that difficulty in mind, I wanted to begin by understanding as much as possible about what it means to Faggin to have a vision.

■ THE VISION ENVIRONMENT

The first element necessary for having a vision in Faggin's model is a stimulating environment. The environment is important throughout the whole "arc of vision," from having one to realizing it. If you're working in a company, that means first of all you have to separate yourself from the larger company environment. "Typically visions are realized by a small group of people, a splinter group—maybe only one or two people. What they're working on may not make any sense to the larger group. So until the vision is brought to reality it has to be kept in a microenvironment."

The problem with the larger company environment stems from its own nature, especially the way it interacts with anything new and different inside it. "The environment is essential to create the conditions for visions to occur. Normally, a vision is not an obvious thing to do. It is nonlinear, a curve ball; it doesn't go along with the way most people think. Once you express the vision, you create antagonism within the very environment that was essential for its creation. You have produced an output different from what is expected, so the environment attacks it. You have to find a microenvironment that will support you within the larger environment so that rather than wasting time arguing with everyone, you can prove your vision works. Then you can use that win for leverage in the larger environment. Once you've got fire, you can take it out and show it to people. But then it's not a vision anymore, it's fire. The vision has happened."

I asked Faggin if Intel's environment had been conducive to the invention of the microprocessor. "Yes. Intel had an essential advanced technology, the silicon gate, which I'd helped develop earlier at Fairchild. The silicon gate was essential to the microprocessor." The idea of a microprocessor was not unique. Other people saw it, but no one else had the advanced technology to do it. Intel also had silicon memories. A CPU has internal registers, with memories inside. Previously, memories weren't random access; they were shift register memory, which is much slower, so a general purpose CPU was not possible. Intel had the technology and the idea. Intel even had a customer who wanted a programmable solution. It was just a question of being in that place at that time. And then, it had to be done.

"We had to believe the microprocessor would change the world. I believed that. I fought very hard within Intel to get them to actually sell it." It was a custom design originally

---

We had to believe the microprocessor
would change the world. I believed that.

---

intended for that one customer, so people assumed it was good only for that customer's needs. It took Faggin nine months to convince people that it was general enough to do other things. It wasn't obvious. They thought it was only good for the calculator-like applications it had been designed for. Then, too, the instruction set was very limited. He took it on himself to show by example that it could do other applications. He was building a tester—for the 4004 as a matter of fact, for the microprocessor—and needed to make a controller for it, a sequencer. "So, I said I would use the 4004 for that, to run the tester to test itself. I wrote a program and did it, and showed it took much less time than if I'd built one from scratch. It was relatively easy. And I could change it easily. So that was the spark that convinced people internally."

By now it may be hard to imagine that Intel, the company known for the microprocessor, had to be convinced that its own invention had any value beyond one customer and one application. The problem wasn't a matter of estimating the size of the market, it wasn't like IBM's initial doubts about the market for computers. In the beginning, Faggin's problem was in proving that the microprocessor had a truly general use. The wonderful irony in his proof was that the "calculator" could run a machine that tested the calculator itself. But the proof also demonstrates just how hard it can be, even—or perhaps especially—for people in exactly the right environment, to actually see something that's different from what we expect.

The microprocessor was easy compared to neural nets. Computers had been around for 25 years before the microprocessor. In 1971, 25 years into computer technology, it was just a matter of taking the same idea and implementing it in a new technology. Neural networks are different. With them, the *idea* was new and different. Both the idea and the technology for implementing neural networks were being developed at the same time, and that takes much longer. Finally a product, the Chinese character recognizer, has emerged and it works very well and is selling. "It is a major feat that shows neural networks are worth it. But it took much longer."

If developing both a new idea and the technolog for implementing it takes a longer time, what in the environment makes such inventions possible at all? I wondered if the combination of different disciplines, say of brain research and computing technology, was part of the answer. "Yes, generally speaking, new ideas come from combining fields that before were separate. The microprocessor combines the idea of the computer with semiconductors. Computers *used* semiconductors, but they *were not* semiconductors." Previously, computers used core memory, magnetic things not made in semiconductors; the CPU was constructed in a heterogeneous manner as opposed to being done all on one chip. So combining the idea of computers with the technology of semiconductors was a matter of coming out with something that integrated what before was heterogeneous.

New ideas come from combining
fields that before were separate.

■ THE EDGE

Faggin's discussion of the way a combination of different disciplines can lead to new ideas led him to make a point that captured much of what I'd been hearing him say about the kind of environment where new ideas, new visions, come from.

In my first meeting with Faggin, he talked about visions being on the knife's edge between what is possible and what is not. Later on, he said that any revolutionary product or idea is at that same knife's edge. It is important to note that he is saying both the idea itself *and* the person who comes up with such ideas must be at this edge.

One of the edges in the field of neural nets is the current progress in research on the brain. It was some of the results

FEDERICO FAGGIN ON CHAOS THEORY

There is an even more general principle, which is one of the insights chaos theory has provided. Creativity happens at the interface between order and chaos, just at that very fine boundary. If there is only order, you have a crystal in a rigid position. Nothing happens. At the other extreme, molecules bounce all over the place like in a gas. And nothing happens there either. At the interface is where everything happens: between air and earth, between sea and shore. Life evolved at the interface, maybe between ice and water. It was an interface between order and chaos. If you want to encourage vision, this notion indicates that creative people can neither be too orderly nor too much with their heads in the clouds, changing their minds all the time. They have to be something in between.

in brain research that first inspired work on neural networks. Faggin points out that neural net technology has now caught up with our basic knowledge of how the brain works, so progress is slower. There is no new brain information to inspire new work. Our present knowledge of brain function constitutes probably only 1 percent of what research will yield, however, so new ideas will be coming. The field of neural nets will expand as we learn more about the brain.

There was a different edge involved with the microprocessor, one that acted to force progress. As Faggin explained, there was a 25-year history of computers that work on the microprocessor could make use of, so it went much faster. Pent-up knowledge allowed the explosion to occur. But that was a unique set of circumstances. "Usually, revolutionary visions progress like neural nets. Lasers are like that, too." So, in Faggin's view, this edge in the world of ideas is mostly something you have to push against, even if once in a while it pushes you.

The edge Faggin has in mind is not, however, simply between the known and the unknown. Another way he describes the domain of vision is the edge between science and philosophy. "Science deals with the predictable, the known. Philosophy deals with things that are softer, unknown, undefined. Visions exist on the edge where both meet." So this edge in the world of ideas is better understood as standing between two kinds of knowledge, one more like order and the other more like chaos, not simply between knowledge and nothing.

There is also a critical edge you have to find in the everyday world of work and living. Faggin repeatedly stressed that visions have to be "on time," and "made real." Otherwise they don't count. For a product, that means the technology that goes into the design of the product and the technology that goes into making the product have to be ready; you have to be able to produce it at a particular cost point; people have to be willing to accept the product, and so on. It isn't enough to push ahead in the world of ideas, find that edge between science and philosophy, and then think of something new. You've got to bring it into the real world at the time when the world is ready and will actually use it.

Visions have to be "on time," and "made real."
Otherwise they don't count.

That requires, first, an accurate reading of the real world and the forces in it, and, second, the ability to deal with these and all the frustration they create. The ability to read the world accurately is another skill that is more "philosophy" than "science," more intuition and feel than fact. Then the ability to act on this world calls for working at another edge, this one more internal and behavioral, the edge between "persistence and pigheadedness." You have to deal not just with ideas but with "people as they are, their emotions and all their complexity." You have to be able to spend nine months convincing Intel that its microprocessor should be sold, and usually it's harder than that. As Faggin said, the time it took him and Synaptics to achieve the success of the

Chinese character recognizer, some 12 years, "tested my distinction between persistence and pigheadedness."

The internal edge you must find if you want to make a vision concrete involves much more than persistence and pigheadedness, however. In Faggin's experience, it seems to require that your basic mental and emotional temperament be on the edge between chaos and order. Your vision work must involve a balance of emotion and intellect, intuition and reason, feeling and thinking. If you want to realize a vision, you must cultivate both sides.

I asked Faggin if, in his own career, he had consciously sought out these edges that he said were conducive to vision and creativity. "No, but I have known intuitively all my life that I need an environment that values what I value, which is why I'm here in Silicon Valley." Why does Silicon Valley have such a high rate of invention and innovation? The environment attracts like-minded people and provides stimulus to innovate. "I could not have done what I've done in Italy. My innovation there would have been more artistic, but I wanted more technological innovation. We self-select." Because the world is open, people can choose the place where they can give the most. "I have reached my potential here; I could not have done so there. And an artist in Silicon Valley would probably be better off going to Italy."

■ AHA: PATTERN RECOGNITION

If the environment is critical to having a vision, so is the skill or talent that seems to lie behind the moment of inspiration. The environment alone can't do it all, nor can the sensitivity to be stimulated by that environment. "Vision is a talent. If someone can only do it once, maybe they didn't really do it, maybe they got too much credit. Some people are good at articulating the vision of others. It's difficult to tear the vision process apart, but those who've only done it once are probably more the implementors. In general, a person with high skills in visioning tends to keep at it for life."

FEDERICO FAGGIN ON THE
IMPORTANCE OF FEELINGS

Feelings are like a tremendously compressed amount of information. Like when you dream, there are feelings. When you wake up, if you want to figure out what the dream means, most of the information is in the feelings, condensed there. If you want to solve the puzzle, you have to stay true to the feeling. The critical thing is to avoid being mental. The *feeling* must guide. The whole meaning of your life can be condensed in a feeling.

Feelings are also part of business. When I've screwed up, often it was when I didn't trust my feelings. But feelings, like everything else, have to be educated. Nothing is worse than intellect without feeling. It can lead to things like Nazism. Feeling without intelligence leads to aberrant religions. I've learned over the years to have a dialogue between feelings and intellect. In science, intuition can easily mislead you, which leads some people to throw it out. But Einstein used it to imagine time and space in a new way. Feelings are connected to reality in a way that's not understood. In time, with dialogue between intellect and feeling, everything rises and both powers are enhanced. There is no question that feelings have a connection to reality which is much more powerful than we give it credit for.

Much of what we do is based on repressed feelings. Repressing says, I don't want to know. Awareness is about being awake, a process of allowing all that you are to be seen and accepted—by yourself—which means loved and allowed to be expressed. Including parts you don't like, your shadow, to make this work for you. So, that's a vision of living a life worth living. Ninety-nine point nine nine percent of my education was about falsification in one way or another. When you get to the point that life seems meaningless, that's when you can start stripping away the layers of falsification.

Part of the talent for visioning must involve competence in both "science" and "philosophy." When Faggin spoke of chaos theory, after we'd discussed a number of examples where creativity seemed to be associated with a boundary between order and chaos, he said the idea that new information is created at this interface is very powerful. Particularly so because it has a mathematical apparatus behind it. It's not just a thought. "It comes out bottom up, so to speak, by noticing what happens." What Faggin said about this theory seemed to apply equally well to his description of the inspiration in a vision. At least one possible sequence of discovery—for example, noticing what happens in an experiment or observation without understanding why it happens that way—is bottom up. Then you need something like the order of a mathematical apparatus to fully recognize and represent this new pattern.

This bottom up learning is also characteristic of the way neural networks work. They aren't programmed to perform tasks, they are built to learn how to perform tasks themselves by recognizing patterns. So there is a similarity between the way Faggin perceives the vision process and the content of the vision for neural nets. Given Faggin's long work in the field of neural nets, it may not be surprising that many of the examples we discussed echoed this approach. The similarity may simply indicate a long and current association with bottom-up discovery as opposed to the more deductive, top-down method typical of traditional computer programming and artificial intelligence. But it may also be part of a more general relationship in which vision and visioning come to resemble each other.

■ INTEGRITY

The real point in getting to the knife's edge, the importance of a dialogue between intellect and feeling, is that it enables you "to live a life worth living"—personally and professionally. When Faggin said "you have to believe in your vision," he wasn't talking about pretending or manufacturing anything.

I felt he was talking from real experience about an outcome that necessarily follows from the process of having a vision. If vision comes from this dialogue between feeling and thinking you *will* believe in it. You don't have to pretend—the belief is just there, whether you want it or not. It turns out this belief is extremely useful. It helps you in the struggle to make the vision real, but it is almost a by-product. Vision is made up of competence more than confidence.

This vision process springs from deep, real, authentic feelings. "Within the notion of vision is honesty, no fragmentation." That's because vision springs from, and in a way can actually form, your integrity. Aside from their talent for vision and their "desire to find new patterns," inventors like Faggin seem to keep working with and from visions because it makes them feel whole, because it keeps them in touch with and acting from their own integrity. Other people whom the visionary tries to convince can often sense this integrity. It's one of the important reasons—or feelings—behind their conversion to the visionary's new idea. Politicians who claim to have visions are often disbelieved because their so-called visions are seen to be stratagems to get elected without any integrity. The integrity that is part and parcel of a real vision is also part of what makes people feel that working for a vision is worthwhile.

Within the notion of vision is honesty, no fragmentation.

For Faggin, real visions also have their own integrity which is quite independent of the person or people who create them or believe in them or make them real. After listening to Faggin talk about vision for a while, I asked him if a vision exists separately from its creator's or anyone's consciousness of it, rather the way circles and squares exist in geometry separately from anyone's conception of them. "Yes," he said, "that's a fair inference. If a vision works, it's independent of whoever figured it out. I like to think of a vision as a new species, a living thing that grows, develops, and changes—but it's still the same vision. The vision has to hang together, has to make sense. Facing doubt and antagonism can actually be good because they force you to make sure your vision really does make sense and you can prove it." A real vision, in Faggin's view, is like a new species that lives and both changes the environment and in turn is changed by the environment.

I like to think of a vision as a new species, a living thing.

Faggin went on to say, "A strong vision has a way of expressing itself that goes beyond the ability of the person expressing it. This new pattern, new species, somehow has a strength of its own." To use a different image, it's like the new flame carried to the mountain village. It can exist and grow and spread on its own.

■ NOVELTY

One other reason to get to the knife's edge and to engage in a dialogue between feeling and intellect is to come up with something new. According to Faggin, one of the fundamental requirements for vision is novelty. If it isn't new it isn't a vision. The novelty does not necessarily have to be in the idea. Recall that although the idea of neural networks was new, the idea of the microprocessor was not. Many people had it. Neither does the novelty have to reside in the means for implementing the idea. Recall also that semiconductor technology existed before the microprocessor. The novelty of a vision is in what change it brings into the world. The novelty that matters is in the real world.

There's a difference between vision and an idea. To realize a vision, it is essential that you make it understood and real. If Henry Ford had had an idea but no vision, the company wouldn't have existed. "Visions have to become concrete.

If it isn't new it isn't a vision.

Visions can be immature or completed; I bow only to the completed." But this completion is not simply a matter of completing just anything. It's a matter of completing something *new*. "Most people don't understand vision, or stop just at the expression of it. Ninety-eight out of 100 businesses are just mundane ways to make a living. Two percent want to create something new. Usually, they fail. But they have a special place in the ecology of business, taking care of renewal and radiation of the species. The rest are about copying."

Just as vision is not present in every company, it is not present in every leader. In vision there is a novel pattern that is not always needed for successful leadership. To bring to market a revolutionary product takes a different style of leadership than running a McDonald's franchise. Leadership is about providing an organizational and motivational focus for a group of people. Vision is about doing something new.

Not every vision has to establish a brand new industry. "You can talk about vision or visions. For example, if you want to make computers easy to use, that's a vision. To do that, you will need a variety of means, and those are visions. There can be a hierarchy of visions, levels of visions. What is common is change."

Faggin does not see lack of vision in most companies and in most leaders as being bad. I asked him if he thought there were advantages to organizing around vision. He said, "An organization has to have a purpose, like any living thing. To the extent the purpose is understood, you will have a good organization. But I'm trying to limit the meaning of vision. Vision is not just a goal or a plan. It may well be that it's more dangerous to organize around a vision because it may be difficult to convince everyone to go down that road. A simple plan may be easier. It may be better to have a realistic plan than a crazy vision. A vision can create too many crosscurrents in an organization."

He went on to explain why he thought it was rare for an inventor to be running a company, even in Silicon Valley. Inventive skills tend to be different from managerial skills and are seldom found in the same person. Inventing means open-endedness. Managing means closed-endedness, getting the schedule down. Managing is closer to order, and inventing is closer to disorder. There can be a creative tension between the two, but emotionally the demands are very different. The manager has to deal with people, to be much more skillful at handling interpersonal relationships. These are skills and emotions that some people don't want to deal with. For the inventor, the tension is more personal, dealing with the world of things, not people, wondering simply, "Can I do it?"

■ COLLECTIVITY

Faggin repeatedly stressed in our conversations that the vision process is really collective, not individual, from beginning to end. This is as true for the initial phase of having the vision as the later phases of building a movement and making it real. He said, "A vision has a strength that is, in a sense, collective. You can even see it in invention. A bunch of guys may be brainstorming, and then someone says, 'Aha! We can do *this*.' But that someone is not the inventor—it is all the participants, as well as those who came before and contributed the ideas they built on." Vision is a collective phenomenon rather than the work of a lone hero. The story of the hero sells better, but it falls apart if you look closely at any invention.

Vision is a collective phenomenon.

For Faggin, the process of vision, even the moment of inspiration and the recognition of a new pattern, is a collective, social process. The individuals in the process may well need to call on their own intuition and feelings. But their interaction with each other, with the traditions they draw on, and with the larger society are also critical parts of the process. This point is important. The notion that new visions come from a "lone hero" is more than simply a notion that sells. Most people probably can't imagine how visions can be produced in any other way. Perhaps that's connected to the dominant Western theory that knowledge is a belief, and beliefs exist in consciousness, and consciousness exists only in individuals.

The second major step in the vision process, after "having a vision," calls for articulating and communicating it. This step is thoroughly social, collective. Its function is to express the vision in a way that lets a wider audience see and understand it. "If people get it, they begin articulating it, which is necessary for it to spread." And, as Faggin pointed out earlier, the people who actually do most of the writing and speaking may very well not be the original person—or people—who had the vision. This is often the point at which a CEO first enters the picture.

The third step is to create a movement for the vision. The movement is likewise a collective phenomenon, of a group of people who share an understanding of the vision and a desire to see it realized. And the movement is not simply an amplification of the original vision. It is also a process that changes and improves the vision as more people get involved with it. As a vision gains momentum, "people contribute to it and refine it." That seems easy enough to understand, but if all kinds of people start adding to it, how can you keep a vision from being diluted or from losing its integrity? Faggin's sense is that if it's a good vision, the core will stay the same and be enriched by what others bring to it. "If the core is healthy, the interaction will enrich it. When the criticism is outrageous, it forces you to make sure what you want makes sense. As long as the opposition does not go to the point of incarceration or putting you to the stake, as long as it doesn't interfere with your freedom, it's by and large positive."

To gain momentum for the vision movement, people have to really believe it, and that belief is best started with the people who originally have the vision. They have to believe it enough to put themselves on the line. Personal commitment makes a vital difference. "People will doubt you, openly defy you. Where else do you find the strength if not in yourself?"

I asked Faggin if money is a vital part of the motivation in building a movement for a vision. He doesn't believe that if making money is your only goal you can still have a vision. At least not at the same time. For him, vision is about something more—it's spiritual, it's about changing the world. "You have to convince a lot of people to make a vision real. If you want to make money, it's easier to do something that's proven." Vision seems to carry with it its own motivation, and that is what is vital to building a movement.

If you want to make money, it's easier
to do something that's proven.

But once again, what counts is the motivation in a collective, not an individual, not even the individual who first expressed the vision. I asked Faggin if vision always keeps its creator's excitement and inspiration up, and he said, "It's a mixed bag. A person with vision may get discouraged sooner than others. Vision usually starts with one person and then ends up with a social movement. But it doesn't matter if the first one peels away. Just like the microprocessor didn't stop when I stopped working on it."

■ MAKING VISIONS REAL

The final step in the vision process, making it real, is also fundamentally a collective process. And, for Faggin, it's the most important of all. If you don't get this far with a vision, it doesn't count. "The 'first' to think of something, including a vision, gets a disproportionate amount of credit. Credit should go to those who make a vision work, because a vision is like a species that must *survive*." But to become real, a vision is not simply dependent on the people who work to make it happen. It is also dependent on the people who accept it. For new ideas to find fertile ground, people have to be willing to use and accept them. They have to be willing to change. "It's like being willing to use a keyboard to use a computer. In the United States, a lot of people are willing to try the new. It's a more fertile place for these forces to start and spread."

When I asked Faggin what you have to do to make a vision real, he repeated a number of points he'd made earlier. After all, as he said, the vision process is not a simple linear combination of the four steps in his model. He said, "A new vision becomes like a new faith, similar to a new religion. You need people who will contribute to and refine the vision. If you're leading a company, you need to communicate to people why there's a place in the world for us, and what we will contribute to the world. If potential employees don't respond to that, they're probably not who you want. The vision helps people self-select in that way."

While we were talking about building a company around a vision, Faggin told me more about why he likes to work on visions within the business world. He enjoys a company setting because he can go through the whole vision process. I asked him if business also placed limits on vision. He noted that businesses typically want to make money, but there's more to it. Sometimes they're also about making change. Money is like blood—it measures the health of a company. If you have something to contribute, people will pay for what you offer. "Money is a feedback system telling you you're OK." But business is also an intellectual group creating intellectual property and social interaction where people learn to confront issues in a constructive manner. "A company is all that, but it's also a mirror for people to learn—including spiritually. A company's responsibility is only to be the mirror. Using that is your own personal responsibility."

For Faggin, the school was more in management than in technology. He did most of his envisioning in his late twenties and early thirties, and a little bit more when he was older, but always in the environment of starting or running a company. "The growth I experienced—and this is why I chose this path—was more emotional than intellectual. Because of the way I grew up, I was intellectually mature in my mid-twenties, but emotionally I was very immature." It was very difficult for him to adjust to the way things were done and how people compete in the world of business. "All this was tough. But I'm glad I did it because it was what I needed, personally. It had the biggest payoff, I could grow the most."

Once a company has been formed, Faggin says, it's important to find the focus, create a flame that can spread. Resources must be focused where they can make a difference. A new microenvironment must be created that is conducive to the vision, to the spark. If the site is receptive, that's good enough. It isn't possible to do everything at once. You have to start small, with that spark. If the time for the idea has come, the process of adoption will be rapid.

"How do you know if the time is right? You don't. It's like the difference between persistence and pigheadedness. How do you know? That's wisdom. You have to know the difference. It comes back to your internal sense—which can also be wrong. You have a sense of where the future is, some intuition or psychic feeling that has no logic, no reason, it just is. At most, that sense can be corroborated by logic, but it often defies logic—like quantum mechanics defies logic. Yet, that's the way the world is. Some people say the future is out there and you can tune into it, glimpse it a little bit, even if not clearly. They have some sense of it. I'm not saying I believe that, but some people claim it's true. The world is bizarre enough, who knows? Maybe some people can do that. Look at artists like Mozart—by three or four he could compose music. How is that possible? There is more to life and consciousness than we know; there are so many things we can't explain and can't dismiss. Vision belongs to that class of things."

There are so many things we can't explain and can't
dismiss. Vision belongs to that class of things.

■ FAGGIN'S VISION

Faggin said again and again that visions are about a change in the world. I asked him what change he is trying to make in the world with the visions he has worked on. His answer resonated with the purpose I'd heard behind his discussion of microprocessors and neural networks and vision in general. It evoked in my mind the Promethean image of the gift of fire suggested earlier. He said, "There isn't only one. At different stages, I wanted to make different changes. What is common is change for the better: ways to let people work more productively, have a higher standard of living, so they'd have more room for personal and spiritual development."

Chapter

4

Simulate, Sell, Surf: Joe Costello, Chairman and CEO of think3

Engineers all over the world use tools made in Silicon Valley to turn their ideas for new products into reality. Before they manufacture a computer, a car, or even a cardboard box, they first design it and analyze it and plan for its manufacture using computer-aided design (CAD), computer-aided engineering (CAE), and computer-aided manufacturing (CAM) software. Although these computer tools have been widely used only since the 1970s, in that short time they've become indispensable. High-tech products could not exist without them. It takes smart tools to make smart products.

Until the fall of 1997 when he resigned, Joseph B. Costello was for 10 years the president and CEO of Cadence Design Systems, the world's largest vendor of Electronic Design Automation (EDA) products—which are computer-aided design and engineering tools used for making electronics products like microprocessors and memory chips. Under Costello, Cadence grew to nearly a billion dollars in annual sales by taking the lead on the second wave of technology in EDA and then doing something no competitor had done before: Cadence rode out the second wave and then managed to take the lead on the third wave. These changes in technology, usually also accompanied by changes in the cost and revenue structure of the industry, had wrecked most of the earlier leaders. They didn't use vision the way Costello does to constantly simulate the changing world so he can act quickly—and intuitively—when he needs to sell employees and customers on getting out in front and aligning themselves to make their own beneficial changes.

Earlier companies that had pioneered the EDA industry in the late 1970s—Calma and Daisy, for example—looked spectacular for a short while. They grew extraordinarily rapidly by selling their design and engineering software combined with their own proprietary computer hardware. But they wiped out as the industry shifted to the next wave of technology: software only, sold to run on standard UNIX workstations. Cadence picked up the pieces (literally, by acquiring what was left of the pioneers) and learned a lesson. When the next technology wave came along—with more powerful, extensive, and integrated software, often running on PCs—Cadence made the transition and was still the industry leader in 1999.

But after 10 years in this intense business, Costello got bored. He left Cadence, amid rumors that Apple Computer wanted him as their new CEO. Michael Milken, the ex-junk bond king, asked Costello to join him in a new venture in education and training called Knowledge Universe, which Milken had started with his brother Neil and Larry Ellison, chairman of Oracle. Although the press reported that Costello had joined Knowledge Universe as vice chairman, and although it was through Knowledge Universe that I first contacted him in late 1997, in reality, he told me, he never really did join. Using a term he used often in our conversations, he later said that he and Milken just didn't have enough "alignment." Accustomed to being in charge, Costello wanted to be CEO of Knowledge Universe or nothing at all. He said, "I told Michael that he could be the archbishop of a grand new cathedral in education. It would be his place, and he could come and speak anytime he wanted. But I wanted to be the architect with full authority and responsibility to design and build it." In the end, Milken—used to power himself—wouldn't give up that much control.

Costello and Milken parted amicably, and Costello started looking for another place to put his considerable energy. For Costello, in early 1998, that meant making a three to four million dollar investment in each of two companies he joined as chairman. The investments keep him keenly interested. He says even in sports he needs to have some money on the line to keep his interest high. And the positions as chairman, with virtually no day-to-day operational responsibility, allow him to focus on strategy.

One of his investments was in a wireless data company in Minnesota called Racotech. The other was in a little known company in the automated design field—only this time in what is known as *mechanical* design. Mechanical design tools are used for automobiles, airplanes, and similar three-dimensional products, as opposed to the rather two-dimensional electronic products like microchips and printed circuit boards. One set of tools is used by mechanical engineers, the other by electrical and electronics engineers. This new company was Cad.Lab—fittingly renamed think3 late in 1998 when Costello also became CEO. For me, the timing and the circumstances could not have been better. When I sat down to talk with Costello from late 1997 to the spring of 1998, he was in the process of developing his vision for Cad.Lab. I had a chance to question him in real time as he applied what he'd learned about vision to a new company, to see this vision in the process of its creation.

■ SURFING BIG WAVES

The image that captures Costello's vision for Cad.Lab, and what vision means for him, is Costello, surfing a big wave. The huge wave rises, appearing to be 30 feet or more from its trough to its curling peak. Another wave, just as large, is already rising some distance behind it. The one in front is collapsing in thunderous, explosive confusion on the beach. And there is Costello, tall and lanky, driving his surfboard down and across the concave face of his wave, away from the curl, moving with the quick, sure, instinctive fluidity of a cat.

As you watch Costello, you can feel what he feels—the tremendous power of the wave, as if a huge invisible hand has grabbed you, pushing you forward. You also have an immense feeling of freedom and control, because you know what you're doing. You're surfing by feel, by intuition, not really thinking at all. There's no time for thinking. Before you ever ventured out on that wave, before you built the special board that's just right for these waves, you thought a lot. In your mind, you simulated riding the wave again and again and again. On your personal computer, you modeled the wave and the board you were designing, maybe using virtual reality goggles to maintain a real world feel for what you were doing. You analyzed all the forces, all the problems you'd have to avoid. You developed a deep understanding of the fundamental dynamics of the board on the wave. And out of all this thinking and simulation, you brought not just a sense of what you had to do, but a deep passion. Nothing would stop you.

You knew you couldn't do it alone. Making surfboards required skills you didn't have. So you started telling others about the wave and what it would mean to ride it. In telling them, you brought them into the world you'd been simulating. You let them see what you saw and asked them to tell you what they saw. Several people noticed things you hadn't. All of which led you to avoid some mistakes that might have proved deadly, and helped you improve your board so much that other people started thinking they wanted one just like it. They wanted to ride the wave, too. Eventually, you got the help you needed. Now, you are surfing.

Costello uses surfing as a metaphor to describe what it's like to a run a high-tech company. But the image also resonates with his model of vision, with his specific vision for Cad.Lab, and with his style.

■ MODEL OF VISION

Costello became interested in vision as a result of his interest in leadership. As the leader of a high-tech company, he wanted to be able to choose good leaders to help him. So, this Yale and Berkeley trained physicist did what he seems to do out of habit and temperament: He developed a theory of leadership. The theory turned out to be all about vision.

There are three parts to leadership in Costello's model. A successful leader has to be able to:

1. Create and articulate a vision.
2. Sell that vision to others.
3. Execute the vision, with an absolute commitment to seeing it through.

All three parts are necessary, and they have to be in balance. If a leader can't do and balance all three, he or she will fail.

According to Costello, "People tend to fall for the salespeople first. Sales with no vision and no execution is just an empty suit. At first a great salesperson can really get you going, get everybody's motor running. That tends to be the least satisfying miss. And there's a lot of that out there: Salesmanship with no substance."

Sales with no vision and no execution is just an empty suit.

There *is* a lot of salesmanship with no substance in Silicon Valley and beyond, and the emptiness isn't always apparent at first. Most Silicon Valley CEOs seem to come either from a technology or a sales background. The pressure in the Valley to grow fast may put salespeople under tremendous stress, but it also rewards them with a tremendous amount of money and power and with a clear path to the top of a company. People with strong sales skills are often put in leadership roles. Even those who are technologists have to take a leading part in sales. Either way, the result is too often just what Costello indicated, an empty suit.

"Then there are people with good visions and no communication skills," Costello said. "They can't sell worth a damn. That doesn't work either, because you really have to create a critical mass of energy behind something. Usually, if it's a good idea, you need many people to make it happen. I'm sure there are a lot of people with visions who can't sell them. They complain when someone else succeeds with what they'd thought of first. But so what? They couldn't sell it. So they didn't get anywhere. You can't do it by yourself."

This rings true as well. Would-be leaders with substance and vision but no sales skills don't seem able to bring changes into the world. The best technologies and the best new ideas don't sell themselves, no matter how good they are. Whatever else it is, business is not a meritocracy of ideas.

If salesmanship without vision doesn't work, and vision without salesmanship doesn't either, that led me to wonder if there is something special that distinguishes selling vision from selling anything else. "I don't think so," Costello said. "Or maybe I should say: If you can sell a vision, you can sell anything. I don't know if the other's true. I don't know if a good product salesperson could necessarily sell vision."

According to Costello, it doesn't matter what you're selling—you have to have passion. The best salespeople, of anything, have passion. You could be selling used parts at an auto wrecking yard. If you're passionate, they sell. "So, in that sense passion may be the key ingredient. Because of the nature of vision, you're trying to convince people that the world can be different. Well, you better be passionate about that because if you're not, you're not going to get anywhere."

You better be passionate about that because if
you're not, you're not going to get anywhere.

Passion. That's the energy I'd felt radiating from Costello beginning the first time I met him. At first he seemed almost shy as I explained what I wanted to discuss with him. But as soon as we began to talk, he lit up with what can only be described as passion about his work and how he goes about it. When he described some of the ideas he'd convinced Cadence and the EDA industry to follow, it was clear his passion was at least one reason why he was convincing. Costello is a man who can sell his vision.

The last component of Costello's model is absolute commitment to execution. Again, there are people who have a great idea and sell it like crazy, but then never seem to get anything done. Costello considers them dangerous—they can get you really excited, really ready to get going. Then nothing happens. "It's always a series of disappointments that get in the way. They don't get the right people put together. Or they don't keep their eye on the ball, they get interested in other things. There's all types."

It takes an absolute commitment to make your vision happen. If it's a real vision, you're painting a picture of the world that is different. You will have setbacks. Some things won't work, some wrong choices will be made. The world will change somewhat. People will say no to you. And there will be people who want to crush you and kill your vision. "Some of the people closest to you are going to lose faith and that's going to disappoint you. All kinds of stuff. The only thing that keeps you going, through all of that, is if you really have a vision. If you really do see a different world out there."

The only thing that keeps you going is
if you really have a vision.

Costello offers a sobering dose of reality about vision: There are indeed people who have and sell others on their great new ideas, but who never seem able to bring them to fruition. It is especially this last part, making ideas real, that I wanted to understand. That's why I'd chosen to talk with CEOs and other business leaders instead of inventors or futurists or scientists. I wanted to know what it takes not just to have a vision, but to make it real, make it happen. Vision itself, because it works at changing the world, will bring up countering forces that will make implementing it even harder. Some of these forces will be aimed at you, the visionary, personally, and will be very difficult to bear. But if vision is the source of some difficulties you face, it is also the source of the energy and commitment to overcome them.

In every way vision is central to Costello's model of leadership. As he said, "If you don't have a vision none of this works. Is vision real? I think it's extremely real." For Costello, vision is not a vague or faddish business term. Vision isn't a moment of inspiration or a dream. It is the art of using your head, your heart, and your will to change the world.

■ BACKGROUND ON CAD.LAB

When Costello joined Cad.Lab in early 1998, it was an 18-year-old company, a leader in the mechanical design market in Italy. Italian design in automobiles, furniture, appliances, clothing, and other products is often the envy of the world. And because Italy is such a hot design market, Cad.Lab had to build a very good product to serve it. But Cad.Lab had never marketed its products outside Italy, except for a small effort in France.

Two years before, Cad.Lab had a rude wake-up call. The Americans were invading Cad.Lab's turf. Parametric Technology, the current world leader, was the main aggressor. Other companies, like Computervision, were also attacking. The men running Cad.Lab saw this American invasion and they looked at the American products and they were amazed. "They said to themselves, 'This stuff is crap! This is what people are using outside Italy? We can do better than this!'"

Five years earlier, Cad.Lab's founders had decided to design and build the next generation product. They decided their new product would run on Windows NT, and it would be object-oriented, modular, and open. It would combine manufacturing with design in a complete and fully integrated system. None of the invaders' systems had these features. They ran on UNIX, not Windows NT. They were not object-oriented and not written in C++. They were not modular, not open. They didn't offer a complete and fully integrated solution for the entire engineering design and manufacturing process. They were all 10 years old.

The worldwide mechanical CAD/CAM market had existed for about 20 years, since the mid- to late-1970s. The last major change was already 10 years old. That was when Parametric introduced one very powerful idea: Instead of drawing everything to exact scale, Parametric's product let engineers draw with dimensioning. It let them "parametize the design," as Costello put it. "And then," Costello said, "they executed ruthlessly. Probably exactly the right term. Ruthlessly. And they had a great run for 10 years." That was the last change. As far as Costello could see, no one was painting a picture of the future.

"So, now I'm starting to feel at home," Costello said. "Because you have an industry that's large. It's in flux. It's like being in your car. When you're on solid ground in your car, try to move it. It's tough. When you're on ice? Whooo! A little touch—BOOOOOM. You can move it a lot. That's where this marketplace is. It's on ice. And that means a small guy on skates, with momentum, can move the whole industry a long way."

Costello became excited again as he spoke. His eyes lit up and he gestured with energy. Remember the image of him riding the wave? It seems to me that part of his excitement and energy is a joy that comes just from sensing and reading the forces he's dealing with. Then his excitement grows as he sees how he can gain some leverage or take advantage of these forces to go where he wants to go—preferably in a different direction from where everyone else is going. Costello likes to change things. But why wouldn't his American rivals be able to make the same moves as Cad.Lab?

He noted that people who have been successful often resist changing the formula that was working. But success is often the seed of failure. At some point, change must take place if a company is to remain competitive. Earlier success can make people wait too long or not even see the need for change. "Parametric set the lead, everybody else followed. You can never change the world following someone."

The industry had to make a platform transition, which is very difficult. "Very tough, I know that personally. I had to move Cadence . . . Well, first of all, we exploited a transition in platform for Cadence to become successful, when people moved off proprietary hardware to UNIX and software only. We made hay. No matter how much people said they were going to go do it, it took a long time."

All the leaders in mechanical CAD/CAM were accustomed to UNIX. They didn't have a Windows NT culture or development environment. "Nothing. So, big opportunity, that's number one. Number two, everybody's sitting on an old code base up there. That second-generation code base—to develop that is hell. And they've lost all their original guys who knew how it worked."

The inertia Costello felt he could take advantage of had many roots. A human tendency to keep repeating what works—until it's too late. A transition in platform that, from experience, he knew would be hard. And an upgrade or rewriting of old and massive software programs—without the original authors to help. These are all real forces in the world of mechanical design, forces that Costello had experienced, not abstract numbers about market share or return on investment. One other thing I noticed: Costello was by far most interested in the company he saw as the current market leader, Parametric. He wasn't looking for a nice niche where he could survive or take on one of the weaker competitors. He was thinking in terms of beating the biggest competitor of all.

What was Costello's first priority, given his early assessment of Cad.Lab and its situation? "They needed sales and marketing help. They were not on the map, outside of Italy. I'm focused on one thing: put 'em on the map." Reasonable enough. But did vision have anything to do with the sales and marketing help they needed? Or with putting Cad.Lab on the map?

Cad.Lab was missing a piece, he said. They intuitively knew the right kinds of product features. In general, they were headed the right way, guided by their customer experience, but the positioning of the company was all wrong.

"The market divides into two pieces, basically. There's the high-end guys: Parametric Technology, SDRC, Unigraphics, CATIA, et cetera. All UNIX. All $25,000 plus per user. Closed systems. There's the low end: Autodesk and a couple new guys, SolidWorks, Solid Edge . . . About $4,000. All Windows. Much lower functionality. No improving. Everything on the high end is UNIX, everything on the low end is Windows. Cad.Lab: $12,000. Right in the middle. In every way it's right in the middle.

"So I said to our guys, 'Look, one of two things. You either hit the sweet spot, like, whoa, no one figured out this is exactly where everybody wants to be, or you're positioned in no man's land.' Truth is, they're positioned in no man's land. No one wants something right there."

Ah, but where should Cad.Lab go to get out of the middle, out of no man's land? From my early discussions with Costello, I had the clear impression he wanted to challenge the high end directly, take on Parametric Technology. That appealed to his competitive spirit. But this was still early on in the process of forming his vision for Cad.Lab. He hadn't announced it in public yet. He was still working on it. What was he doing, if he was following his model of working with vision?

■ SIMULATE

The first part of Costello's model calls for creating and articulating a vision. In this case—as CEOs frequently do in Silicon Valley—Costello joined a company that already had a product and already had an idea where it was going. It may already have had a vision, even if a piece was missing. So he wasn't inventing or creating a vision from scratch. But Costello still went back to the first step in the process. The first step turns out to be mostly about simulation.

To build a model he could simulate in his head, Costello relied on the resources closest to him. He talked at great length with the founders of Cad.Lab, who after all had been in the industry for 18 years already. He read the reports of

JOE COSTELLO ON SIMULATION AND VISION

One of the fundamental dynamics is, you simulate. With vision you're trying to build a new reality. You have to build your own picture of it with as much detail as you can. You're an artist of the mind building this abstract concept, first for yourself.

It turns out these worlds are hard to create. It depends on the scale, but generally they're hard to create. Sometimes you think, "This is really cool, but. . . ." Forget it. It was a fun idea, but not worth it. Then you find one and, "Wow! Imagine that world! Wow! That's cool!" Then you start filling it out. Start playing with more pieces of it. And you make sure it makes sense. Is it a neat world? Is the world a better place? What's the world going to look like if these things come true? What is it that changes? Are there any funny side effects? Are there too many conflicts? But once you get excited about it, then you've got to say, "Great! That's the world I want."

Now let's compare it to where we are today. What does it take to get from here to there? What are some of the fundamental obstacles? How are you going to drag this world to that world? You can begin to see the dynamic, after you've done a lot of internal simulation. A lot of times, people don't do that with vision. They don't do enough simulation.

respected industry analysts like Charles Foundalier. He read what financial analysts had to say. He read a report for Cad.Lab written by Regis McKenna's marketing consulting company. He read the financial reports of all his competitors.

As he was developing a picture of what the marketing and sales strategy for Cad.Lab should be, he worked with the salespeople in Cad.Lab. They were close to customers, and so their reactions would be a good test. They liked some of what he had to say, but were doubtful about other parts. Disagreement or doubt prompted Costello to study more, ask for more data. He talked with the engineers who wrote the software programs for Cad.Lab, hoping to learn something that would give him an edge in the competition he was gearing up for. "Most high-tech execs don't know what they've got!" he said. "They really don't know what they have because they don't talk with their engineers enough."

Most high-tech execs don't know what they have because they don't talk with their engineers enough.

Finally, after he had a good idea of what Cad.Lab had to offer and where it should go, Costello would start talking directly to customers, to get their input and their reaction to his ideas. Logically, in the model he was building, the customers and their needs come first. "It starts with the customer," Joe said. "What do they really want? What are their real needs? Then you ask yourself, 'Where are all my obstacles? Competitors?' It gives you the lay of the land. 'Aha! There's my best shot! That's my angle. There's the landing spot. That's where I'm going to go.'" Costello began by looking at the customer from Cad.lab's point of view and by looking at what Cad.Lab had to offer them. Only then did he go talk with real customers.

The picture Costello was forming, the world he was simulating, didn't come from thin air. And it didn't come primarily from him. It came from what he read and from all the people he was talking to. "I'm no genius," he said. *"They* told *me!* I just listened up to what they were saying." Some of it didn't make sense. He ignored that. But some of it did make sense. The market needed to be shaken up, but no one had stood up and said so, because they all had vested interests and were protecting themselves. "Now by the way, that was a strength I had at Cadence. We had vested interests. I still would speak the truth. That has some negatives, but it's worse *not* to be truthful. No matter what pain you suffer in speaking the truth, it's better than the opposite."

No matter what pain you suffer in speaking
the truth, it's better than the opposite.

■ THE VISION

Now came time for the results of Costello's simulation. I
asked him to explain Cad.Lab's vision and positioning. "This
whole market can be reduced to a very simple picture," he
said. He drew a graph, with price on the vertical axis, increasing from bottom to top, and function on the horizontal
axis, going from a simple two-dimensional drawing on the
left to more complex, three-dimensional solids modeling on
the right. "This is 2D in the lower left-hand corner, with less
function and low price. And up here in the upper right corner you've got 3D. The 3D market has been split among four
players: Parametric Technology, CATIA, SDRC, and Unigraphics. The 2D market is basically all Autodesk." That was
it, nothing else, and it had stayed that way for 10 years. There
had been some consolidation in the 3D market, and growth,
but nothing significant had happened.

Costello saw a change coming in the 2D market. What
had been priced at $3,500 was now available for $400 from
Visio, a company in Seattle started by some of the founders
of Aldus. And they were only one among several, which was
the natural thing. It had been 10 years—same function, no
change in price. The whole world was standardized, the gold
standard being AutoCad and 2D drawing. "It blows my mind,
but that's what everybody used. That's what you exchanged
data on. Government agencies used it."

Suddenly 2D customers were wondering why they
couldn't have 3D. They had been using PCs and Windows; if
they wanted 3D, they had to get a workstation from Silicon
Graphics or Sun or someone like that. They couldn't step up
to 3D with the hardware or software they had. "Our whole
goal was: new gold standard. Or better than that: a platinum
standard. The platinum standard was going to be Cad.Lab

and 3D. Same price point as AutoCad. Runs on a PC and Windows. Why would anyone work in 2D when they could work in 3D using the same platform? It was a natural stepping stone. Now everyone could do all their work in 3D."

That was the solution to Cad.Lab's positioning problem and the first expression of its vision. To move out of no man's land, Cad.Lab would not move up in price to directly challenge Parametric. Instead, it would move down in price to where Autodesk was the standard. But it would offer the kind of functionality that previously was only available from companies like Parametric. That way, Cad.Lab would challenge both leaders in the mechanical CAD/CAM market.

■ SELL

The next step in Costello's model calls for selling the vision he articulated. In addition to passion, the simulation he's done provides focus and purpose.

"If you've done the simulation right, then it's not so hard to sell your vision. Because no matter who you're interacting with, there's something in it for them. I'm talking about a world we're going to be in together. So, whoever they are, I can start showing them what it's going to be like for them."

If you've done the simulation right, then
it's not so hard to sell your vision.

In the sales process, Costello focuses primarily on the different world his vision contemplates, not on the particular product he wants to sell to help create that world. The different world has to include other people and their needs and desires. At a minimum, his customers have to like his vision too, for themselves, so he uses their input to improve the vision. Selling and simulation must be closely linked. You need to go back and forth between them.

JOE COSTELLO ON SELLING

Your model gets *much* more detailed as you interact in the sales process, because you learn things really quickly. You can't do it all yourself. Selling is as much a piece of building the vision as when you're doing it yourself. Your model gets better. You start learning more about it from other points of view.

All right, now I'm testing this against you, OK? You start telling me your view. If I can really get you into it, I've infected you with my vision, right? Now we're both looking at this new world, we're both talking about it and imagining it. It doesn't matter if you don't like it, that's OK. That's actually good. *Why* don't you like it? Oh, good. Gee, it's going to be bad for these people, and they're hostile because of *that.* Now you've got to make some decisions. Are they hostile for good reason? If so, you should modify your model. Or is it just resistance? People aren't comfortable with change just because of fear—usually it's fear or greed.

That whole process is super powerful. That's why selling, good selling, is exciting. Because not only are you convincing people of what you see, but you can see just how good your vision is. Sometimes visions die during that phase. You realize, "You know, it was better for me, but it was too personal. It doesn't really have enough stuff." And you can see why. Sometimes a vision doesn't appeal to enough people. Sometimes there's too much resistance. It's not the right time. All these things have their own time.

Selling is also experimentation for Costello. It is a method he consciously uses to improve his vision. And he doesn't mind getting negative reactions to his sales efforts—he views people who don't like his vision as the best sources for learning more and improving it. The important thing is to improve and spread his vision, not to be right.

Just 30 days after his appointment as chairman was announced, Costello began selling his vision for Cad.Lab in public. At an important industry conference called Daratech, he announced Cad.Lab's vision. For him, this presentation was a test, a simulation. And, he said, "it resonated." I wasn't surprised Costello had felt ready and willing to go public in so short a time, even though many executives would never have done that. Earlier, while we were discussing simulation, he had said, "I guess you could go out and test a vision separately from selling. But you might as well move right to stage two, right? In the interest of efficiency, put them in parallel. Start convincing the right people. You can fall flat if the vision's not quite fleshed out enough. So you do want to make sure you test it until you're really confident. Then you go after the *big* obstacles between you and getting it done." Linking simulation and sales as closely as Costello does requires some confidence, but it has the merit of moving the process along quickly.

The confidence and passion that come from vision also help attract people's attention. Soon after Daratech, Cad.Lab went to a big manufacturing trade show in Chicago. Costello didn't want to set up a small booth and give away brochures and pens with the company logo on them, which is the normal routine at these events.

To take another step in putting the company on the map, Cad.Lab gave away a hundred Palm Pilots, digital cameras, and TVs at the trade show. To receive one of these prizes, attendees had to be wearing a Cad.Lab T-shirt so that a Blues Brothers character might come up to them and give them a prize. Cad.Lab gave away 4,000 T-shirts and got 4,000 leads in return. The floor of the trade show became a sea of these shirts. And on the plane ride back to Santa Clara, Joe saw people still wearing them, still chanting the Blues Brothers chant they'd used at the show. Cad.Lab had gotten some attention.

In solving the market positioning problem Cad.Lab faced, Costello simultaneously brought more focus and logic to the company's sales efforts. Before, Cad.Lab had been trying to sell to everyone. When you're in the middle, in no man's land, anyone looks like they might be a customer.

Cad.Lab's salesforce would try to sell to the low-end customers. But naturally, that was a struggle because they didn't want to pay a higher price. The salesforce would also try to sell to the high-end customers. But they wouldn't believe in Cad.Lab because it was "this weird, funky company." The salesforce would partner with anyone who got their attention. "They were all over the place," said Costello "until I told them, 'That's our sweet spot.'"

Once Costello convinced Cad.Lab's salesforce of the new vision, they could identify the potential partners they really wanted and get their attention. They made it a clear and top priority to work hard and closely with Toyota, an extremely important customer Cad.Lab had managed to penetrate before rivals like Parametric could do it. That customer alone would give Cad.Lab tremendous credibility in the marketplace. And they would work at bringing 3D to the 2D world.

Costello explained that the new vision also helped Cad.Lab focus its product development efforts and be more decisive in completing the transition to the new computing platform it had chosen. The engineers stopped all UNIX development, although Cad.Lab still provided products on UNIX. Costello believes in making your commitment to the future. "Place your bets and go like hell! This is not a wild risk, why hedge your bets? And you can't do that if you're the other guys. See, I also like to do things other people can't do."

Make your commitment to the future.
Place your bets and go like hell!

All this work in selling Cad.Lab's vision is part of what Costello calls "getting alignment." You have to understand alignment if you want to understand vision from his point of view. During our first conversation when I asked him what he looked for in selling a vision he said, "You've got to get alignment of all the parties." When I talked to him while he was still introducing himself to industry analysts and testing his vision before going public with it, he told me the alignment had started. Now it was time to align internal people—sales, engineering, marketing people. "We'll start getting alignment there. Then we go execute." Focusing the salesforce on the right customers and the engineering team on the right projects was part of this internal alignment.

More than that, alignment is an important result Costello seeks in selling his vision. It is not an overstatement to say it's the main goal of the sales process. He believes alignment is about amplifying your power by having other people share your vision and promote your vision. "And by the way, every time they do it they *add* to it. Once they're on your team, they have great ideas. You don't have the only good ideas. Start adding. They ask questions and make suggestions and you think 'That's a good one.' Reinforce it. As soon as you reinforce the good idea they *really* feel a part of your team. Right? Your idea is better. Now they're invested in it."

Alignment is about amplifying your power by having other people share your vision and promote your vision.

The effort Costello put into getting alignment from within Cad.Lab itself raised a question in my mind. As chairman and managing director of Cad.Lab, he was the boss. Why not simply give the order: *This is the new vision, now go execute it!*? I've seen it done that way elsewhere. Costello laughed when I asked him. "In knowledge-based companies, you can't order people to do anything." What may have worked with assembly-line workers when Henry Ford started his company, or with coal miners, doesn't work in modern knowledge-based industry. "You don't order anybody to do anything. I used to tease people. They'd say, 'You're the boss. You can do anything you want.' I said, 'Really? Try it someday. You try being the boss someday.' You can't do whatever you want. If you are not thinking vision and selling people on it so it becomes *their* vision, you just can't be effective."

Costello believes the corporate structure we've had for the past 25 to 30 years—what he calls the post-industrial model of organization, which is basically just a modification of the old industrial model—is going to die. It won't fly going forward. In his view, we have to come up with a new structure, and the thing that will bind people to the modern corporation is vision. "It is *the* most important bond that people form. It's their reason for joining an organization or group. It's the vision. I think it's the single most important piece, it's the magnetism. And that's true for any group of human beings. I don't care if they're a country, or a state, or local group, or the NRA, you name the organization. Any group of humans. The bond is the vision. I think companies have been too much *not* that."

The thing that will bind people to the
modern corporation is vision.

Costello identifies two components that bond people in the modern organization: the vision of *what* and the values for *how* something will be done. "If everybody owns those, you're free to make all your own choices. There are a lot of underlying mechanics, like project teams and organization, but that's the execution piece."

For Costello, selling vision is simultaneously a series of experiments and an effort to achieve alignment. The result is a better vision and a group of people united by the same purpose.

■ SURF

Having developed his vision through simulation, and having sold it to learn where he could improve it and to get alignment, Costello and Cad.Lab were now ready to execute their vision. Make it real. Since Costello was focusing much of his energy on sales and marketing issues, I asked him what marketing channels he planned to use to communicate Cad.Lab's vision. It was then that he raised the metaphor of surfing big waves. Not just any surfing, but surfing *big* waves like those that rise in the winter on parts of the north shore of Oahu, or off the coast of Half Moon Bay near Silicon Valley at Maverick's break. Surfing these big waves is as different from ordinary surfing as climbing Mt. Everest is from walking up a hill in San Francisco. Not many people would even try.

I asked Costello what marketing channels he planned to use and how he planned to use them. He asked if I'd heard about the recent K2 Challenge—$50,000 to the guy who surfed the largest wave. He has a collage of the guy on the winning wave—an unbelievable picture. He put it up because he thinks that running a high-tech company today is a lot like surfing a big wave: You've really got to be prepared. "These guys don't just wander out into the surf. People who do get in trouble. So, you've built your skills, you've thought through carefully how you're going to attack it, how you're going to get out there, how you're going to set up, where your problems are. You're thinking through the whole thing. Planning your strategy, setting your vision. But once you get on the wave, you forget all that, your mind is gone. Complete intuition. Your mind gets in the way. It's all feel. If you asked me whether I thought I'd crouch or if I'd be standing upright, I'd have to answer, 'I don't know. You tell me after I'm done.'"

> Running a high-tech company today is a
> lot like surfing a big wave.

For Costello in his own work as a chief executive, the homework he does in developing and selling a vision is ultimately aimed at a sense of intuition. Vision is a way of knowing what he's doing that:

➤ Starts out analytically as he *dissects* a situation in his mind;

➤ Becomes synthetic as he develops an understanding and a model around an explanatory and fundamental dynamic;

➤ Moves on to a social process of sharing this model and improving it;

➤ And then becomes internalized again, only now as pure intuition.

Vision is analytic, synthetic, social, and finally intuitive knowledge. The point of vision for an executive, for the specific responsibility of execution, is to form and educate and impassion a sense of intuition. Vision is not a plan, but a sense of knowing what you're doing and where you're headed.

How would Cad.Lab get its message get out? Returning to the surfing metaphor, he pointed out that the guy who goes out to ride a big wave doesn't get an itty-bitty sport board suitable for hot dogging, he gets a nice long board. "At Cadence, going into a market where a hundred customers represented 90 percent of the business was very different from Cad.Lab's market where there are a hundred thousand or more customers. So, there are certain things you plan for. But, beyond that, once you get into the big wave, you've got to play it by ear."

The Cad.Lab T-shirts and the Blues Brothers giving away Palm Pilots at the Chicago trade show was one example of Costello playing it by ear. Others would follow, inspired by something he heard on the radio or read in the newspaper, sparked by someone he met with or happened to see. As long as he's moving and learning, Costello is not afraid of making mistakes. "As I told the guys in Cad.Lab, whatever we do, we're probably not right." But *not* having a vision, in his view, confuses customers, confuses engineering, and muddles the marketing message. "You don't know what to do! Which things should we do and which shouldn't we do? Everything looks good or everything looks bad if you're not clear about it. As soon as you get clarity, the tree trims quickly."

Not having a vision confuses customers, confuses engineering, and muddles the marketing message.

Costello's willingness to try things and make mistakes does not mean he's willing to try random things. He doesn't seem to move just for the sake of moving, in the belief that any movement is better than none. Some executives do that, but it's not what Costello's vision-fueled intuition would lead him to do. His intuition also provides him with a sense of understanding of the world he's dealing with.

The intense simulation Costello talks about in developing a vision sounds like it leads to a kind of creative madness. To the point where someone working on a vision would see a different reality than those around him. "Absolutely, it does. *And know that it's real.* That's what gives you this incredible ability to execute with absolute commitment. Maybe it's even a trick of the mind: 'Yes, this is just a temporary state we're going through, I know where we're headed.' Maybe it sounds strange to people, but if you're on a train, you know where you're going to end up. This track goes to Topeka, Kansas. Well by god you're going to get there. There's a certain point when that becomes clear in these things. We're going to get there. For sure."

Trains in the real world are one thing. Bringing a vision into reality is another. Presumably, the world can change in many ways, but it doesn't have to change in the direction of one person's vision. So I pressed him to tell me how he could be so sure that a vision of his would actually become real. "You know," he said, "train tracks can blow up, and there are derailments, and there are forks, and someone can throw the wrong switches so you don't get to Topeka. But with rare exceptions, there is a point at which you know it's for sure. It's as sure as you're going to get to Topeka, Kansas when the line goes to Topeka, Kansas. And it's not just because you have confidence. Obviously, you *are* confident. But it's the dynamics in this meta world, or whatever you want to call it. If you look around at reality there, the forces are just as powerful as two train tracks and the wheels of a train—at a certain point."

There is a point at which you know it's for sure.

Trains on tracks. Surfers on big waves. Both images conjure up tremendous forces. One of the purposes of vision is to come to understand these forces through simulation.

Another purpose is to develop the intuition to work with them, to use them, by aligning with them. None of the men I talked to for this book wants to fight against forces like these. As Costello put it, "I want to get the wind at my back."

■ THE WORLD IN 3D

For Costello, vision is a "picture of a different world." In our first conversation, before he had joined Cad.Lab and perhaps before he even knew of the company, he said something that foreshadowed the picture he would later paint for me. While we were talking about simulating different worlds he told me he'd been thinking and hoping that our technology would become good enough to actually start building those worlds for people on the computer. "Some way to get the feeling of it, a little of the drama. Right now it's words and arm waving, and," he stopped and laughed, "something. Sometimes I can feel it, I can see it, but I can't. . . ."

He told me he used to dream of unbelievable symphonies. When he woke up he could even hum them. He doesn't have any musical training. "I don't know anything about music. And so I was kind of like a dumb person being handed a great oration. I couldn't have translated that . . . I would have loved to be able to write that down."

He explained that he feels like we're very limited as humans today. In his view, lucky ones are decent at selling, painting this new world with words that somehow someone else can catch little glimpses of. "If I could paint some of those worlds, if I could somehow merge myself with artists and start to build pictures of these things . . . that would be really cool. Then I or anyone could get farther faster."

It turns out that this ability to use computers to help simulate the different worlds pictured in visions is very closely tied to the future Costello sees Cad.Lab contributing to. To begin with, Cad.Lab wants to bring 3D tools to the world of mechanical engineering.

In explaining how Cad.Lab would change the engineering world, Costello said we live in and interact in a 3D world.

The only place we live in 2D is when we go to a PC and AutoCad or to a drawing board. We actually force people to learn to create in 2D. Psychological studies have shown that most people are incapable of translating 2D drawings into 3D images. It's a skill that some people have, but most don't. So, he wondered, why would you do that? "It would be different if we all were flat and trying to imagine another dimension. We're not—we're 3D. 3D is actually quite natural. The reason people don't do it is that it has cost too much and the technology hasn't been right. We're going to change the way people do their work. We're going to let them work in a way that's natural, in 3D."

We're going to change the way people do their work.

To anyone who is not an engineer, the change in mental and bureaucratic habits represented by this change to 3D may be hard to appreciate. A little explanation may help. The mechanical engineering process goes through four basic phases:

1. *Concept:* The artistic beginning of the process, in which product ideas are sketched out or, as in the case of automobiles, modeled to decide on style, function, and similar considerations.
2. *Design:* The engineering heart of the process, in which products are drawn or modeled in detail to plan the parts that go into them and to make sure they all fit together and will hold up under expected use and abuse.
3. *Drafting:* The part of the process in which the assembled whole and the parts of the product are drawn in detail to help guide the manufacturing department in actually fabricating and assembling them.
4. *Manufacturing:* Which takes the drawings and develops the instructions and plans for making what they represent, including developing programs for machine tools.

In most companies today, these four phases are distinctly separate. If 3D tools are used at all, they're used mostly in the second—design—phase. Except for certain industries like automobiles and aircraft that use very expensive surface modeling systems, the concept phase uses 2D tools like those offered by Autodesk, or they simply use paper. Drafting is almost totally 2D. So is manufacturing—except of course for the real manufacturing floor where products are actually made. None of this may seem so odd or problematic until you consider how these phases fit together. Or don't.

As Costello describes it, the concept world, whatever they use, is completely divided from the next phase. Once you've got a concept you hand it to someone who's a designer and they say, "Let me see if I can make it." They have to start all over again, using different tools. So, in design you get a drawing of some kind, unless you're in one of the great big auto companies. But in any case, you have to do a translation—say to solids modeling. Then you send it to drafting and what do they do? They take the 3D thing you built and start again—making a 2D version. "The really bizarre thing is that they actually take a 3D thing and reduce it back to two dimensions." And then, when they go to manufacturing, they have to go back to three dimensions.

"To show you how stupid that is, a lot of 2D drawings don't tell you enough to get to a manufactured 3D part. The gap is filled in by humans. And that's what their job is—they're human processors, human CAD packages filling in all the gaps. But what's completely ludicrous is that the part was already completely specified back in the design phase. Completely specified." But all that information has been lost in the translations now required in the engineering process. It's very inefficient. The whole point is to get them all to 3D. "We want to help people move the whole process from 2D to 3D."

In Cad.Lab's system, there are no boundaries. You can sketch, you can draw, you can make elaborate complex surfaces. Make 2D versions and 3D versions. Solid models. "That was the big architectural insight of our founding team. Why not put it all together? In the old days, you wouldn't because the only thing that would run on a PC was in 2D. The only thing that would run on a workstation was solids modeling. If you wanted to do complex surfaces like for a car or airplane, then you needed extremely expensive computers and high-end graphics. So they were three separate worlds. Now, a home PC can run high-end surfacing packages better than what 95 percent of people in the business use. It costs $2,500 dollars. By Christmas it will cost $2,000. So, hardware is no longer a barrier."

What will be the effect of 3D systems like Cad.Lab's on the world of mechanical engineering? Costello sees the 2D world becoming lower priced in the next four or five years, then diminishing in importance. The 3D world will become the new center point. "We get people working in 3D. Much of the high-end world will collapse into the standard 3D, PC world, except for the very highest end, where it's very service intensive."

Costello sees more than just the world of mechanical engineering changing. As he became animated again, he said, "Well, look at us." *[He held up the pen he'd been sketching with.]* "With all of our tools, we're still like cavemen, scratching in the sand. Just a little fancier stick and a little fancier sand. And think about it. We're training a new generation of kids who are starting to get used to receiving in 3D. They're just starting now in video games and stuff. Well, after you get used to consuming it, the next thing is, 'I want to create that way.'"

Cad.Lab, according to Costello, "has found an artist who's really a nut about this. Now people are really starting to work on the question of how you *do* create things in 3D. What tools should be used?" Costello thinks that's incredibly exciting, a brave new world. We live and interact in a 3D world. Our mental model of the universe is intrinsically 3D until we try to abstract. "And then we do this silly thing that translates it into 2D—because it's our only pathetic means of communication. Let's get out of that translation. Let's allow ourselves to create, think, and fiddle in the world of 3D abstractions. These are the things I think will become possible in the next five years."

Our mental model of the universe is
intrinsically 3D until we try to abstract.

■ SECRETS TO SUCCESS

One of the secrets to success in simulating, selling, and executing a vision is to be good at and balanced in all three phases of the vision process. In Costello's view, imbalance is probably one of the biggest problems with leadership. It's what often makes people ineffective. Some people are good at execution once they know what to do, but they need some help to get that initial vision, that initial direction clear.

When I asked him how balanced he thought he was, Costello said he probably feels strongest in the first, vision or simulation piece. It comes most naturally to him. "And the selling part of it . . . You know, they all go hand in hand. If you get really excited about a vision, wow! You can improve your sales skills always. But the truth is, your passion sells like crazy. And if you really really believe in a vision, you can't stand it if it's not getting done. So you improve your execution skills to the level needed to get stuff done."

But he also said he could find a hole in everything—his vision, his selling skills, and his execution. In his role of chairman, everything is different. He's doing multiple things and has to learn to execute differently to do them efficiently and effectively. "So, the place I'm putting effort in improving my own process is execution."

A second secret to success in Costello's approach to vision is the way it involves other people. He sees an amazing difference and subtlety about vision. Two people can say almost exactly the same thing: One is motivating and the other one is ho-hum. He cited his vision for Cad.Lab as an example. In a lot of ways, what he said wasn't much different from what others had said. Certainly people had said part of it. "It's not like I've been in this business forever or invented the thing. I'm still an observer."

Costello defines one difference as the synthesis. Why is the synthesis so important? Like an incomplete thought or sentence, partial ideas might catch your attention, but synthesis gives them bite. "But the biggest difference, what really captures people's attention, is when you involve them. When you present enough potential and possibility to let them imagine themselves being part of it. Show them a world that's bigger and more interesting, more open. If you can open a person's mind somehow, in what you say and the way you say it, that's what sticks."

To really capture people's attention, involve them.

According to Costello, people often don't say what they're trying to say. They don't present a possibility, an opportunity, in a mind-expanding way. They do the opposite—they dissect. He dissects, too, to get to the essence, but then he puts it all back together in a way that, hopefully, opens more space for people. He has always marveled at people who are landscape architects and golf course architects. "They can walk into the most weird, screwed up, odd-looking piece of ground, and they see beauty in it. They see the essence, the nice rolling hill here, and the juxtaposition of the rock and foliage there. They can imagine all the crap going away, the essence still being there, gorgeous and beautiful. And it's mind expanding, it's opened a new horizon, a new vision of things. That's what I try to do—take the fundamental elements and the essence, and then resynthesize, so people see new possibilities. That's the hook, I think, so people see a bigger world."

Take the fundamental elements and
the essence, and then resynthesize.

In Costello's view, many people attempt to dominate, to blur, to close off thought and discussion. At Daratech, he said, everybody talked, typically, about how great they were and how they really had the right idea. "My presentation hardly had anything to do with us at all, until the end. I saw a sea of opportunity and a changing world. I challenged people to look at all the dynamics, the fundamentals. You can just say it, but I had plenty of convincing material and I dissected it enough to convey that thought of a sea of opportunity, of the world as a better place. At the end, I talked about how I thought we fit in and why. But the more important part of the message, what people walked away with, was, 'Wow. It's an exciting world.' If you paint that picture and it's substantive for people, that's what makes the difference."

Chapter

The Next Logical Step: Jim Clark, Chairman of Healtheon, former Chairman of Silicon Graphics and Netscape

If Silicon Valley in the last 20 years of the twentieth century could be symbolically represented by one human being, one of the best candidates would be James Clark. During that time, this former UC Santa Cruz and Stanford University professor founded several of Silicon Valley's most celebrated companies. And he doesn't seem about to stop. Many of the forces that have defined Silicon Valley—including its drive for wealth, its understanding of how technology can create new markets, and its accommodating though sometimes caustic attitudes toward power—are concentrated and whirling within this one man. He has been widely called a visionary for all his pioneering success, though he's not sure the label fits. With considerable energy, he continues to focus on some new domain that interests him, sees the next logical step it must take, feels a sense of conviction about his insight, and then, with a positive attitude, works quickly to take advantage of that next step. Vision powerfully directs and helps energize the beginning of this work, like a rocket sending a satellite into space. But soon after, and with Clark's agreement, other forces take over—with mixed results for the companies though generally positive results for Clark.

As of 1999 when I met with him, Jim Clark had launched three companies successfully and was in the final moments of countdown for a fourth. In 1981, he started Silicon Graphics, Inc. (SGI), based on an integrated circuit he designed and built at Stanford that made 3D computer graphics faster and more affordable. Silicon Graphics has been a major player in computer-aided design and manufacturing and in many fields of research as well. It became known to consumers for making the computers that produced spectacular special effects in movies like *Jurassic Park* and *Titanic*. However, by the late 1990s SGI was struggling as cheaper PCs increasingly offered the sophisticated 3D graphics that only its far more expensive systems used to offer.

In 1994, Clark left SGI to launch Netscape Communications Corporation with Marc Andreessen. Netscape's browser almost instantly became the primary interface for the growing millions of computer users who wanted access to the World Wide Web. In fact, it can be argued that Netscape's browser was the primary catalyst that started the explosive growth of the web. Netscape was so successful and seemed to be so important to the future of the Internet and its combination of communications and computing that it quickly attracted the attention of Microsoft. Microsoft developed its own browser and used all its considerable resources to move Netscape out of the new space it had defined on the computer desktop. Clark believes Microsoft used unfair, monopolistic practices in this battle, but in any case, Netscape lost and gave up its independence when America Online (AOL) acquired the struggling company late in 1998. Nevertheless, Netscape played a pioneering role in the ongoing computer revolution.

In 1996, while still chairman of Netscape, Clark founded Healtheon Corporation, an Internet-based company providing a wide variety of services to the healthcare industry. In 1999, just three years after it was founded, Healtheon expected to earn $100 million in revenue. After an earlier initiative in 1998 was dropped, it went public in February 1999 and its shares immediately quadrupled in price, giving Healtheon a market value of $2.2 billion. This enthusiastic public welcome would have been an astonishing surprise except for the other-worldly pattern set by earlier Internet companies—beginning with Netscape. In May of 1999, some three months after going public, Healtheon agreed to a merger with WebMD, changing the name of the combined company to WebMD.

The same week Healtheon went public, Clark was set to launch a fourth company, MYCFO, to integrate into one system all the financial information and transactions of high net worth individuals like himself. The company was so new that the first day we met at MYCFO's Menlo Park offices, Clark, who is officially a resident of Florida, was introducing himself to a number of MYCFO's start-up employees for the first time. Clark was also considering starting an online, consumer version of this company somewhat later, to be called MYCFO.com.

In launching these companies, Jim Clark has used a similar pattern of vision. He has also followed a pattern of turning these companies over to a CEO—and to other driving and guiding forces—as soon as possible. All of which adds up to three connected fables about vision—and the beginning of a fourth.

■ BACKGROUND

According to Clark, "If you end up being successful, people say you have vision, and if not they consider you a quack." Although vision is a relatively new term as applied to business, in print and in casual conversation, people widely take it for granted that vision lies behind every invention and innovation, as if the effect proved the cause. That is not necessarily true. There isn't a vision guiding every new success, nor a lack of vision responsible for every failure. As usual, the real story is more complex. Jim Clark's story reflects that complexity.

If you end up being successful, people say you have vision, and if not they consider you a quack.

When asked if vision is part of how he thinks about and carries out his own work Clark said, "Vision's a term a lot of people have used since the early 1980s, since I've been in business. It's something that's been ascribed to me, at Silicon Graphics especially. Many people use that term pretty flippantly. I think it applies to the person who's setting the direction, on the assumption they're a little taller than everyone else. I don't apply it to myself, although I do say things like 'I see this coming.'"

Clark is not being modest. If he thought vision should be ascribed to him, or if he consciously worked with it, he'd say so. Perhaps the only reason he's thought about vision is that other people have said he has it. Clark does not think of vision as an art or practice or process that someone engages in, which is how most of the CEOs I interviewed for this book spoke of it and which is how I usually think of it. Rather, he seems to believe it is an attribute or perhaps a special faculty certain people possess, whether as a gift or something earned. Clark is uncomfortable, or at least uncertain, in saying he has it.

"I'm trying to think of some examples that seem to indicate I have it, but I'm not sure they lead to what people refer to as vision. I don't think any of us has that much ability to self-reflect and see ourselves outside of ourselves. We just try to make sense of things. I usually think of it in terms of just putting things together based on my body of experience as opposed to what somebody else's might have been."

Clark's thinking was influenced most by physics. He studied for a doctorate in physics, then switched to computer science in the early 1970s. But he says his physics training has done more to help him understand the world, from a technology point of view, than anything else he's done. Physics is a very comprehensive field. It's mechanics, electricity, electronics, quantum mechanics, and a great deal of applied mathematics. Physics helps you develop some very comprehensive tools for a technological perspective. "I also developed an intuitive sense. Whether I already had that I can't really say. But I know physics gave me a lot of equipment to interpret the world. I think that's one key in my educational background."

Physics gave me a lot of equipment to interpret the world.

In computer science, Clark focused much of his attention on computer graphics, where the geometry seemed to him an extension of the mathematics of physics. But because of his physics background, he never restricted himself to software. He also learned to design hardware. "I really got a kick out of that. I thought it was neat to be able to build things. Build electronic circuits." He worked for a computer company in the summer and learned to appreciate simultaneous design, which is a characteristic of hardware design as opposed to software. Software is very linear; one thing follows another. In hardware, you tend to have lots of linear things going on in parallel. And he said, "You have to think that way. That was a mind-expanding way to think." But Clark never restricted himself to hardware or software. He thinks the reason was, in part, that while in the Navy he was in electronics, he studied applied physics, and both sides started to come together for him.

I asked Clark to describe what he means when he says he "sees" certain things coming. "I just instinctively know certain things are going to develop. I think most of that comes from having assimilated enough knowledge from enough different areas. You get a sense that something is the logical next step. For example, business and technology and marketing and science: I have an understanding of these things at a deep level. I have knowledge in enough different areas that I can see how things link together."

One other quality also emerged during his academic work. "I found that when I was in my best moods I was a great inspirational leader. I learned this at Stanford." He said he'd never been a leader, always a loner. At Stanford, he had an attitude change related to his divorce. Many things were going on, Clark told me, that culminated in a "psychic twist" that told him to be more positive in life. "I noticed a change almost immediately. Students began to gravitate toward me. I collected a group of about six or seven students and I said, 'Why don't we start a company?' and they said fine." The company was Silicon Graphics.

■ SILICON GRAPHICS

"When I came out here to Stanford, it was hard to pigeonhole me. I was in the Electrical Engineering department, and I wanted to learn how to design chips. So I learned how to design integrated circuits and I built a chip. This was the chip that eventually became Silicon Graphics. I never had any business experience, but I had a kind of innate instinct. If you're a good observer, you realize that companies are composed of certain constituents. There's a financial officer and all that. I put all that together and wrote up a business plan." That was how Silicon Graphics began. And that was the one company about which Clark feels most comfortable in being called a visionary.

When Clark describes how he started Silicon Graphics, it sounds almost casual. In fact, it was intense and purposeful. "I created it. I caused it to happen. I think it was conviction and a positive can-do attitude and collecting people with a similar attitude around me. People said I was a visionary because I seemed to know where I was going." He believed 3D graphics

---

It was conviction and a positive can-do attitude and collecting people with a similar attitude around me.

was important to the world. "I could see that, and you can call it vision if you want to." He saw it from a pure business perspective and knew people would buy the product. It was a tool for chemists and people doing 3D design. He said, "The world *is* 3D, so why wouldn't everyone want it? That was the basic vision I built Silicon Graphics around. If I've ever had a vision, the most significant one was that, because that was my company. I was with that company for 12 years."

Behind Silicon Graphics was a vision to put 3D graphics technology into more widespread use. It was all too expensive. Clark figured, make it a chip, make it cheaper. After he built the chip at Stanford, he went out and tried to license it. "Evans and Sutherland and DEC and all these people just stared blankly at me and asked why you needed that." Finally he decided he'd have to show them why. When he was an academic at UC Santa Cruz, it cost $300,000 to get a basic computer graphics set-up to do whatever research he wanted to do. It was too expensive. "That was what really motivated me, to make it cheaper. So, I guess you could say that was a vision, a pursuit of an ideal."

Make it a chip, make it cheaper.

The vision behind Silicon Graphics involved more than what Clark calls his instinct. It involved Clark's practical experience. He had personally experienced the difficulty of acquiring an expensive graphics computer while a professor. And before that, while still in graduate school in Utah, he'd worked for Evans and Sutherland, which makes high-end graphics systems, and so he also knew from experience there was a market for such systems. Beyond instinct and experience, the vision also involved his belief in an economic principle: He knew there was a small audience, mostly academics and R&D types. He sensed that all that was needed was to bring the price down. He reasoned that if there were terminals and workstations that essentially had a free 3D capability (because it was added in with the cost of the integrated circuits), software developers would develop applications that would use the capability. Clark knew from experience there were people who would pay for the high end. He explained, "I wanted to bring the high end to the low end. There's always a price-demand elasticity." In other words, cheaper 3D graphics would create a larger market.

Cheaper 3D graphics would create a larger market.

But Jim Clark's vision only launched Silicon Graphics; it didn't guide the company from there. He was the founder, not the CEO. "I was more interested in the success of the business than in running it. If I'd gotten the right operating officer, I think I could have done it. But I was just too timid to take the total responsibility and I wanted someone else to be the fall guy. I also wanted someone else because I thought they had more raw leadership to offer than I did." Silicon Graphics brought in Vernon Anderson for two years as the company was just getting started, and then brought in Ed McCracken to take it from there. McCracken was CEO, Clark was chairman. Over time, it became apparent the two had different ideas about what Silicon Graphics should be doing. And, as CEO, McCracken's ideas won. In actual practice, Clark's vision became irrelevant except as a source of friction between him and McCracken.

From the very beginning, Clark's idea of low-priced 3D graphics ran into difficulty. At first, it simply cost more to build the systems than he had hoped. But then it became difficult to convince SGI to focus resources on bringing the cost down drastically. "I erroneously thought I'd be able to bring 3D graphics to the low end, to personal computers, much sooner." It took years, for all kinds of reasons. One was just inertia. When a company starts doing business at a high price point, it doesn't move very readily down market. It's much easier to start with less power and lower price and add power later. "It wouldn't happen without an intense management effort, and there wasn't that effort. People were quite comfortable collecting 60 percent gross margins. They didn't want lower prices and therefore lower margins."

I asked Clark if *he* wanted to build products for a lower price. "Absolutely. All the time." In fact, he explained, if they had, Silicon Graphics would be much better off today. Sun Microsystems did and they got the market share for the UNIX business. The PC got the market share for the rest of the world. SGI was marginalized out of the business with its specialized graphics products.

The future for Silicon Graphics that Clark saw was not the one that led Silicon Graphics, despite his being a "very vocal" chairman advocating it. Why didn't his ideas prevail? According to Clark, people spend a lot of time doing what they've been doing. They don't spend much time doing what they haven't been doing. So in Ed McCracken's mind, getting to a lower price was an evolutionary process that would take years. SGI's management didn't want to sacrifice performance. It would have taken a dedicated three-year effort to produce the lower priced product that Clark wanted. McCracken was dedicated to getting product out every year and a half. So McCracken wouldn't commit the R&D because he didn't share Clark's view.

Clark wanted to have mainstream workstations that happened to have 3D graphics because then people would develop applications for them. 3D began creeping into CAD and other applications in the 1990s because the PC became powerful enough. "If it's there, there are certainly people who will use it. But forget 3D for a moment. I knew that real-time graphics was important. Instantaneous feedback, a real-time ability to pan and zoom and look at things. Since you have to do that in 3D in order to have 3D, we used to say 'If it doesn't move, it's not 3D.' You just design software differently when you have 3D in the system. You design with the user in the loop and that connects the computer to the person."

To make his point, Clark drew an analogy with a computer's user interface. You push a button and something happens. Imagine if you pushed one of those buttons and it took 10 seconds before something happened. Those were the kinds of delays 3D graphics faced in those days. The only place you could get instantaneous feedback was in 2D. That left out a whole set of applications. "You can't look at a 3D object without being able to move it around on a screen. Real-time 3D connects a user more intimately. I just felt that instinctively and preached the gospel for many years until finally SGI began to make lower priced products. And then they began to grow in the market. Two-thirds of the revenue started coming from the low end."

Real-time 3D connects a user more intimately.

The problem Clark saw was not just that a low-end strategy fit better with his ideal of ubiquitous, interactive 3D graphics. The problem was also that a high-end strategy, though perhaps doomed to fail in the long run, works for a while. So SGI didn't adopt Clark's view because a different view was producing good results. He explained that the high-end strategy is seductive; it hides the forthcoming collapse. He drew an analogy to a healthy building being eaten away by termites. One day, without warning, the building collapses. "In the end, all these ubiquitous programs on the PC like AutoCad become dominant. Eventually the high end just vaporizes, goes poof! You become marginalized, pushed to the tiny top of the pyramid." SGI was committed to that strategy. Then they bought Cray Computer, which epitomized it. And that, said Clark, was a disaster. "It's just the nature of a high-end thinker. So the big lesson I walked away with was, I wanted to be in a volume business. I also wanted to be out of the hardware business. That's a dead end. I didn't want to be at the high end of anything. I didn't really leave to do the Internet. I left to do something new and to *leave* Silicon Graphics."

Jim Clark left Silicon Graphics in March 1994, not quite 13 years after he founded it. He said that in advocating his own views against the contrary views of Ed McCracken, the two grew to dislike one another. Their enmity was no secret, but that was not the only reason Clark left. It was also no secret that he felt cheated by the way the venture capitalists who had funded SGI divided up the ownership pie. He left

Silicon Graphics feeling a bit cheated. "I wanted a real success. In economic terms." As an academic, he had thought that trying to make money was dirty. He was "a purist." But he came to think the economic motivation in business has to be number one.

Clark's economic motivation seemed to raise a contradiction. That same motivation led SGI to its high-end strategy. It led to making a lot of money in the short-term, but prevented the low-end strategy that Clark wanted and that over time proved to make more money. But the emotion behind Clark's argument about money has a much more personal than

---

JIM CLARK ON MONEY AND MOTIVATION

If making money isn't the number one priority, then the entrepreneur won't do the right things to make money, to make the company successful. And business is about making money.

The pure and simple metric of business is whether you're making enough money to sustain yourself. The company has to be self-sustaining at some point, or it's a black hole. By definition, companies are economic entities that become self-sustaining. Which means they make money. So if money isn't your goal, you shouldn't be in business. The people who own part of the company get to share in the wealth. And that translates into money in your pocket. By simple Aristotelian logic, if you're not interested in money in your pocket, you're probably not going to make a successful company. You shouldn't start it in the first place—you should stay in academia. I'm economically motivated. And Silicon Graphics wasn't a very big economic success for me. I didn't have a big enough piece of it by the time it saw the light of day, and I didn't get along with the CEO, so I just quit. I'm motivated by economics.

communal focus. He was talking about something that affected him more than his company. He was also making it clear that he felt worse about not having a great economic success than about his ideas not being implemented. It was enough that his ideas got the business started, but next time he wanted a bigger piece of the pie.

■ NETSCAPE

According to Clark, Netscape was really the vision of Marc Andreessen. Andreessen saw what was happening with the Internet, what could be done. Clark wanted to make a business out of it. And so, Clark explained, he taught Andreessen a little about business and Andreessen taught Clark a lot about the Internet in a period of about two months. And they both realized they had to get running if they wanted to be out in front and make things happen, because the Internet was about to explode. "That was vision. And there were many people who thought I certifiably belonged in the asylum. People thought I was nuts. Larry Ellison was quoted as saying, 'You can't make money on the Internet. The Internet's too slow.' There was all this babble coming out of people's mouths, and Andreessen and I were just saying 'Great, I hope they keep thinking that.'"

Clark was motivated, as he said, by the desire to have a big personal economic win. But he could also see what was coming: that the Internet was going to be an explosion and was going to change the nature of advertising. "You can call it vision, but it's only common sense to me. I didn't think of it as vision as much as a conviction that the computer revolution is still on-going, maybe only just starting when coupled with communications. This was in 1994. I went out and talked to all the magazine companies. I even got investments in Netscape from five publishing companies. So, I saw all this stuff unfolding."

You can call it vision, but it's only common sense to me.

Clark could see things unfolding around the Internet, but he was also reluctant to be Netscape's CEO, even though that would have been one way to ensure his ideas were implemented. "I ran it for the first year, until I could recruit someone. It appeared to be such a harebrained concept that it would have been hard to recruit anyone in the early days. I met Jim Barksdale in the summer of 1994 and started recruiting him. It took me about six months and then he came on board in January of 1995." As at SGI, Clark did not want to run the company, but he continued to have ideas about the direction it should take.

At Silicon Graphics, Clark personally had a sense of knowing what he was doing and where the company should be headed. From his academic background and from his brief experience working for a computer graphics company, he developed both a sense of how things fit together and a conviction about where they were going to go. At Netscape, Clark's sense of knowing what the next step would be only began to take shape after collaborating with Andreessen.

The intuition came from Andreessen. But Clark began to realize the web had a tremendous, rapid growth rate. E-commerce hit him immediately. The $50 billion catalog business. Catalogs have to be mailed to you; you have to call the company or fill out an order. To Clark, that was a natural. Just replace catalog sales. Newspapers. People prefer to read a real newspaper. It's easier. But it's not really suitable for classified advertising. It's too hard to search. Eighty percent of the money newspapers get is from classified ads, but to Clark it was just logical that classified ads would go online, away from newspapers. "Their sources of revenue are going to decline. I felt that as an absolute conviction. I also felt you could buy music online. I wish I'd thought of books." Books are natural for online because you can read samples—it doesn't require a lot of bandwidth. You probably also need to let people sample music, and that takes larger bandwidth. "I came up with the idea for an online rent-a-CD. Why should people buy a CD if they can rent one for 50 cents? I came up with economic models for that. AtHome Corporation and these companies that have the bandwidth will be able to deliver music on demand."

Clark said he hired people in the first couple of months of Netscape to put together examples for *Rolling Stone* magazine to come online so people could see what it would look like and how it could be done. "I tried to convince Jann Wenner, the publisher of *Rolling Stone*. He basically wasn't aggressive enough, so I walked away from him." Clark met with and eventually recruited some newspaper companies to invest in a corporate round of financing. That's where he saw the value at the time. "In short, I saw the value of a portal. I was thinking of the consumer."

I saw the value of a portal. I was thinking of the consumer.

Jim Clark, at the head of Netscape in 1994, was thinking of pursuing the kind of strategy that Yahoo! and other portal sites were to pursue. He even put resources behind his ideas, hired people to make them real. But that's not the direction Netscape took. When Jim Barksdale came in, suddenly the money was coming from elsewhere—from businesses that wanted internal intranets and so forth. "So we got focused on delivering products to those customers and basically abandoned the work I'd done focusing on the consumer. It's too bad, because later they were sorry. Yahoo! came along and developed a consumer portal. You can talk to all the people at Netscape now and they wish they had listened. But let's face it. They were making booming revenues in the enterprise business. You can't be all things to all people. Since Yahoo! and all these consumer-oriented portals came around, Netscape has turned around and tried to enter that niche. But they're not very good at it. AOL will probably help that."

In a history that echoed what happened at Silicon Graphics, Clark had convictions about the direction Netscape should take, but those weren't the ideas held by the CEO. As with SGI, the actual strategy followed the money: Netscape paid attention to where its revenues where coming from at

JIM CLARK ON NETSCAPE'S
MISSED OPPORTUNITY

In retrospect, Netscape wishes they had gone after the consumer. But in January 1995, we had a lot of revenue from the intranet business. You can't convince anyone you're doing anything wrong when you're growing like that. Nor did I think so. I was just upset when they flushed the group I'd put together that I called the Content Group. It would have been the online marketing part of our presence in the portal business.

They gave away the search business to Yahoo!, and that helped Yahoo! establish itself even more. I used to have short conversations with Barksdale about that, asking why we were doing this. I'm greedy—I want it all. Why did we give it to them? He said, "We're not, they're paying us." But the payment was hardly in proportion to the value. I would have had us at least take an equity stake in them before I let them come into our portal for free. Get a 20 percent equity stake before we let them be our search engine. I would have been a little more mercenary.

But one of the things I learned from my experience at Silicon Graphics was that I got to the point where I butted heads with McCracken so much that I eventually developed a real negative point of view toward him. And he didn't like me. So we basically became enemies because we had different points of view. I decided I was never going to do that again. If I hire someone to run a company, he's in charge and I'm not going to go in and raise hell. It could be I backed off too much to the other extreme at Netscape. But all I will do is voice an opinion if I'm not running the company.

that time and focused on those customers. Despite his convictions, Clark agreed. He wasn't looking for a way to make his ideas real as much as he was looking for that big economic win. He also didn't want animosity between himself and Jim Barksdale.

Had they been followed, Clark's views would have taken Netscape in a different direction, but he's not bitter about it. "Netscape was a big win, no matter how you cut it. It's just that at the stage when the company could have hedged its bet a bit, it made a hard overbet to enterprise sales. I'm talking hard over: There is *no* money in the consumer business, there *is* money in the enterprise business, *that's* where we're going." Jim Barksdale made an ironclad decision that was followed right up by Marc Andreessen and there was no debate. "And I thought, 'How do we know there's no money there?'"

Clark believed the advertising model *was* viable. He spent a lot of time in the early days of Netscape talking to advertising agencies. He was the evangelist, trying to convince them to "go out and bring their Procters and Gambles along," convince their clients to convert their advertising to a web-based medium. Netscape didn't develop any advertising salespeople, although they had sufficient revenues to do so. "We didn't have to be profitable, the industry didn't expect us to be. We could have just gone out and spent some money on that. It was unfortunate we didn't, and the reason was that Barksdale went hard over. So did Andreessen. And we were making a lot of money. It just ran counter to my own gut instinct. I didn't think enterprise sales were bad, but we were running up against Microsoft, Lotus, and IBM in that space. The other space was untapped."

■ BATTLING MICROSOFT

If Netscape had followed Clark's ideas it might have become a lot more like Yahoo!, and it might not have butted heads with Microsoft, at least not so hard. But it did. Clark thought it was inevitable. "I've despised Microsoft for a long time. I admire them, but I despise their tactics and business practices. I despise the fact they don't create things. They tend to just suck it up from someone else. There's nothing illegal with that, it's just that business ethics don't exist at that company. Ethics are necessary in the world and in business. Business is a form of economic warfare. But in warfare we have the Geneva Convention; there is no Geneva Convention in business. Microsoft takes advantage of that." In Clark's view, once Microsoft gets the upper hand, the company mercilessly crushes everyone. Clark had no doubt that Microsoft would come after Netscape. "I knew it was going to happen from the beginning. That's why we just ran like hell. We said we've got to get out there and build enough market share."

Netscape made the browser ubiquitous to protect itself. "Without having done that we wouldn't have had a chance. If Microsoft controlled the browser today, Yahoo! and all the other companies would be squeezed and marginalized out of existence. People don't get that, but I know it's true. It's a power that's almost inevitable. It's nice to be a monopoly. There's nothing more pleasant. Because then you get to make the rules."

For Clark, innovation is an ethical requirement. Copying other companies may work better as a business strategy. It may be legal, but it's unethical. "I'm an ethical person. I have a set of principles I live by. I don't copy other people. I like to create something new. I could never create a company like Amdahl, whose purpose was to copy IBM mainframes and sell them at a cheaper price. To me it's like stealing an idea." Clark is not naive, he knows there's nothing wrong with copying as long as you do it legally. Companies are always copying and sometimes they make improvements. But it's just not Clark's style. In his view, Microsoft not only copies but uses its leverage to effectively make other companies unable to compete. "They marginalize practically everyone they want to. Their ruthlessness has been very successful. Their monopoly should be illegal because it stagnates the market. It's like AT&T. Its break-up was a good thing." But Clark concedes that

---

I don't copy other people. I like to create something new.

companies are not in business to allow a competitor to win. As critical as he is of Microsoft, he admits he might have done the same thing, though he says, "I probably wouldn't have been as successful at it."

I asked Clark if he was disappointed that Netscape was acquired by AOL. His answer was unequivocal. "Hell no. Under the circumstances, I think it was great for Netscape. It quadrupled my net worth, which I can't be disappointed about. It's 4X of an already big number, and it gives me complete financial security. No one's going to weep about where I was headed. Netscape should have been something different, but it just didn't work out. The world works that way."

■ HEALTHEON

Clark next seized on healthcare, "the world's largest, most inefficient market." We are all subject to the inefficiencies of that market, every time we go to the doctor or try to make an appointment. He thought somehow there must be a way to lower the costs and make it more efficient.

"And the Internet was exploding. Late in 1994, I developed the conviction that the Internet was going to replace everything. That the entire communications structure of the world was going to run using Internet protocols." Clark thinks data communications is the future of the world; therefore, it seemed a natural thing to connect doctors.

Data communications is the future of the world.

He envisioned Healtheon as a virtual network for healthcare, almost a portal for healthcare, where patients could have secure exchanges with their doctors, where patients could pull up their own medical information. "Your medical information would belong to you, the consumer. Today, the information belongs to the doctor. And if you change doctors, there's the problem of making sure all your information is transferred. I wear glasses. I'd like to have a place where I can just call up my prescription, or consult a new doctor and hand over my prescription. These are the things that motivated me in starting Healtheon."

Clark's approach in starting Healtheon was similar to his initial approach with Silicon Graphics in that his own personal experience, including by then his understanding of the Internet, led to ideas about the next logical step in an industry. His convictions were the primary driving force in launching the company. But he was much less sure about exactly what the company should do. He doesn't think he had a particular vision—just recognition of a "discombobulated world" that doesn't communicate well: doctors, clinics, hospitals, patients, insurance companies. "Everyone's dissatisfied. It was just a conviction that the Internet was going to enable a change in that. It stems from my own personal disenchantment with the system, starting with trying to get an appointment. I have to camp out on the phone to even get through to the doctor's office. A whole bunch of things struck me as inadequate. It's just personal experience."

With Healtheon, unlike Netscape, money wasn't the primary force behind Clark's efforts. But it was important. "At this stage, the economic motivation, although there, wasn't the driving factor. In Netscape, it was largely economic. I thought, 'I can capitalize on this opportunity.' With healthcare it was more like, 'It's a big market and we'll make a big business if we find a way to solve this problem.' It's the mother of all markets." The government spends some $400 billion a year on Medicaid and Medicare. Put another way, 40 percent of the annual medical bill is paid by the U.S. government. "So I thought if we can just get in there and be the first to solve this, we're going to have a real big company. And that excites me, I like that. I like being successful, I like making a difference. I guess that's ego, but it's not bad ego."

I like being successful, I like making a difference.

As was the case with earlier Silicon Valley companies like Fairchild and Intel, when he started Healtheon Clark wanted to apply a new technology to a general problem although he didn't know how that would translate into specific products and services. He had faith the company could learn all that as it went along—a faith that has been tested in each company he's started. "It seems like every company I've started approached a precipice and looked over and almost fell off. It's true of Silicon Graphics, Netscape, and Healtheon. But Healtheon has now turned the corner away from the cliff." And that, according to Clark, happens because you get the right CEO. "One of the things I've learned is you either take charge or you put someone else in charge. I'm not going to take charge because I'm not experienced in the health field." So much about a company is driven by people. The visionary always gets a lot of credit for the initial idea, but Clark gives the real credit to those who actually make the company operate. "All I did was choose a vector, a direction. They mutate the vector around and dodge the obstacles and avoid the cliffs." The key, he learned at Silicon Graphics, is empowering the CEO and staying out of his way.

Either take charge or put someone else in charge.

In Clark's approach, the vital learning process that takes over from the original vision begins only after the CEO and main staff of the company are on board. Once a business is started, a management team, a technical team, and a marketing team work together. They absorb from the system what the market is and what people are willing to pay for. "That's the nature of business. It doesn't always go in exactly the direction you envisioned. I just saw a need to create this virtual healthcare network."

Clark's "instinct" for the next logical step that he gained from physics and that broadened with his experience in business is different from the guidance system that takes over after one of his companies is formed. The CEO rather than Clark becomes responsible for setting the direction, and he uses whatever compass he may bring. But although he's handed over responsibility, Clark still develops his own, second-stage sense of direction. "What's been common in the companies I've started is a strong practical sense that what I was trying to do had to satisfy a problem that people will pay for. That's true of any company. It's hard to say what will lead to success and what might not. A lot of things have to happen right to have success, and only a few things have to happen wrong to make a failure. Just being practically grounded is important. If someone else doesn't want what you're offering, it won't work, no matter how interesting it is to you, no matter how beautiful it might seem." This practical principle of building around what people are willing to pay for is Clark's main guiding principle.

A lot of things have to happen right to have success, and only a few things have to happen wrong to make a failure.

As with Silicon Graphics, Clark employed a temporary CEO between launching Healtheon and bringing in the main crew. Clark was not interested in running the company. He was busy getting MYCFO started and building a boat. But the company and Clark were still learning. "I learned the healthcare market is large and inefficient for a reason. Because it's got so many constituents." All the players in the healthcare system weren't just an opportunity waiting to be connected. Like the Clinton White House before it, Healtheon discovered the players had their own interests that made them separate and disconnected in the first place and that tended to keep them apart. Putting them together, electronically or otherwise, is not so simple.

The man Clark credits with finally finding the people who will pay for his data communications network is Mike Long, the permanent CEO he hired when Healtheon was a year and a half old. "The main picture I provided was, 'let's create a healthcare network. Let's connect the main constituent players.' And it's finally working out. If it hadn't been for Mike Long, this company wouldn't be in good shape today. Healtheon is doing what it should be doing."

As with SGI and Netscape, Jim Clark has ideas of Healtheon eventually finding its main business serving consumers with a high volume, low-end service. He thinks the

---

JIM CLARK ON HEALTHCARE
AND THE INTERNET

What are some of the things Healtheon found that people were willing to pay for as of 1999? Mostly transaction fees paid for by insurance companies. Electronic claims, for example, instead of paper claims, which cost a lot more money. So they'll pay 30 to 40 cents for an electronic transaction. In 1999, I think we'll do 150 million transactions. These transactions are passing through the Healtheon virtual network. They're claims, eligibility checks, and each one represents a transaction for which we get a small fee. We also do prescription refills. Over time we want to keep the database on patients. But there are a whole variety of transactions I can't even begin to articulate: Laboratory test submissions, for one. It's a wide spectrum. Just think of all the transactions involved in your healthcare, all the information you want. In the end, you want secure e-mail between doctor and patient. We're ramping up a consumer portal where people go to find quality information on health and wellness. As traffic builds, we'll get more and more advertisers. These are initiatives from Mike Long and the team there. I don't claim to know much about it. I want to build a place where people will come to find out about health. That will generate traffic and that will generate advertising revenues.

---

biggest payoff is there. But whether Healtheon ever does that will depend on its CEO, not Clark. And that is fine with him.

■ MYCFO

In every way, Jim Clark's newest project, MYCFO, would seem to be the culminating fruit of his work in founding his earlier three companies. It is funded by that work, it repeats many of the patterns of that work, and it is intended to help manage the wealth created by that work. When I spoke to him, the company was in its earliest formative stages and he was still developing ideas for it. Clark was getting ready to launch. "At least for the moment, I'm thinking MYCFO might be a real company. How does a CEO rely on a CFO? The CFO runs the financial side of the company. So imagine this company running the financial side of your life. For now, I have these people here [the staff of MYCFO] doing all that for me." Clark's objective is to move into a set of online technologies so people can do all their financial transactions in one place. Then at the end of the year, all their records will be right there for taxes; they will be kept online on an ongoing basis. The company's initial purpose is to operate for high net worth individuals like himself who are worth $100 million or more. "And we're starting to do that. But there's another company here as well, MYCFO.com, which will be aimed at the low end."

Once again, the company begins with a high-end strategy, but anticipates a low-end strategy in the future. And once again, the company begins from Clark's personal experience. "MYCFO is based on my own needs. It started with my own absolute frustration. I have a bookkeeper. I do things like transfer money, pay bills, buy stocks, and until I set this up, those things were never in one place. I'd get monthly statements from my investment bank and have to take the data and enter it in a spreadsheet. I want an on-going financial statement. I'd like to be able to press a button and get a financial statement that shows my assets and liabilities, who I owe money to, who owes me money, lets me look at my bills, see if all the charges are valid, look at my credit card, keep my current receipts. All in one integrated place. At the end of the year, I want to be able to do my taxes. I want all of that stuff in one place. I like to be tidy."

I like to be tidy . . . I want everything in one place.

To this point it appeared to me that an existing product, *Quicken,* seemed to offer some of the functionality Clark was describing. But he rejected that entirely—*Quicken* isn't integrated enough for him. "I want everything in one place—taxes, wire transfers, everything. I don't want a single financial thing I do not to be in online, right there. That isn't what *Quicken* does. It's not good enough if you have to enter a bunch of stuff manually. It's extremely important to me, and I think it is to everybody. Right now you have to pull all that together at the end of the year and pay someone a lot of money to translate it into a tax form. There's no reason why that couldn't be automatic."

Clark claims that practically all the high net worth people in Silicon Valley have the same problem. Like him, they're often involved in many companies, and have many aspects to their complicated financial lives. "The word we have out is that if you're $100 million in net worth then we can afford to talk to you, and even that is overloading us because we're getting so many requests from so many people." In the process of working on these high-end customers, MYCFO has developed a series of products and services that are people-intensive. "For high-end people like that, you need to have people available on the phone. It's kind of like an investment bank."

At the same time there's a low-end customer MYCFO would like to bring online. That's the customer MYCFO.com will go after. "For that I've got to develop some technology, get some engineers sitting here developing applications and a user interface. That's just getting under way, not really started yet. So I'm going to put some money into this and see if I can compete with what Intuit might try to do."

The high end was already working then for Clark. He was the beta customer. He was funding it all out of his own pocket as the cost of running his business. MYCFO is a Subchapter S company, and at some point he intends to make it profitable and make a profit-sharing arrangement for the people there. "There probably won't be an IPO. Healtheon is becoming less of a concern—it's going public, it's growing, and it requires less of my time. I've finished the boat I've been working on for the past few years, so the timing is right for me to have a new project. I'm 99 percent certain in the next few months I'll hire a team and get things kicked off. I think MYCFO.com is a bigger opportunity than Healtheon, despite the fact that healthcare is a bigger market."

I asked Clark what's driving him with MYCFO. After all, he already has at least one big financial win in Netscape and all the appearance of another in Healtheon. He explained that when he sees a business opportunity it frustrates him to wait for another company to do the right thing. His gratification comes from building a successful, self-sustaining company that employs people. "Like any aspect of life, you get enjoyment from obscure reasons."

If Jim Clark goes ahead with MYCFO, he will not likely be its CEO any more than he was at his other companies. When I asked him why he said, "I'm not good at it. I don't have the attention span or the patience. I don't have the desire to attend staff meetings and coordinate things and meet with customers. It's a hell of a job. You work a lot harder when you do that. Mike Long works much harder than I do. Jim Barksdale works much harder than I do. I just think it's inappropriate for me. I'd rather hire someone else who is good at it."

Unlike many people in Silicon Valley, Clark is not motivated to be in charge, to be in power. And neither is he motivated primarily by vision. He is motivated by wealth and success and has by almost any measure won them. Vision seems to be a tool he uses primarily to establish thrust and guidance at lift-off for his companies. He's very good at that. If he wanted his vision to do more, he would have to find a way to transfer the vision along with the company to the CEO he chooses or become CEO himself. When I asked Clark if his ideas for his companies are important to him he said, "I articulate them, but that's it. People are much more prone to listen to me now that I've had some success. All I can ask is that people listen. But there's no comparison to being on the line, in charge. If your ideas are important to you, you'd better stay in charge."

If your ideas are important to you,
you'd better stay in charge.

■ CAPE CANAVERAL

Imagine you're in front of a computer monitor that can control everything going on at your own private Cape Canaveral in Florida. Outside your window, you can see huge launch pads and gantries that make the few boats you can see out in the Atlantic look like toys. You have the power to send off into space anything you like, anything you decide is worth the effort. You get to decide on your own missions. You wait to make sure you have the conviction that a mission is right, and to make sure you feel positive about its prospects. Then you go ahead. You look forward to the tremendous excitement and power of lift-off. After that you cede control to the crew in the space vehicle and mission control in Houston. Your main role is finished—except that you get to keep a large portion of the material rewards that finally come from the mission. This is the image that describes Jim Clark's approach to vision.

You feel competent to do this work because the physics you studied gave you an innate sense of how the natural forces in the universe work, and through experience you've developed a similar sense for the world of industry and commerce. By now you have an instinct for what should happen next as all these forces interact.

You have mementos of the three missions you've launched so far, gifts from the crews who manned them. One is a computer game running on your monitor right now with movielike realism and clarity. It was for the first mission you pursued, which was simply to make it cheaper for people to get off the earth's flat surface and move about in the three dimensions of space. Before then only organizations or nations with huge amounts of money could explore space. You believed that if it were cheaper more people would use it.

Another memento is a mock-up of a small, one-person spaceship with a large letter "N" painted on its side. You've put it on top of your monitor so you'll see it every time you use your computer. It's for your second mission, which was to develop and prove a simpler and easier way to navigate in space so ordinary people could use the ship to send little packets of stuff anywhere they wanted instead of relying on the mail or telephones. Or quickly go anywhere in the world to find stuff they were looking for.

The last memento just came in and you've put it next to your monitor. It's a wire-framed picture of an old, kindly doctor making a house call to see a child who's ill. It's for your third mission, which was to launch a satellite to connect patients with their doctors and everyone else either one of them needs to communicate with about their health. The satellite just went into orbit and Houston is giving it its first tasks to perform.

But you aren't focused on these mementos right now. You're thinking about a new mission. You don't need the money, but you still get a tremendous thrill out of launching rockets that may do something useful.

Chapter

Guided Natural Selection: Tim Koogle, CEO of Yahoo!

The newest technology to excite Silicon Valley and much of the world is the Internet and its World Wide Web. In just a few seconds, with a click of a button on a mouse the web transparently connects a computer user to untold thousands of other computers around the world—and to the information on them and the commercial transactions they control. Suddenly, anyone can go just about anywhere in cyberspace. This digital universe is so vast that it would be nearly impossible to navigate without a tool like Yahoo! provides. Other companies offer specialized guides, but Yahoo! was the first to provide a comprehensive table of contents to the web, and along with Netscape, one of the first Internet companies to establish a brand name that most of the growing millions of Net surfers could easily identify. Yahoo! became a compelling and natural site from which anyone could enter and explore the World Wide Web. As a result, in the 1990s Yahoo! set the pace in attracting the most users on the web—and the most advertising revenue.

But Yahoo! is much more than a valuable brand and a busy web site and an essential navigational guide. Its birth, again like Netscape's, was one of the catalysts that transformed a quiet, U.S. Department of Defense-sponsored computer network—used mostly by academics and scientists—into a network that increasingly lies at the center of worldwide commerce and communication. Yahoo! has helped create and stimulate the very environment in which it grows, and it seems destined to help shape this environment for the foreseeable future. As I discovered in talking with Tim Koogle, the man who heads Yahoo!, not all this was foreseen; but at the same time it is no accident. Yahoo! has a vision of what it wants to do, and it has an approach to vision that suits a growing new frontier like the Internet. Yahoo! tries to determine its own destiny in a process of rapid and self-conscious evolution. The company, like its signature product, grows through a series of guided experiments in natural selection. Tim Koogle is the man responsible for this approach.

Like many Silicon Valley CEOs, Koogle joined the company after it was already started—although just barely, in this case. Yahoo! began as a rather simple and straightforward directory, a table of contents to the World Wide Web. It was the brainchild of two young Ph.D. students in Stanford University's computer science department, Jerry Yang and David Filo. But, in classic Silicon Valley parlance dating back to the early days of Apple Computer, Yang and Filo "needed adult supervision" to build a company and turn their idea into a real business. Through a headhunter, they found Koogle, who at the time was CEO of a 300 million dollar company in Seattle named Intermec, and who before that had worked nine years at Motorola.

Koogle describes himself as being "spongelike," always trying to learn from what's going on around him. As I listened to him, I constantly heard stories beginning from his early childhood about his asking for and receiving the distilled wisdom of people he respected and admired. At fifteen, his father told him to do what he loved, but be practical enough to keep himself dry and fed. At Motorola he was told about the importance of basic, core human values in building a sustainable business—things like, "Tell the truth" and "Don't ever cheat people." Experienced old hands would tell him things like, "In a start-up, cash is more important than your mother." These words of wisdom, born out of practical experience, are what Koogle seems to have been hungry for and absorbed, far more than anything that came out of his formal education or his Ph.D. in mathematical kinematics.

I sat down to talk with Koogle a number of times from October 1997 into the spring of 1998, during the infancy if not quite the birth of Yahoo! and its vision. In our conversations, I heard him use a number of unfamiliar terms. As in any new field, the people at Yahoo! are borrowing or inventing new language to describe what they're doing. Hearing this new vocabulary in context, an outsider can fairly rapidly gain at least a working comprehension. Much of the vocabulary Yahoo! uses derives either from Silicon Valley's computer culture or from the media businesses it increasingly compares itself to. Yahoo! develops "properties" to put online. The people who develop and manage these are "producers."

Yahoo! constantly plays with this language and with other slang. Maybe that comes from its chosen name as much as anything else. But the words work: They tell a great deal about the character of Yahoo! and the direction it's taking. As is well known, for a long time Filo and Yang carried business cards with the titles "Chief Yahoo!" (Koogle told me Filo had recently changed his to "Cheap Yahoo!"). Less well known is that the woman with the interesting job of Internet taxonomy, the one who develops Yahoo!'s directory categories, adopted the title of "Chief Ontologist." One of Koogle's favorite phrases is "organic uptake," as in "Yahoo! has great organic uptake." I understand that to mean it has an inherent tendency to live and grow and survive in its environment, like a new species that has found a favorable niche. That phrase is especially apt in describing a quality Yahoo! really does seem to have—something vital that its approach to vision takes advantage of and depends on.

■ VISION: FROM DIRECTORY TO MEDIA COMPANY

Yahoo! came to life just as the World Wide Web was first emerging as a communications platform. More and more content was becoming available on the web, and more and more people were connecting to the web to find it. To Koogle and his colleagues at Yahoo! in mid 1995, "the web starts to smell like a medium. And something called a 'navigational guide' for connecting users to stuff becomes core and sustainable. Users really need one. So, the starting point for the vision is: Do this navigational guide really well, embrace the nature of the web as a distributed medium, and continue on to become a major gateway to this new medium."

As I was to learn, Koogle uses the term "medium" in the McLuhanesque sense of a communications technology that uniquely influences its users and the messages that flow through it, and in the popular commercial sense of radio and television and magazines. The specific medium of the Internet largely defines the ecosystem in which he sees Yahoo! trying to survive and grow. Another term I noticed was *gateway*. In early 1998, that was the new term being used to describe companies like Yahoo!. By late 1998, the term *portal* was being used more and more in its place. With the Internet, language like everything else changes fast.

Koogle went on to say, "Even as of mid-1995 when we wrote it down, the vision also said: We're going to build a platform. If we can work really hard and really smart and extend that vision, we might get millions if not tens of millions of people coming through our door every day. And if we do, they will consume stuff, and while they're consuming it they'll leave electronic tracks behind. And we can use that as a true, real-time measure of what is most popular and most needed—and use it as a road sign to guide us toward deeper and deeper levels of content that we ought to aggregate around."

I noticed the phrase "consume stuff," which seemed to be a biological as much as an economic way to think about what people do with the information they find on the web. And, like creatures finding their way to their favorite water holes, these people would leave electronic tracks behind, which Yahoo! could use to understand and serve them better.

Paying attention to where people go while surfing the web traces back to Yang and Filo when they first started building Yahoo!. They did it from the very beginning, using log files. The capability was "built into the bones of their system." It grew out of the way they started the directory. Friends, and friends of friends, and friends of friends of friends kept sending them their favorite sites. As graduate students working on their Ph.D.s, they had to use their time carefully. They simply paid attention to the most popular sites so they could prioritize them and put their own efforts where people cared most.

"But what you could go do with this information to extend the vision . . . Saying, 'OK once you do that, then what is it going to allow you to do?' all that hadn't been put together yet." Tracking what people do and aggregating vertically and deeper in subject areas that are high in consumption brings in "targeted eyeballs" to clients who will pay a higher price for those. Koogle considered this advertising-based business model, which had of course been used in the past, a potentially rich one. "You can also build standalone web properties around themes that people show you, and those would have higher targeting capability. And and and . . . All that hadn't been put together yet."

Koogle helped Yang and Filo put that together. Yahoo! could find clients—advertisers—who would pay to reach its viewers. But in 1995 the culture of the web reacted with skepticism to outright hostility to the idea of advertising. Yang and Filo shared that view. Still, as far as Koogle could see, there was no better way to survive and grow. Subscriptions might work—companies like CompuServe and America Online were trying that—but even magazines and newspapers that charge subscription prices need advertising revenue to survive. Like it or not, natural selection would favor those who could attract advertising revenue—at least until someone came up with a better adaptation.

"So we said we're going to take this directory and we're going to extend it. It's a table of contents to start with. But there are some people who want to do needle-in-the-haystack searches. They'll want to have access to what we'll call *compressed index* and *search engine* capability. So we'll book-end content on the web between those two functions, table of contents and index. But make no mistake about it, Yahoo! set out to serve very well a core and sustainable and exponentially growing need that people have to find information. A single source to come to and find things. That was us." And that was Yahoo!'s vision as of 1995 when it began as a serious business.

A single source to come to and find things. That was us.

➤ Expansion

Right away, though, Yahoo!'s vision started changing, "evolving," as Koogle puts it. For one thing, "it expanded a lot." Like broadcast TV and radio, Yahoo! serves two customers, "one of whom pays and one who doesn't," as he explained with a laugh. Both are vital. Without large numbers of people using Yahoo! for free, the company can't sell advertising. The more traffic the better. So very early on, Koogle decided to take the risk and get into some markets outside North America that had large populations connected to the web. This was very early both for the market and for Yahoo!. The risk was, if he did it too early Yahoo! would be spread too thin and it wouldn't be able to support all its business. But if he got into a market early and the market became very large, Yahoo! would be rewarded with a powerful, perhaps unbeatable position. Yahoo!'s brand would be too strong for a competitor to dislodge it. So, Yahoo! expanded into Japan and Canada, and soon after into Europe. But it did so in a symbiotic fashion, with the help of partners who also benefited from their ties to Yahoo!. The partnering is worth looking at because it's one way Koogle tries to enlarge his own company's power by working with other forces in his environment.

Yahoo!'s expansion was naturally tied to capital. It could only expand as much as could be paid for. But, done right, Yahoo! might not have to pay for all of it. Koogle set out to "capitalize the company in stages that got more aggressive as we were doing it." Things went so well that Yahoo! only needed two rounds of private financing before it went public with an IPO. The first, seed round came from Sequoia Capital and Mike Moritz, before Koogle came on board. Before there was a real business plan. The second round, which was tied to Yahoo!'s expansion, came from corporate partners Koogle pursued.

Tim Koogle is pragmatic and he understands the basic demands of business life. He seems to feel them as keenly, but with as much understanding, as if he were Charles Darwin stranded alone on an island. When he joined Yahoo! he didn't see an operation that was yet following the dictates of survival in the world of business. So he said, "OK, you guys had a million bucks and you've burnt about a half of it already. We're going to start some revenue and we're going to keep the head count really tight. We're going to make this thing profitable. But this is going to be a big game. One thing I've learned in the past is, go raise money when you don't need it. Capitalize the hell out of your business. Even to the extent that you give up a little in dilution. And get ready. Because if you want to play big, play big."

If you want to play big, play big.

This insistence on profits and on capitalization was part of the "adult supervision" Koogle brought to the company. It was required for Yahoo! to survive and have the reserved strength to grow into adulthood. So Yahoo! did a second round of financing in November of 1995 trying to raise four million dollars. It was oversubscribed, so it raised five. As it turned out, the money went into the bank and Yahoo! didn't have to touch it.

The second round of financing came from corporate sources rather than venture capitalists like Sequoia. From

Reuters and Softbank and Ziff. These were more than sources of money—they were also partners, sources of content. As Koogle explained, Yahoo!'s business is building a navigational guide, aggregating the contents of the web. They are not in the business of authoring original content. They stay independent of that, embracing the concept that content is being authored on a truly distributed basis on the Net. There is, he went on, no way to compete with a million—and growing exponentially—sources of original content. "If you try, you should be shot. We're in the business of delivering content, or helping people get connected to content. That has us partnering, big time, with lots of companies. Very tiny to very big."

Yahoo! already had Reuters, which was seeking an outlet onto the web for their news feeds on a worldwide basis. Koogle reasoned that valuations were going up in Yahoo!'s arena, and the business was ripe for real partnerships, lots of them. So Yahoo! did a strategic round, talking to companies as investors, not investors as investors. That led to discussions with Softbank and Ziff. Yahoo! already had a brewing content relationship with Ziff and a brewing content relationship with Reuters. "And so I just decided to craft a strategic set of partnerships."

Koogle's and Yahoo!'s interests in a partnership with these companies was clear. In addition to raising capital, Yahoo! would have more content to offer its users, and a closer relationship with the companies that created the content. "Not only are we linking users to content, but we're tightening and tightening and tightening the relationship between Yahoo! and other companies who are trying to find eyeballs."

But the interests of these partners did not seem so clear to me. So I asked Koogle whether they were really more interested in taking over Yahoo!'s business niche or in taking over Yahoo! itself than in developing a real symbiotic relationship.

"Yeah, we were paranoid. We were a tiny company. Still are, actually. At that time we were just a half dozen people, sitting around, feeling very paranoid. I brought a lot of the paranoia because I've been on all sides of the table. And I know how some of these big companies think. I also know that you ought to temper your paranoia because a lot of big companies have a great deal of baggage. There are things that they say they might want to do that they never can." A company can be prevented from going into a new area by its culture—or by its capital base and shareholders because they would be reducing their revenue and/or cannabilizing their existing businesses. "I've lived in there, and I've watched those guys, and I know that you can temper your paranoia—a little bit. Because there's baggage. It's a *good* thing, excess baggage."

Koogle overcame his natural paranoia by establishing personal relationships with the men who would be his partners. He got to know Eric Hippeau, chairman and CEO of Ziff, directly. He got to know Masayoshi Son of Softbank, directly. And the chairman of Reuters and his first-line executives, directly. "You do deals with people. And you look at the reason for doing business with them and their reason for doing business with you. And you say, 'Is that healthy?' And then you limit their investment so in the end they don't have control. You keep control, financially. You're not going to prevent them from moving into your space, you're not going to prevent them from learning. But they're going to learn whether they invest in you or not."

The partnership with Softbank and with Ziff turned out to be the key to Yahoo!'s initial expansion into Japan, and its later expansion into Europe. "We sat down with Son and said, 'You know, we want you as an investor to help us capitalize this company, but the business relationship also means leverage in international markets.'" Softbank has a lot of brick and mortar to support its trade shows and publishing enterprises. Publishing has a natural infrastructure for advertising sales, and so, Koogle thought, "maybe, if we structure this thing right with Softbank, we can go and launch properties in other parts of the world, in partnership with those guys. Make use of their infrastructure. Not have to invest in that. When we invest we invest light, but we invest in the people who are actually adding value from day one."

When we invest we invest light, but we invest in the people who are actually adding value from day one.

In this way, Yahoo! expanded into international markets while it was still a very tiny company. Through its partnership with Softbank, Yahoo! started a "property" in Japan in 1996 which became profitable in its second month. It went public in 1997 as a partially owned subsidiary with Softbank as the majority owner. The next deal Yahoo! made was in Europe, only this time Yahoo! owned 75 percent. Ziff International, which is owned by Softbank, is the minority equity partner. Once again, Yahoo! used Ziff's brick and mortar—their offices, their financial infrastructure for payables and receivables—avoiding many of the costs that can weigh down a company when it expands into a new part of the world. By the end of 1997, Yahoo! was in Japan, France, Germany, the United Kingdom, Ireland, Korea, Australia, and Canada. Like a small organism hitching a ride on a much larger one, Yahoo! went further and faster than anyone might have guessed it would. That was because Koogle knew that cooperation, especially for a small company, was one good way to survive in the business ecosystem. Through cooperation, Yahoo! raised capital, expanded to new markets, gained new content, and saved time and money—all in one move.

➤ Extension

In addition to growing in size with its international expansion, Yahoo!'s vision was also growing in what it offered its customers. Originally, Yahoo! was a navigational guide—a directory. Then, a directory plus index and search capability. All of that Koogle refers to as aggregation—core aggregation. Yahoo! aggregates the web's contents around subjects. "But, all you have is a tree, a hierarchy. And by the way, what's totally cool about this medium is that now there are cross-links to all kinds of stuff. So there are vines in the branches of the tree, what amouts to a huge web inside the web." In other words, Yahoo!'s directory mimics the web as it creates cross-links based on all the observed consumption patterns. "We draw subbranches over to other subbranches, and stuff like that. That's the basic tree. All the sites that are being submitted are linked into the appropriate places on the tree. And you continue to build with cross-linking. That's core aggregation. All in one place, aggregated. Subject themes. Real simple to get."

Next, Yahoo!'s vision extended into what they call *super aggregation*. Koogle offered this example of Yahoo! Finance: "Suppose you were looking at 20 sites associated with Personal Investing. You look at some of those sites and you get some information content. You consume it, then you go off to another site, come back, and then look at another one, branching here and there. Super aggregation means adding to those sites, which are relatively static, some live feeds that have to do with headline stories, summary news stories, charts, graphs ... things associated with what today's world markets are doing. How's the market today? How'd the Hong Kong Exchange close last night? And how's that rippling through international monetary markets?"

It also means providing access to other services, like buying and selling in real time. You may be making an investment or perhaps selling one. All from the Yahoo! site, you can generate some capital then go plant it in some other money vehicle. At the same time, you can get all the information you need to support these transactions. "You can see this in Yahoo! Finance. It's an example of super aggregation. To the basic tree we've added live feeds and merchant services. It's very cool. I think you just type in Yahoo! Finance, if you don't already have it bookmarked."

After Koogle described super aggregation to me I went to my own computer and looked up Yahoo! Finance. At least in early 1998, it was exactly the way he described it. No doubt the site will continue to evolve and change. That was the basic principle I was hearing from him: Vision evolves, and so the products of vision evolve, too.

Vision evolves, and so the products of vision evolve, too.

Koogle went on to describe one further evolution. Yahoo!'s vision has also extended beyond being a place where people come to find content to a place where people also come to find other people. "Using Chat, for example. In fact, if we enable Yahoo! as a meeting place around content, it can be really compelling. It'll also give us a platform to communicate one-on-one with our users, more tightly. There's a self-reinforcing aspect to lacing in, if you will, communication and community features."

To summarize Yahoo!'s evolution as of early 1998, Koogle said, "We act as a gateway. We've got all these users sitting out here who want to access the world of content on the web." The users come through a navigational guide that funnels them in through the door. Then through partnerships, Yahoo! has added higher levels of value, namely, convenience for the user. And Yahoo! works to give users more and more value by watching their needs, and partnering, and aggregating in more services to what was simply a hierarchy of sites, but now has real content. "So you can see how the vision has evolved. It's bigger. It's way bigger now."

And then I asked Koogle to describe where Yahoo! was headed. He said Yahoo! has always been measured in what they say publicly. They don't want to be using words that sound "too big and high fallutin'" and have them coming off as cocky. They also don't want to be using words that they perceive the world in general hasn't yet gotten their arms around. They don't want to get out in front of the headlights. And they also don't want to tip their hand to the competition. "So we've always been real measured about how we extend the terminology we use in public. We've always wanted to grow this into a very large media business."

We've always wanted to grow this into
a very large media business.

A media business, however, that's web-based. That has no baggage and that provides a very tightly woven, interactive, direct marketing platform. "The economics and the content consumption are so tightly interwoven, it represents a commerce platform and a content consumption platform at the same time, but nonetheless a media company. Maybe a new kind of global network company is what Yahoo! is about."

That's why Yahoo! developed "verticals" like the Metropolitan Yahoo!s and Yahoo! Finance, properties that combine a list of web sites with live feeds of related information and with merchant services that allow you to buy or sell things related to that subject area. That's why Yahoo! watches consumption patterns and continues to plant more verticals. They're a direct analogy to the thematic, standalone properties that a global network business would plant. Entertainment and a sports channel and so forth. "Make no mistake. That's always been our vision, really. I don't talk at that level too much too often because the air's thin up there."

■ HOW YAHOO!'S VISION EVOLVES

As I listened to Koogle describe Yahoo!'s growing vision, I got the impression that in his approach vision grows together with a growing company, and in the same organic way. Vision is linked to a company in the same way that perception, cognition, and intention are linked to a living, growing body. And just as psychological development occurs in steps along with physical development in a growing child, vision grows in steps as a company develops. I wanted to know more about how those steps worked.

"It's an interesting process. Especially in this arena of the Internet and our part of it, which as you know have emerged and grown quite rapidly. I don't think there's ever been this high a rate of change. At least in my experience and all I've read about the history of technology. Really, I don't think the rate of change has ever been this great." Koogle joined Yang and Filo in mid-1995 when they had just a little venture money and "four or five of their buddies hanging with them." They had no written business plan, no revenue. With Koogle leading them, that small group of people tried to cast in black and white a shared vision of what they were going to do.

"We're going to launch off into this space. We know this space is really big. We think our position in it could be big. But we haven't the slightest idea whether or not we can make it big." Today, Koogle explained, there's less tentativeness in the different components of the vision: establish a platform, become a gateway, and so on. Their vision has expanded. They're attempting to foster a culture that develops a vision, "then extends the vision, engulfs more, extends, engulfs, et cetera, et cetera. A natural progression, building on itself."

Foster a culture that develops a vision, then extends the vision, engulfs more.

Extend and engulf. That seemed to capture much of what I'd been hearing. Vision is a matter of deciding where and when to extend. Execution is a matter of taking hold of that area, engulfing it. But at least in a very young company, this process begins with a great deal of tentativeness. It's a learning process. It's like a small child exploring its universe, reaching out its hand to touch and grasp and learn for itself about its new world.

Koogle's description of the extension of Yahoo!'s vision sounded familiar to me. It sounded very much like the way he had earlier described the extension of Yahoo!'s directory and its properties. He said, "Products morph on short cycles here, by the week or month. We put something out and look nightly at whether people like it or not, and then change it on that basis." Yahoo! pays attention to what people watch on the web and how they get there and then gives them more of what they like, through the pathways they like. Yahoo!'s vision grows in very much the same way its product does. The principles behind each are similar.

■ AN ISLAND IN A BOTTLE

Looking at the world and Yahoo! through Koogle's eyes is like looking at an island ecosystem changing rapidly right before you, as if it were a living diorama, shrunk to fit inside one of those large glass bubbles held by a net that you sometimes find near a wharf, the ones that look like big crystal balls.

VISION CYCLES AT YAHOO!

More extending and more engulfing actually happen on pretty short cycles here. It's hallway, to some extent. It's practically a daily exercise in building and sustaining a culture and a vision. We have a real tight team. Part and parcel of having a vision and then going off and executing it is getting a team with great chemistry and a shared vision. Collectively the team has to have a broad enough experience base, but not so broad that you're running really fat and burning too much money. You threaten the viability of an organization by getting too fat too quick. What you'll find—and this hasn't changed—is that we run really lean here. We've grown our head count from six at the time I joined to about 330 people now, I think, over about a two-year period. This is a very leveragable business. It's not a large head count business. Which is the beauty of it.

If you glimpsed inside to see how we operate day to day, you'd find that Yang and a guy named Jeff Mallet and myself have our cubes right next to each other. It's no accident. The three of us pretty much run the business. Between the three of us we've made decisions on all the deals that we've done that affected the company: strategic, raising capital. We operate really tight. During a normal day you'll find us hollering back and forth across the wall, bouncing around inside the cubes, grabbing each other and going off into a little conference room.

We'll put our feet up on the table, and say, "You know, it feels like it's about time for us to extend into the following area, but it carries with it the following kinds of risks, what do you think?" We may not reach a conclusion, but we'll be planting the seeds, planting them again, and planting them again. We try to be pretty connected, pretty organic. Three brains connected at the same time.

(continued)

VISION CYCLES AT YAHOO! (Continued)

I don't mean to imply that only three people here guide the business. By no means. I'm an old veteran, done lots of operating stuff, and I have planted here, in the culture: hire really smart people, drive decisions down as far as you possibly can. But from the standpoint of crafting the vision and taking the next step, we have a really tight group that cycles, literally in the hallway, on a daily basis with each other.

That's the image that captures both Yahoo!'s vision and Koogle's way of working with vision. As you look through the glass you see only one person, apparently alone like Robinson Crusoe. From the field clothes he wears and the net he carries and the way he examines the plant life, you surmise he's a biologist. Indeed, he looks exactly like the young Charles Darwin. At that recognition, you know that this island operates under the implacable laws of natural selection and survival of the fittest.

As you watch the young Darwin you can begin to feel what he feels. You understand that your very life depends on whether and how well you can take care of yourself on this island. You feel with a rush the life and death seriousness of your situation. Survival will depend on your own competence in working with what lives here; your spirits will depend on your own confidence. You've got to learn about this island to stay alive and maybe even enjoy its beauty.

One thing you must observe is that your world has shrunk, as if time and space have been compressed. That's why this island world can fit in a glass ball. Another thing you observe is how fast everything on the island seems to grow and change—especially the trees. It takes a while for your eyes and your mind to adjust to the speed of change. You see a new generation of trees every day, not the maturation of a single generation. The trees are very active, and they seem to be exploring and extending to new parts of the island where they haven't yet taken hold.

As you bring your attention back out to the crystal ball itself, you find it has the power to answer almost any question you ask. When you ask, the ball flickers for a second and then shows you its answer. Between questions, you can see again some of the island trees, their branches laced with vines like those in a Louisiana swamp. The trees seem to reach out and respond to you and your questions. And if you look at the ball at just the right angle, you can see the reflection of millions of other eyes watching the same thing you are.

These eyes are interesting in their own right. Yahoo! pays attention to where people actually go on the Net and how they get there, and then gives them more of what they like and makes it easier to find. And Yahoo! gives them less where they don't actually go and eliminates pathways they don't follow. In this way, the Internet as mapped out in Yahoo! is also a map of the collective and evolving mind of the millions of people all over the world who use it. Yahoo! survives and thrives in its ecological niche in large part by being an accurate, real-time mirror showing what the mass of people are looking at and doing on the web. Yahoo! shows where the collective mind is and where it's going. What it thinks about and how it organizes it. And in the links Yahoo! offers, it even shows the progression of thoughts.

■ DARWIN WAS RIGHT

One story Koogle told me offers the key to understanding how Yahoo!'s vision and its product both grow. During our conversations, Koogle had told several stories about some of his mentors and the lessons he'd learned from them. At one point he said, "In the end, I think everything in the world seeks its most efficient form—naturally. I don't want to get too philosophical, but I think of a guy I knew early in my life. I was young, bending my pick starting a couple of businesses. And I met this guy who'd been real successful in starting a few companies and then taking some of the money he'd made

and seeding other companies. We'd completely blitzed ourselves skiing all day and we were standing next to a fireplace
drinking Drambuie and hot water with a twist of lemon, feeling very relaxed and more and more philosophical as the
evening wore on. And so I looked at him and said, 'If you were
to tell me, young guy, wet behind the ears, boiled down into a
few words, just why you've been so successful, what would it
be?' And he stood back and he said, 'Darwin was right.'"

That was almost 20 years ago, and Koogle has kept the
thought. In his view, everything is part of an ecosystem. Experiments are run, just like when a cell mutates and then
creates a new organism. Mutations are experiments of sorts
and are either supported by their ecosystem or not. If they're
supported they tend to build on themselves and replicate,
and, he said, the same model applies to business. "I'm a Dar-
winist, I believe in natural selection. Human nature is one
of experimenting all the time, with innovation in technology, in social structure, or whatever. The things that are supported grow and the things that aren't fall away. So I think
about business that way."

The things that are supported grow
and the things that aren't fall away.

The experiments and organisms that are supported by
the ecosystem grow, and the ones that aren't fall away. Just
like the changes Yahoo! experiments with in its web site.
And just like Yahoo!'s vision as it grows and extends toward
the media company it believes it's headed for. Failure is as
much a part of this process as success. In fact, "it's good to
fail. It's the best way to learn hard lessons. But the key is that
you *must learn* so you know what to do different next time."
In this way, Koogle's approach to vision seems to be less a
matter of long-range foresight or even of trying to make particular changes in the world. It seems to be much more a
matter of playing out a hunch or a well-informed feeling
about what might allow you to grow in your environment,
and then paying very close attention to the results. Vision is

being keenly aware of and taking initiatives in a process of natural selection that governs business just as much as the natural world. You take something that wants to grow and you guide it in its interaction with the world around it. As Koogle said, "Vision just directs and shapes a little bit the organic expansion of a company."

> Vision just directs and shapes a little bit
> the organic expansion of a company.

■ EXPERIMENTS IN NATURAL SELECTION

With the model of an ecosystem in mind, Koogle's vision comes into sharper focus. And so do a number of his operating methods. But the model also raises a number of questions, one of which is just how far into the future vision can provide any guidance. If vision is something that extends a little bit each day and then changes based on feedback and extends a little bit more the next day, perhaps in a different direction, is vision really limited to one day's work? The answer is, no, but most of your conscious attention should be paid to daily vision.

Koogle believes that a certain balance is required in starting, growing, and running a business—whatever stage it's at. You need a vision that's large enough and grand enough so that there's something more than just tomorrow that people are working for. Something that people inspires people. "That's really key. I think human nature, especially on the West Coast, here in the Valley, demands to be in a space where there's no lid, a place where you don't feel shackled."

On the other hand, Koogle believes people will be able to embrace larger and larger chunks of a vision that is inherently uncertain to the extent they feel confident. Individuals come to work with different levels of confidence, depending on how they've been raised, what life has dealt them, their genetic makeup and basic chemistry, what happened yesterday.

"Confidence is a very interesting thing. It's related to competence. They self-reinforce—or not—depending on experience. If you've been confident enough to go and do something you hadn't done before, and nobody else had, and you achieved something with it, then you've gained experience and competence. And you've also gained another level of confidence. You are able to embrace less certainty, which is the hallmark of most entrepreneurs."

Koogle emphasized that people aren't born with this confidence and competence. You hadn't run a business when they slapped you on your behind when you were born. You have to work your way up. "It's true for organizations, too. Organizations are full of people who have various levels of both competence and confidence, and they have to be brought along."

In Koogle's approach, long-range vision creates in himself and his employees the feelings of inspiration and freedom. These feelings attract and energize people. Short-range vision creates other feelings: confidence and competence. These feelings allow people to grow and do more and ultimately fill in the "space with no lid" in their ecosystem. But it is the short-range, daily vision that Koogle seems to pay most attention to.

Koogle believes that in business you have to be very practical. The benefit of proceeding by steps is that it allows a company, at whatever stage it is in, to be very careful about its use of time. You try to put your time where you can get the biggest benefit. That is an exercise in trying to cull out from all the things you could be doing those things you really should do, based on the highest rate of return today. The company has to balance today's payoff against a large vision. So you achieve a few things now, to build people's competence, and then extend the vision. Then people feel confident *and* competent enough to extend and extend and extend what they reach for.

"I've done turnarounds, I've done shutdowns, I've done growth companies. And I know the value of establishing order. Figuring out the priorities. Lining those up. Ticking them off. Extending the vision. Relisting priorities.

Ticking those things off. Because organizations, small or big or huge, really do need a roadmap. You have to be more anal or less anal at any given stage in development, but there's a lot of value from it."

Koogle believes vision has to be "granular." As the vision grows, it becomes more granular, more specific. "In growing a business, you need to have a big enough vision for a number of reasons we've already talked about. But you've also got to have the granularity so that there is something people can execute against, truly build a business, and build their confidence. So you can expand to the next level and the next level."

You've got to have granularity so people can execute.

Although Koogle may spend most of his time focused on the daily struggle to survive and grow in his ecosystem, long-range vision does enter into his active thoughts. "Both things happen: You expand to the next level because, if you execute well, you've got great commerce happening and that fuels payroll and you can support the growth of the business. People's confidence expands and they're able to take in the bigger vision. It's very practical. You always need to walk back and forth between two lines: one granular enough to allow execution, the other nongranular enough so the vision doesn't put a lid on people, doesn't overly constrain them. A vision has to be big enough to be exciting but not so big that it is daunting—or unattainable."

To Koogle, these are very fine lines demanding precise choreography. "It's very interesting. As you build a large organization, you have to build the way to process the vision into it. I hate talking in layers, but fact is people look up to the top of the company for direction. The vision gets cast there. And then the organization that is built, hopefully, is one that takes that, and creates the granularity from it. And executes it."

As part of its role in a daily dance with short-term vision, long-range vision is also present in Yahoo! as a kind of subconscious metaphor in Koogle's and his colleagues' minds. From the beginning of our conversations I noticed the regular use of terms and ideas from the media world in addition to the computer world Yang and Filo and even Koogle came from. The long-range vision for Yahoo! is to become a full-fledged media company, in the specific medium of the Internet. That vision provides many of the terms with which Yahoo! thinks through its daily vision, and it provides the fundamental direction for all its daily experiments in vision. In the biological terms of an ecosystem, long range vision at Yahoo! is also a matter of *emulating* another species and its methods for surviving. Why take the risk of inventing something entirely new when proven models exist for you to follow? Hence, a business model built around advertising, efforts to build numerous "properties" that attract targeted "eyeballs," and so on.

■ CULTURE AND VALUES

As I was coming to understand vision from Koogle's organic, Darwinian perspective, I began to wonder what would keep vision in power, actually leading an organization. Fear, greed, ego, lust for power—many other forces besides vision also exist in business. And in many companies, despite what their PR says, those forces rule. How can you be sure that vision is really present in a company at all? And if it's there, how can you make sure it, rather than other forces that compete with it, rules?

One answer goes back to Koogle's emphasis on making sure vision is connected to daily work, that it's about actionable tasks. At every stage in a company's growth, he explained, you need to ask what the structure is and whether it's capable of taking the next level of "ungranularity" and processing it into actionable items. That's critical. Otherwise the organization doesn't have enough people in the right places, with the right experience and confidence and competence, to process a vision down to actionable work. "Then: disconnect. The company collapses over time."

Another part of the answer to having vision and empowering it comes down to values. Koogle said he witnessed that while working for Motorola. "Core values are fundamental to building anything that's sustainable. I was raised with well-rooted human values, and fortunately throughout my business career I've gravitated toward working with people who shared those." At Motorola he found the same thing. At the top—quality people who not only had good fundamental human values, but also had very large visions and knew how to build visions on top of those values.

Core values are fundamental to building
anything that's sustainable.

"You do hear about values and business as if there's a natural built-in contention between the two. But there are companies that are founded on the belief that they don't have to be. And Motorola is one." He told me he was fortunate enough to have a lot of access to the people at the top there, very bright people with a global vision based on human values. "From watching I learned a lot of business principles, I saw people who ran very large enterprises who stuck to their values, and wove vision and values together."

To say that vision depends on values is to say that people, especially founders and top executives, have to *want* to do the right thing and they have to *want* vision to be in power. Initially, it's a matter of choice. Then over time, vision and values have to be woven in as part of a company's culture. "With sound values, greed and ambition and all those other forces take a back seat. With a strong culture, peer pressure will continue to moderate those forces. If serving customers is foremost in everyone's mind, negative forces are kept at bay and people's focus is on the outside instead of inside the company. You need feedback that tells you what you're doing really serves a need. If that's your focus, you can keep to your vision." Everything will change for a company over time, but the good ones don't change the way they do things. They keep their principles and values.

■ DISINTERMEDIATION

I asked Koogle to look ahead at the changes Yahoo! and the web might make in the world. After all, while the Internet itself changes very rapidly it also seems to be changing the world around it. Yahoo!'s ecosystem is changing the world's ecosystem. He said, "Yahoo! plays a very central role in what's been called disintermediation. It's actually one of the reasons we've been able to get such a following out there, such a user base."

Naturally, disintermediation for Koogle is best understood as a change in an ecosystem. As part of the economic ecosystem, there has always been an intertwined flow of goods and information. One very important part of the information flow concerns the goods themselves and the companies that make them. At any one point in the world's history, there's an equilibrium in this flow, which is largely determined by the physical channels established to handle it. Before the web, the global distribution and flow of information was mediated by the available technology:

➤ Letters sent through postal services;

➤ Magazines and newspapers printed on daily, weekly, or monthly cycles and then shipped to their destinations;

➤ Telephone calls or faxes, sometimes to parts of the world in very different time zones.

With the web, distribution of information becomes much more immediate, and consumers play a much more active role in obtaining it. Anyone can get up-to-the-minute information from anyplace on Earth, straight from the source, without being forced to go through countless intermediaries. That's disintermediation. And that will change the world of commerce and information.

With the web, the information channels for commerce have contracted; now people can go directly to whomever holds the information. The same thing is starting to occur for products; consumers can not only shop around but order

TIM KOOGLE EXPERIENCES
DISINTERMEDIATION

Last Sunday afternoon when it started pouring rain, instead of going out and having coffee I decided to go learn a little bit. I'm a car freak, was a mechanic early on. In half an hour I was able to get an incredible amount of information on the evolution of Jags, something I've been meaning to learn about for a long time. Within half an hour, hitting a couple of sites in the UK and one in Scotland, I had aggregated some information about service providers there. One guy had some photos . . . And I pinged across to Norway where a guy has a stable of vintage cars and has strung together their history. Back over to the United States on a couple of sites that looked at the evolution of the different Jaguar power plants. And back to how Ford had acquired the company and all this sort of stuff.

So, within a half an hour, not only was I accessing information in at least three or four different countries, but I was able to learn a lot I hadn't known. Series One and Series Two and Series Three releases, and why that had happened and what the performance of the different ones were, et cetera, et cetera. Now, three or four years ago, what would I have had to do? Go to the library. Hope that they had an extensive collection of books that were relevant. If not, talk to a librarian maybe. Write away to another library, possibly, and ask that they either photocopy or send copies of books. Maybe then I would go to the bookstore to see what else I could get. Call some friends. If I was looking to buy some parts to rebuild a Jag—which I am—then I would call my uncle who I know lives close to Pennsylvania, which ends up being a center for parts collections and stuff. The whole thing would have taken, probably, a month. At least.

Think about it. Disintermediation has occurred. That's kind of cool.

goods directly from manufacturers. Dell Computer is one good example. Already in early 1998 Dell was selling millions of dollars worth of computers a day directly to consumers over the web. "The whole food chain is inevitably shortening. And it's all about disintermediation."

The whole food chain is inevitably shortening.
And it's all about disintermediation.

Direct consumer-to-manufacturer contact didn't seem entirely new to me, given, for example, catalogue sales, so I asked Koogle how the web made this relationship different. The big, fundamental difference he sees is that the web allows the consumer to "time and space shift everything." That is, you no longer have to call an 800 number and order a catalogue through the mail and wait for it to arrive. You can have direct and immediate access to the manufacturer's online site, no matter where you are, no matter where the manufacturer is, no matter what time it is in either place. Consumers can become much more independent and powerful by taking advantage of these changes. Individuals can work from their own individual needs and desires, and look for exactly what will satisfy them. The limits established by the old physical channels no longer exist. In effect, space and time have shrunk for consumers.

Far more changes are coming. More large shifts in the distribution channel for pure information about goods and services. More changes in the sales process and distribution channel for the goods and services the information refers to.

Products that are themselves packaged information can be distributed directly through the medium of the web. That includes software, of course. You no longer have to buy a floppy disk and a manual at a store—you can simply download both. The same is true for images and sound files. Koogle believes that it's only a matter of time before videos and books can be downloaded as well. "Anything that you can create in electronic form can be downloaded immediately and not necessarily physically distributed."

Large sections of the distribution and sales channels involved with either information or goods and services are going to "get sliced out" by the web, and what doesn't get sliced out will have to change. Retailers of all kinds, the wholesalers and transportation systems that supply them, the financial services that support these channels, the manufacturers who build and inventory products—almost all will be affected. The marketplace will not be the same as it was before the web.

According to Koogle, there's very little commerce that couldn't be supported on a web-based model. "It all depends on whether there's a viable business model that will support a given class of goods. Or on whether a basic human need for physical touch and feel are part of the buying, the decision-making process itself."

Take food, for example. Food for immediate consumption. Koogle described some experiments that have been run by Peapod and companies like it. They allow consumers to go online and order food for delivery to their homes. Branded, packaged goods seem to work especially well for consumers, since they already know what brand of peanut butter or bread they like. But it's not yet clear that there's an efficient model for fulfilling these orders, for physically gathering and then delivering them. It's not yet clear, to Koogle at least, that companies like Peapod can mark up the price enough to support their costs or come up with other efficiencies that make a premium price unnecessary.

Clothes are another example. In Koogle's view, there are many kinds of clothing that people could easily buy over the web, especially standard branded items like jeans and T-shirts and underwear. If you know your size and you're familiar with the brand, you could easily order goods like that over the web. You could look at your computer screen and check out different colors and styles and order what you want. But before you buy you'd probably prefer to look at and try on other clothes.

In general, however, Koogle contends that "because you're slicing costs out and reaching a broader audience, those two things should more than offset delivery costs."

More and more goods should end up being sold in volume over the web, just like books and computers are already.

Even cars—according to Koogle, cars are already emerging as a large market on the web. Many people get the information they need to make their buying decision straight from the web, even if they also still rely on word of mouth or testimonials from friends. They can get more information online—including information on where they can get the best price—than they used to be able to get any other way, and they can get it much more easily. Before the final step most people will still want to get behind the wheel before such a major expenditure. But they will have even less reason to put up with the sales process at traditional car dealerships.

Koogle also believes that something that might be called *reintermediation* will also occur. It all goes back to what he learned over twenty years ago: "Darwin was right." Some firms and industries were able to do business because the old physical channels forced consumers to go through them, even though they didn't add much value. Now, consumers won't be forced to use them. "That low value-add position in the food chain goes away." The only way these firms will survive is if they find a way to add value back in.

Take the case of jeans. Koogle thinks stores like The Gap may be forced to think more about the viability of physical stores and what makes the in-store experience superior. Maybe a little more service in terms of educating people about upcoming products. Something. Car dealerships will need to find *something* to truly add value. With all the access to the information they need online, people will demand the next level of value in physical stores. "And that's healthy. That's what'll happen. So I think reintermediation will occur, too. We think about this all the time here: What can we do to enable commerce? What can we do to add value?"

We think about this all the time here: What can we do to enable commerce? What can we do to add value?

Chapter

Imagine and Create a New Whole: Bud Colligan, former CEO and Chairman of Macromedia

One of the newer technologies to emerge from Silicon Valley between the rise of the personal computer and the Internet is actually an amalgamated set of technologies called *multimedia*. As the name implies, multimedia brings together on a computer many different media, enabling text documents to contain video and sound, for example, or enabling computer applications—mostly games so far—to combine sound, animation, video, and text. For creative people, this integration offers a wider palette with which to create. For the consumer, all these artfully combined media can produce a richer experience, and possibly communicate better, than plain text can. The company that has done most to make all this possible is Macromedia, headquartered in San Francisco in the Silicon Valley outpost known as *multimedia gulch*.

Multimedia requires authoring tools just like plain text requires editors or word processors. That is, computer tools are required for capturing or creating and then editing the text, graphics, sound, video, and animation that go into a document or game or web site. And tools are required to integrate all these media into a final output. Without them, multimedia wouldn't exist. So when Macromedia began offering a set of these tools in the early 1990s, it made possible a whole new means of creative expression, and a whole new industry.

Under John C. "Bud" Colligan, Macromedia's CEO from its inception in 1992 until 1997 when he stepped back to the sole job of chairman, Macromedia's approach to vision resembled the creative process its products enabled, and indeed the process of Macromedia's own formation: Vision is a process of stitching together more-or-less existing pieces to form a new and better whole that goes on to interact with its environment. The original idea of the vision is usually the work of one or two creative people, but after the idea is implemented it continues to evolve in response to market and technology changes—and in response to critical feedback from the audience the creative work is aimed at. Over time, this evolutionary response works to get the implementation of the vision right, although it may also go so far as to completely change the original creative spark.

When I sat down to talk with Colligan late in 1997 he had just stepped back to become chairman of Macromedia, and both he and his company were at the end of a cycle of creation and evolution. *[Not long after we spoke Colligan resigned as chairman.]* I found him in a mood to reflect on Macromedia's vision and to think out loud with me in drawing some human and business lessons from his experience. Macromedia and Bud Colligan have been real pioneers. That isn't always a pleasant role. When the company seems to be making all the right moves, its stock soars. When some moves don't work out, the stock plummets. Colligan has experienced both. "You're the hero one day and the you're the dog the next. But, you know, you weren't as smart as they said you were before, and you're not as dumb as they say you are now. It's a matter of executing, because people believe results more than they believe speculation."

One other unpleasant part of being a pioneer and leading a high-tech company in Silicon Valley's environment is the time it requires and the impact that has on personal and civic life. To the extent that vision motivates such disproportionate devotion, it has to share in the blame for the problem—and share in the solution. At one point during our conversation, Colligan's young son walked by on his way to a backyard playplace. As we talked briefly about children Colligan said, "Well, that's really the reason I've just cut back. I'm going part-time now at Macromedia, just as chairman. I hired Rob Burgess to be president and CEO because two years ago I said to myself that this just can't keep up. I was working 70 hour weeks all the time and my kids were growing up and all those hours were killing my family life. It's a real problem in the Valley. I've resisted having a pager, even though a lot of people in the company have them. It puts you on call all the time. It's got to stop somewhere. Kids don't wait for you while they grow up. So I'm his room parent now. We're just going to do things differently . . ."

I asked Colligan if this was part of a dark side to vision, that people can become so devoted to making some change in the world that they lose perspective on other things that are important as well. He thinks that's true—it takes a huge commitment to make these companies a success. There's also a perverse culture in the Valley that values the visible signs of success more than the invisible relationships and commitments people make to their family and their community. "Just look at the high divorce rate in Silicon Valley. Look at all these lists in *Upside Magazine* and *Vanity Fair* and *Forbes*. It's becoming a little bit like Hollywood. There's a cult of personality—Larry Ellison, Bill Gates, and so on—and of the trappings of success. Starting a company in itself is all-consuming, and

BUD COLLIGAN ON CHANGING PERSPECTIVES

As you pull back from a company there's a certain affirmation. People tell you what you meant to them, or what they miss about you not being there as much. For me personally that was very affirming. It gave me a lot of confidence that I have some qualities and capabilities I can bring to any group of people in the future. You can read these books about Larry Ellison, Bill Gates, Steve Jobs: There is a tremendous need in these people to be accepted, to be affirmed. You would think, "Gee, someone who has so much and accomplished so much: How come they just can't get it that they're very capable?"

There's obviously a whole psychological aspect to this. But it's also true that when you're in positions of power it's very hard to get straight and objective information, whether it's information about your business or about yourself. How do you really find out what your strengths and weaknesses are and which things are working and which aren't? You have to be pretty self-aware. A lot of these successful people frankly aren't that self-aware. They just do things that end up working and they're able to drive people and so on. So sometimes you get a lot when you step back from that and you're able to look at it more objectively. People no longer have an incentive—you can't question their motivation because they really don't want anything from you anymore. So for me, stepping back a little was a real positive experience and one I appreciated.

then there's this cultural veneer that lays over it. . . . Hopefully, as the area gets more mature, people will settle down and see they've got to get back to the community and participate in the schools and try and create a stable environment for their family."

Hopefully, people will see they've got to get back to the community and the schools and their family.

■ BACKGROUND

Macromedia was formed in 1992 by a merger between Authorware, Inc. and Macromind Paracomp. Colligan had been president and CEO of Authorware since 1989, and before that he'd worked at Apple Computer, which he joined in 1983 as a new Stanford MBA. According to Colligan, a man named Michael Allen had the original vision for Authorware. Allen's vision—and Authorware itself—grew out of his work on a system called *Plato* at Control Data Corporation (CDC).

Plato was a groundbreaking, computer-based training system developed in the 1970s and 1980s, using CDC's large mainframe computers. And then, Colligan said, when the Macintosh came out Michael Allen saw that it presented incredible possibilities for education. Education didn't have to be confined to text. For the first time you could add voice and graphics. "Allen said, 'Gee, just think of what this could be if the computer could talk and if there was more interactivity and you could simulate things graphically,' He could see the educational possibilities there." Simultaneously, Colligan was working with Bill Atkinson on similar issues with Hypercard at Apple Computer. "We were developing Hypercard as a kind of Rolodex, and we said, 'Gee, we could use this to control a video disc, we could integrate questions with elements of video. Biology could really come alive if you could start seeing all these images on a screen.' And then Allen and I started working together. Eventually, they recruited me to be CEO of Authorware. So, we had a shared vision that evolved at two separate points and then joined up and went forward."

When Colligan joined Allen at Authorware, their shared vision was focused on education and training systems. But they faced problems as they moved away from Plato's world of mainframe computers. Before CD-ROMs, distribution was very difficult. Basically they were developing applications that could be deployed in a limited LAN or a classroom environment. At American Airlines they did a big project: 300 hours of stand-up instruction were translated into 152 hours of interactive multimedia learning on computers for about 50,000 of their 90,000 employees. "They would run through a couple of computer labs we had there for them. It was very successful. The employees had a very positive feeling toward our system. They liked it better than stand-up instruction. Their learning was measured to be higher. But it was very localized. It was a brute force way of doing it."

In fact, Colligan explained, the marketplace was not engaging sufficiently for Authorware to build a big company based only on that technology. In 1991–1992 they knew it was necessary to get more critical mass. To have and consolidate the resources necessary to grow the company rapidly, to pull more of the various pieces together, they merged with Macromind Paracomp. "And that led to the notion of a studio which would bring all the pieces of multimedia together. We would be the defining company for bringing all the pieces together and marketing them to our customers."

That's where Macromedia's vision began in 1992. But the pioneering company faced more than a few surprises as it worked to implement it.

■ MACROMEDIA'S VISION

Colligan believes that a vision changes over time. There was a clear vision for Macromedia that everyone understood in the beginning: "We were building a set of creative tools for designers and developers to build beautiful interactive content." In the beginning that was primarily on paper and CD-ROM because those were the media of choice, and now the choice has quickly evolved to the World Wide Web. "The vision for the company was to be the absolute leader in being able to translate people's ideas into reality, into content. If they could imagine it they could do it. If they could think of something brilliant in 3D or video, we provided the bridge between their thoughts and what appeared to a consumer, whether that was a game or an educational story or whatever."

If they could imagine it they could do it.

The specific representation of Macromedia's vision was to build a family of interconnected tools that would not only do all those things but that would also be a great value, have good price performance, be excellent at work flow, be the most efficient tools for people to use. "And so we built this concept called Macromedia Studios which was an animation product, a video product, a sound product, a graphics product, et cetera, and all the facets were linked in a common architecture." There was an authoring tool at the center that could take media from each of these various editors, integrate it, and make a production. And then the World Wide Web hit. "And it was like skkkktttgggg! It surprised everybody. And the Macintosh platform declined. Those were big big changes for us. We really had to go back and examine our vision very, very carefully."

The CD-ROM market had taken off for Macromedia, but when the web came along it didn't continue to grow at the rates it had before. And then the Mac platform declined dramatically. "At first when the Mac declined we were able to withstand it. Our sales kept going up. We thought our product was really good and maybe we'd get through this. But eventually just the sheer numbers of how far the Mac was falling impacted our business."

I asked Colligan if the decline of the Mac and the leveling off of the CD-ROM as the medium of choice for designers had as big an impact on Macromedia's vision as on its business. Did the vision specifically include the Macintosh and CD-ROMs? He said it didn't. They had two key notions in their vision: *author once, publish anywhere* and *source and center*. "These were part of our vision and part of Macromedia Studios. We would not only provide the products but also the service, the user groups, the academic programs—everything that supported our customers."

Author once, publish anywhere.

When I spoke to Colligan, Macromedia had just had its user conference and they talked about their vision going forward. "We said, 'You know, our vision really hasn't shifted that much. We are still about creating the best tools to allow people to take what's in their mind and convert it to a medium, publish to a medium.'" Fifty percent of Macromedia's sales were on the Mac, and so the Mac's declining marketshare hurt. And the company had taken the notion of Macromedia Studios to a very detailed level where it had either bought or developed products in all of the categories. "But we had made a mistake, and we decided afterward that we really shouldn't be in a market where we couldn't be the number one or at least a very strong number two product."

Macromedia had thought it could be like Microsoft. When Microsoft threw Powerpoint into Office it was in last place, but today Powerpoint is all there is. They put Harvard Graphics and Persuasion out of business because Powerpoint was free everywhere and it was free for a long enough period of time that eventually that business stopped being viable to Microsoft's competition. "We were hoping to do that on the creative level, but we don't have Microsoft's wealth or staying power and so we need to focus only where we're the very best."

Colligan said, "Our vision was right: 'Author once, publish anywhere.' But our tactics weren't right for the Internet." Macromedia's products were not all developed for the Internet initially. So it had to retrofit some of its products to output Shockwave. Shockwave itself was first downloadable and then Macromedia improved it to streaming Shockwave. But the company also had to work on some new, base-level Internet products that were designed from the ground up to publish to the Internet. So, Colligan argued, "Our vision has sustained us and in many ways has not changed. But there are some practical realities to platforms and publishing media. The tactical implementation of your strategy may go off base. Then you have to go back and acknowledge that although the overall concept is right, you've made some mistakes in the way you've been implementing some of it. It's not often you get both a major platform change and a world-changing event like the Internet in the same year. It was a lot to go through all at once."

As Colligan explained how Macromedia's vision changed over time I wondered whether the vision also represented a desire to change the real world in some way. And if so, why was this change good? "Well, there are a few things. Anytime you're a tools maker you have to look at the end product that is built with your tools, and you have to look at the process by which people use your tools because both are an outcome of what you do." Macromedia's tools enable their customers to take their inspiration and translate it into something useful. Examples Colligan cited were designing ads, whether on paper or on the web, to communicate benefits to people; an educational program teaching math, reading, or writing, or tutoring people learning to type; and entertainment.

"And then on the end user side, what's good just relates to our human experience: It's fun, it's joy, it's feelings of satisfaction about learning something, it's increasing knowledge. It's easy to work in this area. Because it's clean, it's modern, and it helps people."

From the very beginning and through all its evolution, Macromedia has had some product and market focus on education. That seemed to be an enduring part of the company's vision. "We've always had a real soft spot in our heart for education. That is certainly something that motivates us and our vision. We really believe these technologies are good for people, they're useful, they can help create change." The Internet makes a big difference in what Macromedia can do for education.

We really believe these technologies are good for people.

On one hand, he said, the Internet "smacked us on the head." On the other hand, it was the fulfillment of the dreams they had for 10 years about educational computing. The infrastructure to deliver it hadn't previously existed. Now there are numerous start-ups trying to build curricula for virtual universities that will make interactive multimedia learning available anywhere in the world—as long as you're connected to the web. Companies are also getting serious about deploying educational intranets within their own companies to keep track of their human capital, train people properly, and understand what kind of skills and resource base exists internally—because most people don't know. Most of these educational programs are being built with Macromedia's tools.

"And with the Dreamweaver product that we just introduced at the user conference, one of the things we're building is a set of HTML-based learning templates." Director and Authorware, used frequently as authoring tools, were conceived before the web, so the file formats and the file sizes are larger than ideal. "Yet people still use them actively because we've come up with Shockwave and compressed it and figured out how to stream it. But we want an HTML-based solution as well because that's the lingua franca of the web." And Macromedia acquired Solis, which is a learning management system for tracking all the students or employees following a course curriculum. "So yes, learning is a very big part of our agenda. This is an important part of our business."

I asked Colligan about how that market had changed and whether the company may also have made a mistake in pursuing additional markets in the first place.

He said that even with the CD-ROM it was very hard to distribute educational programs. Now, the Internet has blown the opportunity wide open and put an infrastructure in place that makes that possible. Now numerous start-up companies focus just on education, and older companies are narrowing their focus back to learning only. "And we've had to go back and look at ourselves and say, 'Can we still be the supplier of all things to all people—all creative people, our customers?' The answer is, we're still going to pursue the learning agenda and we're still going to pursue our video and authoring agenda, but we're not going to compete in areas where we're not the number one player."

So, because Photoshop was by far the number one imaging product, Macromedia decided it could invest its resources better elsewhere. And in 3D the company couldn't see a way of making money over the next several years, so again it's going to invest its resources elsewhere. "But learning is a core piece, even in Director, which has been much more of an animation product. A lot of people use it to explain and illustrate concepts."

Colligan went on to say that Macromedia thinks there's a real synergy between learning and entertainment, even though most people would say they're completely different. "The best learning is entertaining! We don't want drill and kill programs." When Macromedia's user conference comes together Colligan said he often hears a common complaint from educators. They'll come up to him and say, "Gee, we really feel bad that you guys spend so much time showing us this glitzy stuff produced with big budgets. We don't have those kinds of budgets in education."

The best learning is entertaining!

And to that Colligan replies, "Peace! I know you don't have those kinds of budgets in education. But we think you will learn a lot from seeing the production values, from understanding how these companies approach entertainment, and from knowing the kind of fast-paced stuff that appeals to kids. Because what you're doing doesn't work! So, you need some of their values." On the other side, Colligan believes that companies like Electronic Arts and Broderbund, which came up through the entertainment side of software and are now trying to pitch their products as educational, need to think more about their learning objectives. Do their products really have a strong educational content? Does *edutainment* really teach people anything? "I think there's great synergy here, not so much between markets, but from each group learning the strengths of the other."

In business, one very often hears hopeful talk about synergy. Less often does the synergy actually seem to exist. I asked Colligan how Macromedia tried to make synergy between its educational and entertainment customers actually happen. "We create physical forums. We're having one down in Australia soon, and we have one in Japan, and we're having one in Europe in January. We've kind of gone around the world with physical forums and seminars. But there are also virtual forums. We do that through our web site, which is available now in multiple languages. People can come together, and we have chat and e-mail capabilities there."

I asked Colligan if he could envision a time when Macromedia's tools would be so easy to use and so productive that large numbers of educators could use them to create effective educational programs. He explained that a lot of them do that today.

"Our tools are sufficiently easy for many people who are motivated. However, I think the biggest impediment to more generalized usage of these tools is the time and cost required to develop meaningful content." Colligan sees a broad scale of production values and quality: Hollywood movies, television, and documentaries on one end; people who do weddings, and home or semiprofessional afficionados toward the other end. And then there are people who never edit anything they film. "I think that great content still needs great thinkers and very talented media professionals to put everything together. To do that, you have to amortize your investment across hundreds of thousands or millions of people."

Colligan believes that between the publishing companies and the media companies there will be sufficient budgets and talent to produce the high-end products that have to be amortized. It's all the other productions that intrigue him more: People who have web sites right now that are all just text, or text and graphics, and who want to teach you about flowers, or how bees make honey, or whatever. They'd like some information processing tools that make producing that easy, and make it easy for someone else to access what they've done and go through the information in an interactive way. No one's really cracked that nut yet. It's a hard nut to crack. "That's what some of our learning templates on top of Dreamweaver are about."

Colligan became more impassioned the more he spoke about education. He went on to say, "This is the true use of the Internet: for distributed learning that's prepackaged, but also for courses taken online in real time where perhaps 200 people come together simultaneously on the web." For these courses, Colligan envisions a virtual whiteboard and a queue

---

This is the true use of the Internet: learning.

---

of students, and each person's computer is capable of giving and receiving input from instructors as well as the other students. And there's a window where instructional courseware can be put up and where new materials can be developed quickly—even the day before. Faculty members today often come to class with an article they've photocopied, or some current event from a paper that's relevant for the course they're teaching. What Colligan would like to see are programs that make it easy to process information into knowledge relatively quickly. "This has always been the big bugaboo in educational computing. It just takes too much time to organize and format information into some kind of insightful presentation. We're working on that and other people are working on it too."

■ COMMUNICATING CHANGE

After Colligan had described the changes Macromedia has gone through—its merger, the decline of the Macintosh, the switch from CD-ROM to the Internet as the preferred distribution medium for content—I wanted to know how he worked to get the whole company to adjust to and fully comprehend the changes it had to make. How does he let them know where they're headed and how they expect to get there?

Colligan answered, "I communicate a lot. I think people like to follow me because I emote. I lead by that. People know the way I feel, and I tell them honestly the way it is. I've learned this. I wasn't always this way. I've learned more and more how to be a leader." As the company got bigger, when he couldn't just talk to everyone anymore, he would hold monthly communications meetings. He would also send companywide e-mails every couple weeks, or every week when it was important. He let people know, "This is what we're doing, this is where we're going, this is why we're doing it, this is why what you're doing is important." He said he tries to communicate those things constantly, and that all his managers have to do that as well. But he said that communication is one of the things that starts breaking down as you get bigger unless you pay a lot of attention to the problem: How do you replace the personal communication processes with institutional processes that can work as the company grows?

Colligan also found that the physical things he would do are important: being up in front of people, being up in front of the industry. "I'm really identified with Macromedia. People think it's my company. I don't want to do these appearances like there's a cult around me, but so that people think there's a leader who takes responsibility and has a vision for where the company's going. Ideas. It all starts with ideas. What's our big idea, and why is this different?"

It all starts with ideas. What's our big idea,
and why is this different?

According to Colligan a company is very much a living organism. It goes up, it goes down. It has good quarters, it has bad quarters. Macromedia had gone through a difficult period the past year. Every great company has gone through difficult periods. How do you get through those? If people are in your company just because you're paying them the most, or because the work at the moment is interesting, you're in trouble. If the project they're working on is not interesting for a while, or they get bored because it's the fourth or fifth rev of the same product, or if they think some other company is doing something more interesting, they'll leave. Silicon Valley is the culture of the Grass is Greener Somewhere Else.

Colligan believes, "You can't just be about making the quarter and about successful financial results. People want to believe that you're doing something that's good for humanity, that's good for customers, that leads to people being satisfied and happy with what you do for them." According to Colligan, the more you can get a feedback loop going the better, whether it's thanks and appreciation from management or whether it's money or stock. But Colligan has found the most effective feedback is not money but human

---

People want to believe that you're doing
something that's good for humanity.

---

appreciation, saying thank you and recognizing people publicly. Those go much further than monetary compensation. "We all have monetary compensation, we all have stock options, and sometimes they're worth more or less. Oh, people do make monetary calculations. Fundamentally you work to better your families and yourselves, so if at some point you see a huge opportunity, yes, I'm not saying that doesn't matter. But given a relatively level playing field for monetary compensation, then what matters is how people feel." Does the management of this company care? Do they treat their employees well? Do they separate themselves from their employees?

On purpose, Macromedia has always had a culture where everyone was in a cube, there were no privileged parking spaces, and people were compensated based upon the job they did, not seniority or who they were or who hired them. Benefits were increased every year as the company could afford more. "It was clear that we valued the employees. We also had a monthly pizza day—the company paid for the pizza and subsidized drinks. Some of these things are standard in Silicon Valley, but it's what you do."

Every year—except 1997 when it went to Silverado— Macromedia would have an off-site at Pajaro Dunes and everyone would come together and Colligan and his managers would outline the company strategy. But they also had time for recreation and getting to know each other, and they had a talent show. "When we merged Authorware and Macromind Paracomp, a lot of the talent show was basically about that. There was one blues song that went about a half an hour long—everyone in the company could get up there and come up with their own four-line blues jingle, to the cadence of the music. And people came up with incredibly creative and sometime very pointed remarks about management because we'd just mooshed these two companies together and a lot of people were unhappy with their new positions. It all came out. It was a huge cathartic experience and they felt safe doing it. It was okay."

Colligan thinks all those open communications and open-door policies end up being part of a company's culture. "The result is that people feel ideas are what govern, not other things."

Ideas are what govern, not other things.

Given how much Macromedia's markets and technologies have changed since the company was founded, and given how Macromedia has had to evolve in response to these changes, I wondered whether all this movement had clarified the unchanging parts of the company's vision. And I wondered whether Colligan sees a new change on the horizon. He thinks people see clearly that their business is about serving the needs of creative professionals. That has never changed. "But we've also started thinking very hard about what our business means for consumers. With the web we're downloading a hundred thousand copies of our Shockwave and Flash plug-ins every day. And so we've got a relationship with people we've never had a relationship with before. They know about us, they come to our site, they use our technologies every day."

That raised new questions for Macromedia: How could the company make more money from these consumers? How could it have a meaningful relationship with these new customers that is mutually beneficial? "Right now, they get everything, but we don't get anything in return. Right? So we're going to launch a Shockwave-enabled content service in November [of 1997] called *Shockrave,* and it's going to be about the best Shockwave content on the web, about community, and about some value that we can bring to them because of our relationships with other companies."

Despite everything the company has gone through, Colligan thinks it's important to say that everything hasn't changed, they're not a completely new and different company. "It's important to say to your staff, 'All this work you've

> This is a new-products industry, and we've got to be
> building the products that people want.

done is important, it's good, it's meaningful, it helped us get where we are.' But it's also important to recognize what has changed. We've got to adapt if we want to survive. This is a new-products industry, and we've got to be building the products that people want."

■ IMPORTANCE OF IMAGES

One of the implications of working to make a vision real is that certain ideas—ones that express a vision—must rule instead of other forces like fear or greed or politics. I asked Colligan to tell me more about how that can be made to happen. "People want to know 'What's the larger context?' We used to have a thing we called *the wheel,* which showed all these media editors as the spokes and an authoring tool in the middle. That served as a very useful framework for many years for the company."

But then Macromedia started getting rid of some products. They'd filled the whole wheel with their own products or those they acquired. "People would say, 'What's the new wheel?' They even called it that. 'What's the new wheel, Bud?'" Colligan and his staff started talking in terms of a new cube framework, which was about the design, delivery, and display of digital media that would take Macromedia beyond desktop tools to systems that would enable media to be delivered. "The real emphasis in the industry was shifting away from actually creating content to delivering content, because the Internet was so big and performance was so important on low bandwidth networks." Macromedia had to start thinking of themselves as being in the server business. That would change their distribution channel, which in turn would imply fundamental changes throughout the company. Big changes.

"Through this company off-site, we said, 'OK, here's the new strategy. Really, our vision hasn't changed, but with the

Internet the premium on performance and on playback has changed dramatically. Multimedia is not all on CD or on disc anymore. It's over a wire, and we've got to become really good at getting our bits to go through that wire. That isn't going to be easy because multimedia applications tend to create big files. Sound and animation and video are huge files compared to text. They're not exactly tailored for the Internet.' So, the company needed a whole reeducation. We're going through that right now."

Macromedia went quiet while it began its reeducation. Then at its user conference two weeks before I sat down with Colligan the company started going public again. "We made a lot of announcements and we said, 'Here's where we're going.' And now that has to be reinforced consistently throughout the company and with the public."

Colligan and I talked for a while about how he planned to reinforce Macromedia's message with the public. We had already talked at some length about how his user conference offered one channel for communication. Now he mentioned several other important channels, especially design. A company communicates its vision, he explained, through any communications it does, whether it's verbal, what its packaging looks like, what kind of press releases it puts out, or what its web site is like. Design communicates.

"In fact, I think one of our major failings is that, even though I came from a background of world-class design at Apple Computer in its early days, I tried to do things too cheaply on our packaging and things like that. A lot of times when you're bootstrapping a company you try to do things cheaply." Colligan now felt that Macromedia needed to articulate a look in its design that was as good as its products. The company had just recently done that. It had Neville Brody, a world famous designer in London, redo all its design. "But I should have done that five years earlier. I didn't. You know, a lot goes into your brand. And a lot of what goes into it communicates who you are and where you're going. You have to ask yourself what a package says about this company. Does it say that we're kind of stodgy, don't really have good design, really don't know how to use color? In our business that's

---

You have to ask yourself what a package
says about this company.

---

particularly important because we sell to designers and they evaluate us by what we look like."

■ EVOLUTION

After we'd talked for a while about Macromedia's vision and the ways in which it had both stayed the same and also changed in response to changing conditions, I asked Colligan what his experience may have taught him about vision in general. For example, how has his experience helped him interpret the visions of other companies and the ways they've changed? He said, "I think Bill Gates would say Microsoft's vision was 'one person, one computer.' That's been their sustaining vision. But now the Internet and wireless communications are giving us the capability of having one person, fifteen computers. We're wearing pagers and we've got cell phones and increasingly these are going to be connected to the Internet."

Colligan had just gotten back from Agenda where he'd seen a new little credit card-sized smart card in which you can put up to 2,500 addresses. Eventually it's going to have wireless communications as well. And the Palm Pilot was taking off. "So, is Microsoft's vision still 'one person one computer?' I don't think so. I think their current vision is enabling that one person to go out and search and retrieve and communicate on a worldwide basis, regardless of how many different devices it takes to do that."

Colligan thinks visions evolve based on changes in markets and market conditions that no one can project. "We can project out a few years, but the world-shaking changes—I mean that seriously—that have gone on here in the past two or three years have had a profound impact on how everyone thinks about their business. I don't think anyone really foresaw that, not to the extent that it's happened."

Visions need to evolve according to Colligan. But they also need to keep some things constant. With few exceptions, he doesn't think you can say, "Well this is what we were doing, now let's change completely." As one exception, he mentioned Hughes, a business that had lost its way and had become seven different major businesses—all unrelated. They were acquired through an acquisition frenzy and eventually they all sputtered down and were not very interesting. Armstrong came in and took a 15 billion dollar business and cut it to four billion and said, "This is our mission, this is our vision now." That was a radical departure. "But I think that happens more when you go in and you're fixing a company. If you're talking about a successful company that has an idea that keeps growing . . . I think visions do evolve, but you can still see the same strain through everything you've done in the past."

From what Colligan was saying, it began to sound as if visions are somehow rather passive, reacting to changes in the larger world around them. But visions are also proactive, they create changes. He believes a proactive force is clearly a part of vision. In a lot of ways, he said, many companies' visions originate from seeing the way things are and knowing they could be different or better. You're building on a human need or on a process that exists—but what you're going to do is radically different.

Colligan mentioned Jim Von Ehr, the founder of a company Macromedia purchased that built a graphic design product called Freehand. Von Ehr is now working on a product in nanotechnology. Nanotechnology is about building and being able to control small machines that are made out of atoms. They're so small they're imperceptible. But these machines, which can consist of millions of atoms, have more processing power than millions of computers today. And you can make machines that make more machines, and through this duplicative function over a very short period of time you can create more processing power than is imaginable today.

According to Colligan, these machines will be able to do incredible things, solve problems that we think are completely unapproachable today. When Von Ehr talks about it, it seems like it's a hundred years away. "That takes a lot of vision. Von Ehr has it—he's sure that although we can't see it, we can't even imagine it, it's there. It's somewhere out there and he's determined to figure out how to get it done. Maybe he won't be able to do it, but he's aggressively pursuing a far out, incredible vision. It's all been research up until this point, just far out research. But he's trying to make a company. He believes his is the first nanotechnology company. It's pretty wild."

Colligan explained that when we spoke about vision earlier he was talking much more in terms of a strategy and a vision for a five to ten year timeframe. He does think in a lot of visions, particularly in those that end up being sizable businesses, there is groundbreaking work and a belief in something that is 10 or 15 years out that not very many people believe in when they're first involved. Macromedia had a vision of what was possible. Colligan thinks it was grounded in things people could see that were not quite there, and in a desire to bring it all together for customers. In nanotechnology there's vision, but as yet there's no semblance of anything that presently exists and it may take another 30 years to make it commercially practical.

■ SOURCE OF VISION

Colligan's approach to vision relies very much on one or perhaps a few creative people to initiate it. But many people are generally required to implement the vision, and the response of large numbers of people contributes to its all-important evolution. So I asked him to describe this movement from the initial creators to the larger numbers who must make the vision work. "I think vision, the process of seeing things that other people don't see and seeing what's possible, usually originates in the mind of one person." And then that

---

I think vision usually originates in the mind of one person.

---

person expresses the vision and rallies other people around. Over time the vision is adopted and is evolved by a group.

Colligan used Macromedia as an example. Norm Meyrowitz is the company's chief technology officer. He came out of Brown University. Colligan worked with him when he was at Apple running the education market, and Meyrowitz had developed something that was very much like the web called Intermedia which was a Hypertext system for faculty members to use to build educational courses. "So he had a vision for that. He just never got connected to the web as a way of linking to everybody else's resources. That was the breakthrough there." Since Meyrowitz got to Macromedia he has been able to keep thinking about the possibilities of the technology and what implications that has for the company and for its vision. "So he's an integral part of evolving the vision. As people buy into your view of the world, it ends up being evolved and articulated and transformed as it goes along."

How do you get people to buy into your new view? Colligan believes there are few leaders and many followers, so getting people to buy into your vision is not so hard. People are looking for something to believe in, particularly if it's a good vision, if it's helpful to humanity. In his view, people want something that's bigger than themselves—they want to be part of a successful group. "So, I think you get people to buy in by being enthusiastic, by articulating what's possible, by appealing to their notions of goodness and of creation. . . ."

You get people to buy in by appealing to their notions of goodness and of creation.

■ NEW IMAGES FROM OLD

Imagine an artist at work in a large studio, perhaps part of an old warehouse on the edge of a city. Piled on the floor and hanging from scattered hooks or nails on the wall are all kinds of odds and ends, enough to make the studio look like a junk collector's dream. There are parts of bicycles, old cars, ice wagons, saddles with long stirrups, rowing sculls with long oars, and all kinds of smaller things in boxes and bins. All these are things that have had other uses at other times and places. But as the artist moves through the studio, selecting different objects, he finds new uses and new combinations for them. This is the image that captures Colligan's approach to vision as well as his vision for Macromedia.

In the middle of the studio's floor, just beneath a skylight that highlights it with a ray of sunlight, stands a large work the artist has recently completed. It looks like something Marcel Duchamp or Robert Rauschenberg might have made. Its general shape is of a large wheel, and it rises all the way from the floor to some horizontal beams at ceiling height.

The center of the wheel is an old writing desk, turned on its side. The spokes of the wheel are made out of various kinds and sizes of stiff electrical wire, mostly black, though some have more colorful orange or blue insulation. The outer rim, like a waterwheel, is an assemblage of rather discreet, boxy pieces somehow welded together to make a rather smooth circle. There is a large Victrola record player followed by a reel-to-reel tape recorder and some loudspeakers. Then there are several televisions, all showing different old cartoons. Then there is an old television camera followed by a movie camera with the big round housings for its film and a VCR. And then the final section of the wheel is a series of computer monitors showing what look like a collection of some of the artist's earlier work—paintings, pieces of sculpture, sketches and drawings.

But as you look at the wheel it isn't really the pieces you end up paying attention to as much as it is the overall effect. Somehow out of all these mostly boxy shapes the artist has created something definitely round. In fact it looks so much like a working wheel and has such a feeling of dynamism that you expect it to roll away, right out the door. With a feeling of admiration for the artist, you also feel that maybe you could do something similar. You just have to find the right old pieces and have the imagination to see them joined together into something new.

Chapter 8

Let Science Lead: Art Levinson, CEO of Genentech

While semiconductor and computer technologies have de-fined Silicon Valley in the twentieth century, biotechnology may very well define it in the twenty-first. As electronic extensions of our human capacity to process information, computers and the Internet have changed and will continue to change many parts of our lives. But biotechnology stands poised to change our lives at a more fundamental, cellular, and genetic level. Biotechnology will let us not only read our genetic code and the genetic codes of any other living creature, but increasingly rewrite at least some of that code to suit our purposes. Biotechnology gives us the awesome opportunity to process and change the information on which life itself depends.

Although the science of biotechnology can trace its roots at least as far back as Gregor Mendel's experiments on flowers in the nineteenth century, and although some of biotechnology's production methods go back to the earliest civilizations and their fermentation of beer, as an industry biotechnology began almost yesterday, in 1976. In April of 1976, Robert Swanson, a San Francisco Bay area venture capitalist, and Herbert Boyer, a biochemist at the University of California in San Francisco, founded Genentech, the very first biotechnology company, intending to exploit the results of a new breakthrough in genetics called *recombinant DNA technology*. Boyer and Stanford geneticist Stanley Cohen had pioneered this new field earlier in the 1970s when they successfully transplanted genes from one biological species to another, thus *recombining* their DNA. Although it got away from it for a brief and unhappy period, Genentech's approach to vision was to let this science and its related technology lead the way in discovering new drugs.

One of the many potential applications of recombinant DNA technology was the idea that you could alter the genes in some widely available organism like E. coli bacteria and use them to produce a therapeutic drug, a protein, that may be hard to find in economic quantities in nature. Using just that technique, in 1978 Genentech cloned the first drug based on DNA technology, human insulin. In 1982, it marketed the first approved bioengineered drug, human growth hormone. By 1998, Genentech had pioneered more production techniques—and many more drugs: it had eleven of the approved drugs derived from biotechnology, and it had over a dozen more in the pipeline.

Along with its successes, Genentech has had to overcome the difficulties most pioneers face. And other difficulties of its own making. The company had to learn that doing great science isn't enough to bring a new drug to market; the science has to be backed up with clinicians who know what to do with a new drug, and marketeers who know how—and to whom—it can be sold. The company found that the traditional sources of funding for Silicon Valley start-ups—venture capital and eventually a public stock offering—are not as well suited to biotechnology's longer, more capital-intensive, and FDA-regulated product development cycles. Especially not at this still-early stage of the industry when profits are scarce. Of over a thousand biotechnology companies in the world in early 1998, Genentech was one of only about a dozen that managed to make a profit. So Genentech also pioneered what has become the norm in its industry: It sought funding from established pharmaceutical companies. In 1990, the giant Swiss drug company, Roche Holdings, acquired a majority stake in Genentech. And in 1995, Roche and Genentech agreed to terms whereby Roche would acquire the remaining shares by 1999.

Nineteen ninety-five turned out to be an important year for Genentech in several other ways as well. Genentech's sales and marketing practices came under criminal investigation, and in the aftermath its board of directors forced the resignation of the CEO, G. Kirk Raab. According to a *San Francisco Chronicle* report on July 14, 1995, "Raab had been one of the most prominent business leaders in the industry, a well-known figure in Washington and on Wall Street. But he lost favor amid questions about his personal ethics and leadership. Some of the most unsettling issues involved the company's aggressive marketing of Protropin, a bioengineered hormone used to treat growth disorders in children. A top Genentech sales official faces criminal charges in an alleged bribery scheme designed to increase sales, and the U.S. Food and Drug Administration is investigating the company's marketing practices. Federal prosecutors continue searching for criminal evidence in company records. But neither Raab nor Genentech has been charged with any criminal wrongdoing."

Genentech immediately named Dr. Arthur D. Levinson, a scientist, to replace the high-profile marketeer Raab and to take the company back to its scientific roots. Levinson had been the head of Genentech's research and development efforts since 1990. He joined the company in 1980 from the University of California at San Francisco, Herb Boyer's home, where he was doing post doctoral work in microbiology. Before that, he earned his Ph.D. in biochemistry from Princeton. Along the way he has written more than 80 scientific articles. So his scientific credentials were—and are—impeccable. But in 1995, many people wondered if a scientist could run as large and complex a company as Genentech. By March of 1998 when I met with Levinson in his office in south San Francisco, Genentech was still prospering more than its rivals, so the answer certainly appears to be that he can manage the company very well indeed. However, my interest wasn't in his skills in general management. After Genentech's acquisition, after all the success and all the pain it had gone through in its first 20 years, I wondered whether this important company was guided by a vision. If so, I wanted to know what Genentech's vision was as it prepared to enter and perhaps profoundly change the twenty-first century.

■ SCIENCE, SCIENCE, SCIENCE

Genentech has gone back, over the past couple of years, to the roots of the company, to the vision that Herb Boyer and Bob Swanson articulated in the late 1970s. And that is to be a company that is based primarily on sciene. They aspire, said Levinson, to be "the leading biotechnology company, based on scientific leadership." It's their conviction that with this leadership, the company will develop great drugs.

"We've said these same things over the years, but I think we went through a period of doubt when we asked ourselves, 'Is this really possible?' There are 1,267 biotech companies out there right now. Can we really be *the* leader? Is it really a path to success to base your whole strategy on scientific leadership?" Levinson had been at a trade association meeting a couple of months ago with other CEOs from the industry. At the executive board meeting one of the CEOs stated to a very senior FDA official that her company *knows* now that you can't successfully run a biotechnology company with "this dream of having it based on scientific leadership." In her view, you just develop products, you *tell* your employees what to do, and you make sure that they do it. Levinson was thinking, "Boy, she's off base."

"But it's not the typical model that companies use to carve out a path for success. I think we're quite unusual that way because we really fundamentally believe that out of scientific leadership *will* come success, as long as we approach it in a relatively goal directed way, with some focus. So, that's

---

We believe that out of scientific leadership *will* come success.

what we want to do. Scientific excellence is the underpinning of the whole deal."

There are several important parts to Levinson's argument. One has to do with the value of leadership, despite the difficulty of achieving it against so much competition around the world. With leadership, Genentech can obtain patents (in 1998 it held 3,100 patents worldwide, and had more than 2,000 pending) and either gain a protected headstart in the market for its new drugs or sell their rights to other companies. With leadership, Genentech can more easily attract top scientists to work for it, and it can create a more powerful brand image. That much seems straightforward and obvious enough. What may not be so obvious is Levinson's emphasis on the field in which Genentech seeks leadership: science. He is saying not only that most other drug companies do not have the same vision, but also that they don't even base their work on science. In a highly technical field like drug research, what's the alternative? Isn't the whole drug industry one of the "knowledge industries" we hear about? What was that CEO talking about when she said the industry had learned that basing its work on science was just a failed dream? Do she and most other drug company CEOs really just tell their employees to go make the products they tell them to make?

"Right. Right. And why doesn't that work? Well, there's a role for that. I think it's fine if 80 percent of the companies do it that way." But, Levinson believes, a company doesn't attract exceptional people with that business model. When he arrived at Genentech in 1980 he was considered a bit of a heretic. He had been well regarded, doing good work as a graduate student and a post doc, and the typical approach would have been to take a position at MIT or Harvard and do academic research. "That's what the good people invariably did. The third-rate people would go to work for a drug company." According to Levinson, that was because drug company work was boring. They just screen a hundred thousand or a million compounds and see which of these compounds on a random basis would fit into a certain keyhole—and that was the beginning of a drug.

"Now that doesn't mean it's unimportant work. It's extremely important work and it's led to really wonderful drugs. I'm not disparaging that in any way. But it's not intellectually exciting." What Genentech and a few other biotech companies have set out to do is to bring in the very best people. Let them follow their own nose. Let them decide what projects to do and carry them out in a goal-directed but fundamentally basic fashion, so that they advance the state of knowledge in their field. "Out of that knowledge we believe will come opportunities to develop important drugs. That's been our model in the past. And we're going back to that model. We're seeing real scientific success out of that."

Bring in the very best people. Let them
follow their own nose.

Despite his emphasis on science as opposed to the brute-force screening of compounds, there still seemed to be a large element of chance in Genentech's approach. Or an element of faith: If you hire bright people and put them on the cutting edge of science, then good things will happen. Levinson seemed to be saying that Genentech didn't tell it's scientists, "That's the hill we're going to take!" Instead it was, "Come and do interesting work and we'll find out what hills are out there." But Genentech's approach is not that open-ended.

"I think management does have a responsibility to define, to some extent, what hills we're going to try to climb. It was true in 1980 to say that we were taking it on faith that good things would come from science. But having lived through that, and having seen us hire extraordinarily talented people, and seeing the success that came out of their efforts, I don't think it's a matter of faith anymore. The concept is valid." Genentech has demonstrated, and continues to demonstrate, that if you bring great people in and give them a lot of freedom, good results occur as long as their energies are channeled in a way that ultimately will lead to drug development and commercial success. "We have validated that method of operating, but it's still not widely adopted."

■ FOCUSING THE SCIENCE

But *how* does Genentech channel the work of its scientists? And how does it achieve this focus while still allowing its scientists the freedom they want? It ties back to their vision, Levinson told me. They had a scientific vision in the early days. The first priority was to hire the best people, let them do what they wanted to do, and watch what happens. It became clear over the years that the company was able to capitalize on an important observation very well *if* some company infrastructure and marketing strength was established in the area.

He cited some examples. Genentech became very good at developing drugs in the cardiovascular area—for heart attacks, stroke, and vascular disease. They also became very good, based on their growth hormone work early on, at developing drugs in the endocrinology area. But, Levinson said, they were *not* very good at developing drugs outside of those areas, because the infrastructure, the expertise that's required to do drug development beyond what might be a brilliant scientific or clinical idea, was not in place. Nor was the structure necessary to execute the complex development path that leads to the approval of a drug. "So, we stumbled, and sometimes we stumbled fairly badly, when we tried to develop a drug where we had no particular expertise in the associated functions: sales, marketing, clinical—whatever was required outside of the scientific discipline that led to the breakthrough discovery."

Genentech decided it had to pay attention to that first, but at the same time it didn't want its people to feel too restricted—it had to keep the fundamentals that make for scientific excellence. Over a period of a year and a half or two years, through a top-down driven exercise at the highest levels of management, the company defined areas it believes hold great promise over the next 10 to 20 years from the points of view of scientific inquiry, technological advances, and medical need. "One was vascular and cardiovascular biology, which we were already in. We see many other approaches for success there. Second, we also reaffirmed our commitment to endocrinology. We see many opportunities there. And the third one, which was relatively new for us a couple of years ago, was oncology."

These three fields are still very broad. To see how Genentech works within them I asked about the third and newest field, cancer, which involves Levinson's own background as a cancer biologist.

"It's becoming very clear that through our efforts and the efforts of scientists throughout the world, we're gaining great insights into the molecular mechanisms of cancer. Cancer is a horrible disease. It is a tremendous unmet medical need. But it has essentially been approached with a sledgehammer." Levinson explained the approach has been to develop a drug that kills cells that divide, but the drugs don't discriminate between a normal dividing cell and a cell that's dividing because it's cancerous. That's why chemotherapy makes people sick: It kills all the normal cells that must divide in order to keep you alive—bone marrow cells and many others.

So a few years ago Genentech decided that cancer was an important area that could produce tremendous success for the company over the next 10 to 20 years. The company decided to build up expertise in oncology. It hired scientists and clinicians, and built up a sales force in advance of the first product so it would have the right contacts. "We did all that so that once we had our first big opportunity to be successful—with Rituxine, an antibody for the treatment of patients with non-Hodgkins lymphoma—we'd be ready to go. And we were. Over the next six to twelve months we hope we'll have an approval for something called Herceptin, which is a drug, a monoclonal antibody, for women with breast cancer. That looks really good."

That was how Genentech got into the field of cancer. The company took what Levinson describes as a "visionary position" and said, "Oncology is going to be important and here are the reasons why. Within that context, scientists, go do your stuff. We're not going tell you what cancer to study. We're not going to tell you it has to be breast cancer or prostate cancer or any other. We're not going to tell you how to do the experiments. But we have a fundamental belief that if you do good experiments, good things will come out of that."

If you do good experiments, good
things will come out of that.

The picture I was forming was that within the three areas of cardiovascular biology, endocrinology, and oncology, Genentech's scientists really did have great freedom, unlike those in most biotechnology and pharmaceutical companies and very much like those in a university. The only thing I'd heard that might counter that freedom was the top down decision to focus on those three fields. Asked to explain that process further, Levinson told me that the decision was made at the executive committee level, which involves him and six or seven colleagues. It was also made by reaching down into the organization, relying on teams of people who had what the committee thought was the necessary expertise: Clinicians who understood unmet medical needs, scientists who understood where the scientific opportunities were going to be, and people from sales and marketing who could assess the commercial opportunities.

"We really wanted to get all three components integrated into the process. There could be great scientific opportunities, but if there's no medical condition, who cares? We made that mistake in the past, many times. We've also made the mistake where the clinicians will say, 'God, this is a terrible disease!' and we say 'Okay, lets go at it,' but the scientists don't have a clue what to do. Well, that doesn't work either. And then the third piece, of course, is the commercial assessment, which is largely a function of the unmet medical need. But we still have to have that input, 'Can we sell it? What's the reimbursement environment like?' "

People from the three areas worked together over six to seven or eight months, regularly updating the executive committee on their thought process. In the end, the committee debated: three areas? two? four? include cancer? exclude cancer? The final decisions were made by the executive team, but the actual recommendations came from a grass-roots level.

As I was gaining an understanding of the way Levinson and Genentech had produced their current vision, I wondered if and when they may challenge it again and modify it with more experience. At three to perhaps five years—even a few days in the case of companies like Yahoo!—the new product development cycles in high-tech Silicon Valley companies are typically much shorter than for biotech companies, where new drugs may require fifteen years or more. How does that affect the frequency with which Genentech reviews its vision?

Their vision looks out a good ten to fifteen years, Levinson explained. A five-year vision in their field would not be taken seriously. "That's not a big enough space to work in to get things done in our industry. Still, it's good to do a reality check every year or so to make sure that your vision is consistent. I'm not talking about communication. I mean that your vision is consistent with where the company in the field and the science are going." He thinks some companies have made mistakes with a vision they treat as a given, as if the company has to have that vision always, forever. Vision is not something that should change every year, according to Levinson, but perhaps every ten or fifteen years it should be changed. "You certainly have to change your operating plans, perhaps every three to five years. And you don't want to cast aside your core values on a regular basis. But that doesn't mean that they're cast in stone and should never be challenged either. I think it's important to step back every year or two and just say, 'Okay, here's our vision statement, here are our values, here's our operating strategy: Let's start from scratch and see if they're still right.'"

It's good to do a reality check every year or so to make sure that your vision is consistent with where the company in the field and the science are going.

Genentech takes a three-day off-site meeting every year. And virtually ever year, a look at their core values and their vision is high on the agenda. "We review the operating strategies every year, automatically. But we also spend a lot of time with the culture and vision stuff."

■ IF SCIENCE LEADS . . .

As I listened to Levinson describe Genentech's vision of scientific leadership, I became more and more curious about what that really means, especially what it would mean to make that vision real. Genentech's vision is not a picture of a specific change it wants to make in the world. It's more indirect than that. Genentech's vision is of a process, one it believes will ultimately produce unspecified but beneficial changes. It has a process vision rather than a content vision. In part that means that scientific knowledge, as opposed to random screening, is the base from which Genentech works to develop drugs. In part it also means that science, as opposed to marketing or finance or some other management discipline, leads the company. How is this done?

One thing that helps is for the leader of the company to be a scientist. "I think, everything being equal, it's a clear advantage. Certainly companies not run by scientists are and have been successful. I wouldn't want anybody to think that it's a prerequisite for success. That would be ridiculous." But if a company is to stand on the power of science, and the direction of science, it's hard for Levinson to imagine a hardcore business person inspiring or leading that commitment.

"I've always been amazed at how few scientists run drug companies. There have been a few: Roy Vagelos ran Merck for many years. Great guy. In something like five out of the seven years he ran the company it was the most admired company in *Fortune*'s annual poll. Wonderful guy. He knew what science was about. He was a great scientist himself, and he moved Merck forward in major new ways, very successfully." A business person running a company can be fabulously successful—but Levinson's not sure he or she can be fabulously successful at constantly innovating at the scientific level. The problem is, a company like Genentech has to make fundamental choices: Is it going to go after oncology with this approach, or go after neurology with that approach? "You can try to make sure that you hire the very best people to make these decisions, but in the end there's got to be a real gut check. You have to ask yourself, 'How do I know I'm hiring the best person?'"

Another big issue is the long lag time in science. It takes ten years to know whether research is failing or succeeding. It takes many, many years even to come up with a drug idea. Once you have the idea, it can be seven to twelve years before the drug finishes a Phase Three clinical trial. "So, you're making your best bets on who you should hire to run research, to run development, and if you don't know science you simply can't do as well. I like to think that I know how to do that. I like to think that other people with strong scientific backgrounds also know how." Over the long run, Levinson simply believes that a drug company that is led by people who have some scientific insight has to do better, assuming that they're competent in the other things management requires, than a company led by somebody who's "clueless" when it comes to science. "The way the field is moving now—and it's not just biotechnology, it's computers, electronics, and many others—in your gut you've got to have some sense of where things are going." That's why he says, if anybody's going to turn Apple around it'll be Steve Jobs. "I don't know if he can do it. But I'll tell you, if anybody can, it will be him."

In your gut you've got to have some sense
of where things are going.

So companies in complex and fast moving fields have to be led by people with an educated intuition about their field. And if that field is science, then the people most likely to have this intuition are scientists. But to realize a vision of science it takes more than just a scientist as leader. Even more importantly, it takes a commitment to hiring great scientists.

Genentech does a number of things to attract top scientists. One of the most important is giving scientists a great deal of freedom. Genentech's scientists are allowed to spend 30 percent of their time on their own research. They are also granted sabbaticals to study anything they may wish—or simply to rest. And, to maintain their standing among peers— something vital to most top scientists—they are allowed to publish their work as soon as possible. This publication policy was insisted on by Herb Boyer very early in Genentech's history. The company decided that since it wanted to make hiring top scientists a top priority, its legal department would simply have to figure out how to move faster in obtaining patent protection. At other companies, the legal tail more often wags the scientific dog, and timely publications are discouraged.

Among all the policies and traditions Genentech has formed to attract scientists, none stood out in my mind more than the apparently simple policy of not telling its scientists what to do. This approach is strikingly different not only from most other pharmaceutical companies, but most companies period. Like the CEO said to the FDA, standard business wisdom says you have to tell your employees what to do and then make sure they do it. A Silicon Valley CEO who would no doubt agree was quoted as saying, "I spend most of my time trying to find out what my employees are really doing, and then I figure out what they should be doing." One result, no matter what industry or how high its technology, is that employees cannot guide their work by what they know. They aren't expected to know what they're doing, they're expected to do what they're told. At best, this tends to constantly reduce the knowledge power available in the company to the knowledge of the one person ultimately giving orders. But if science is truly what leads a company, and if you want to multiply the knowledge available to it at least by the number of minds that work there, then science, not a system of sergeants giving orders, must be the guide. Without that you cannot realize a vision of science. You cannot even attract top scientists.

One other implication of putting science in power in a hierarchical corporation is that communications take on added importance. The corporation may not be a scientific democracy, but it needs to win the hearts and minds of its scientists—and its other employees.

When I asked him about this, Levinson agreed, saying "It's hard for me to imagine that you can overcommunicate. I think many companies have some really wonderful policies, procedures, and intentions, but 90 percent of the people in the company don't know about them. Management thinks 'this is what's important,' but if they looked they'd discover nobody understands it." Over the past couple of years Levinson thinks he and his staff have done a pretty good job communicating: through e-mail correspondence from him to all the employees, through Genentech's internal web site, and through all-employee meetings and staff meetings with smaller groups of people. "It's very important that all of our people understand what the vision of this company is. And if you were to survey 10 random people, I think they would have a pretty good sense of it."

It's hard for me to imagine that you can overcommunicate.

And then, Levinson told me, the process has to continue to the next level down: What is the operational strategy for succeeding with this vision? How are we going to be successful? "We worked very hard a few years back, in 1995, developing a plan for success with this vision. You can click on my page on the internal web site and you can see a full elaboration. Any employee can do this, and a lot of employees have actually accessed it." On this web site people can see exactly what the four main elements of Genentech's operating strategy are, related to its sales approaches, product development, strategic alliances, and its short- and long-term financial objectives. "I think most employees in the company can tell you how we're trying to be successful, and what our benchmarks are along the way."

Another example Levinson cited was that in 1995 he addressed all of Genentech's employees and put it on the web site to let them know, "Here's what we want to achieve in 1996, 1997, 1998, 1999, and the year 2000. Here are our specific financial objectives." They didn't make all this information available to the financial community. They considered that proprietary information. But they wanted the employees to know what was important.

One of the key elements in this communication had to do with science. As a company Genentech has historically spent very large amounts on R&D—50 percent of total revenues. "If you do the math, you don't have to be a genius to understand that at some point as our revenues increase we can't keep putting 50 percent of revenues into R&D." For 20 years the company had been doing that. But it recognized in 1995 that in order to meet its 2000 objectives it had to break that mold. "That was something we knew a lot of our people would hate to hear. But, better that we let them know two and three years in advance than to surprise them in December several years down the road: 'By the way, we've just done the budget, and guess what, we're taking R&D from 50 percent to 38 percent of revenues.'"

Levinson allowed that it would have been a good short-term decision to keep that decision quiet and not have any rumbles. "But we said, 'That's not the way to manage a company.'" So as soon as Levinson and his staff were confident in the strategy, they had it approved by the board of directors. Within a week, he was out communicating to all employees: "This is it! We have two years to get ready. But here's what we're doing." And more importantly, "Here's why we're doing it. Once people understood why we were doing it, and that the 'why' was essential to get us to where we wanted to be in the year 2000, there was a tremendous amount of buy-in. Some skepticism, but I think we've been through the transition phase now. I think the vast majority of people say, 'Yeah, it was a tough thing to do, but it was necessary, and good for us for doing it.'"

■ CONNECTED EXPERTISE AND INFRASTRUCTURE

In addition to connecting its scientific vision to operating plans, Genentech has learned it has to connect its science to the associated marketing, clinical, and manufacturing expertise and infrastructure required to bring a drug all the way to a market that can use it and pay for it. How does it do that?

"One of the things we do all the time, and I think any company has to do, is to ask, 'What is rate limiting for our whole development process? Where are the rate limiting steps?' You can't simply assume that they're always in a particular area of the company. It's easy to think, 'Well, let's just wait for the research scientists to come up with the idea.' That can be rate limiting, but for us it's not at all. That's a tribute to our research scientists." One good example of that is the way Genentech first started producing its drugs. When Levinson arrived at Genentech in 1980, it was not entirely clear that you could create an economically viable process to produce human therapeutics using E. coli bacteria. In theory you could use the E. coli as the factories to produce the drugs but it hadn't been done before. When Genentech's scientists demonstrated that with growth hormone, and with insulin, they could do just that, it provided tremendous momentum to the young company.

Another example Levinson cited was his early project to develop a vaccine against Hepatitis B. Well over 200 million people are afflicted with this disease. It's a terrible disease that causes a high incidence of liver cancer, among other problems. "Nobody could produce the vaccine in the bacteria, so my group and I started asking whether or not you could produce it in mammalian cells. That was considered ludicrous at the time because most people couldn't imagine using mammalian cells as the factory for production. How could you ever do that on an economically viable basis?"

Levinson and his team started working, and started making some breakthroughs, and everything seemed to be working reasonably well. They ran their results over to some of the manufacturing people, who did a very detailed analysis and came back and said, "Ah well, nice try. But this is economically toxic. You won't be able to produce the drug at these levels because our manufacturing cost will be $2,000 per dose." If Levinson and company had just accepted that they would have folded up their tent and forgetten it. "But what we and Bill Young *[the head of manufacturing at the time]* and others said was: 'Baloney! Let's keep working and figure out how to manufacture it and reduce the cost from $2,000 down to $100, or whatever it might be.' And to their great credit, because of the direction and the scientists that they had, they figured out how to do it." Genentech now has more production going on in mammalian cells than in bacteria. "We've had breakthrough after breakthrough, absolutely stopping conventional wisdom in its tracks. As I said, in 1981 nobody thought you'd be able to do this. It didn't take very long before the world changed their mind on it. We had a three-year head start because we were first."

We've had breakthrough after breakthrough, absolutely stopping conventional wisdom in its tracks.

The end result of the manufacturing group working to find a way to implement a scientific discovery at an economic price was another pioneering achievement for Genentech. It also reflects a change in the way Genentech connects its scientists to its other operations. In this case Levinson's group didn't throw their discovery over a wall to the manufacturing group like design engineers often do in companies that don't practice concurrent engineering. "We worked very closely together. The research scientists with the process science folks with the manufacturing people, all of whom played an important role in contributing to incremental breakthroughs that eventually led to success." It was a team-oriented approach. Many companies have isolated islands of expertise that don't communicate. In Levinson's opinion, Genentech itself had been that way until it learned the painful lesson that it doesn't work well.

When he took over Research and Development in 1990–1991, one of the biggest problems Levinson thought Genentech had was that the scientists weren't talking with the clinicians. The clinicians were up the hill at their facility, the scientists were down the hill at theirs, and there was almost no communication between them. When scientists were working on a research project, it didn't occur to them to ask a clinician several key questions: If I develop this drug would you use it? Would you know how to use it? Would you know how to evaluate it in a clinical trial? "The questions were never asked. I could give you a number of unfortunate examples where the scientists would do heroic work for three, four, five years. Do what was thought to be technologically impossible. Claim success. And then say, 'All right, Doc. You go do it now. It's obvious that I've done my part.' And the physicians would look at it and think about it. And they wouldn't know what to do with it."

Levinson's number one priority when he became head of both the research and the medical affairs groups was to make sure Genentech never embarked on a project that involved a serious amount of work at the research level unless a physician said, "You know, if you're successful, I know what to do with this." The scientists weren't looking for the physician to tell them how to do the project, just that he or she would know what to do with it. "That became a prerequisite. I wouldn't fund anything on any single project that involved more than one or one-and-a-half head count of effort, or the full-time equivalent, unless a physician said it made sense. I insisted on it. And once you insist on it at the top, it happens. If you don't, it *never* happens."

Once you insist on it at the top, it happens.
If you don't, it *never* happens.

■ EXCEPTIONAL LEVERAGE

So, you have a place where scientists want to come work and where the results of their work are tied to a system that can take a new drug all the way to the market and to patients who will benefit from it. Is there any particular advantage to doing it this way, as opposed to the more traditional screening of compounds? Does science have any advantage over brute force?

Levinson clearly believes there is a real role for random screening of drugs. Good things can come out of that. But it's not who Genentech is. "You've got to ask yourself what motivates you and what inspires you to work. I think we have a style that appeals to certain people, people who like scientific inquiry and the freedom to pursue it. That's very very good for us and we can be successful. I fundamentally believe that in this environment, an exceptional person—and I don't know how the math works out—might be more productive than 20 unexceptional people combined. Now that's not true on the factory line. An exceptional person might be 20 percent more productive than an average person there." The heart of Levinson's argument is that a single breakthrough idea completely changes how the world thinks about things. And if you're the company that has the breakthrough idea, and if you can capitalize on it, you should be able to do wonderful things with it, as opposed to reading about it in somebody's patent filing 18 months later, and then trying to figure out how you're going to get around their patent. "We want to be the kind of company that attracts the exceptional people who are committed to this type of research. We hope we can channel their energies, a little bit, in a direction that in the end would help people and that could allow us all to make a living and then reinvest money back into more research. That's the vision."

A single breakthrough idea completely changes
how the world thinks about things.

The traditional approach in the drug industry has been a brute force, random approach to find molecules that either activate or inhibit what you think is going to be an important target in the human body. "You do this massive screening. You use robots. It's very repetitive. When you think you have something that might work, the chemists work on it to try to make incremental improvements. It's not a process that really advances knowledge." Levinson believes this kind of work is extremely important and leads to very important drugs, but it doesn't open up new vistas. It doesn't give you information you could extrapolate from to make a new breakthrough in a related area.

"If we, for example, make a discovery—the observation that angiogenesis, which is the process of blood vessel formation, is essential to support the growth of a solid tumor—that's a profound observation. Because that says if you can stop new blood supply from feeding a tumor, you might have a therapy. Well, tumors might use different mechanisms to bring in a blood supply. That seminal observation can potentially be used to attack three dozen different types of solid tumors—if they all have the requirement for blood vessel growth. So from that basic insight, that original breakthrough, a lot of other things can be done as well. That's the leverage you get from basic science."

That's the leverage you get from basic science.

Another example Levinson mentioned was the work done by his post doctoral advisors in the mid-1970s. They discovered that cancer genes exist within all of our cells. Normally they're silent. So cancer is not caused, typically, by a virus or some mysterious phenomenon. It's caused, for example, by an X-ray zapping one of your nucleotides at a gene that, when miss-expressed, tells that cell, "Hey, time for me to divide." And nothing can stop it. "That is hugely important, because it says cancer fundamentally is genetic. And if it's genetic we can then ask what genes are involved. And if we know what genes are involved we can ask what the products of those genes are at the protein level. And then we can ask how we kill the protein. That's an idea. That's a big idea."

■ THE FUTURE

The exceptional leverage science confers on biotechnology carries with it potential risks as well. Not since scientists developed nuclear power—and perhaps especially owing to the troubled history of that field—has the public been simultaneously so excited and so frightened by a new frontier. At the time Genentech was founded in 1976, .public concerns led government agencies at all levels to consider a wide range of controls. Immediate fears largely focused on the possibility of newly engineered bacteria or some other life-form escaping the laboratory and doing great damage to human health or to the ecosystem in general. Laboratories involved in biotech research promised a variety of safeguards, and over time that immediate fear has quieted down. But related fears continue, some well-founded, others not. Levinson and Genentech try to address these public concerns without becoming embroiled in unproductive side issues.

"There are a lot of doomsday scenarios out there. If you go to an international meeting on AIDS, for example, you'll see people picketing and saying 'This is a government conspiracy,' or 'This is a CIA conspiracy,' or whatever. Just for the sake of argument, let's assume that someone would actually want to develop an HIV-type virus. *We scientists wouldn't have a clue how to do that.*" People who are not scientists don't know whether Joe Scientist can go to the lab and create a new AIDS virus. It turns out it's impossible, according to Levinson. The industry is trying to use genetic engineering and the knowledge of the genome to develop drugs that help people. "We are probably a lot less sophisticated than people think we are. There's much less power here than the general public believes. Much less. I don't think we're pushing the envelope nearly as much as the science-fiction writers or the politicians might imagine."

There's much less power here than the
general public believes.

Levinson acknowledges that they raise important questions that he wouldn't want to trivialize. He cited cloning as an example. What are the right policies? As a company Genentech has decided to stay out of the debate, in which some of the arguments are highly complex and there are numerous different legitimate points of view. "Generally, you don't get a lot of credit with the group for agreeing with them, but you get a lot of headaches if you disagree with them. So, we'd rather just stay out. Our mission is to focus on developing drugs that clearly help people. And that's kind of full stop."

Even though a vision of scientific leadership is more focused on a process than on any particular result of that process, I wondered what Levinson sees his company and the industry accomplishing in the next 10 to 15 years.

"I answer this with some trepidation, because science always progresses in a discontinuous fashion. Incrementally things get more efficient and things move along, but every 2 years or every 10 years something utterly unexpected can happen that changes the whole curve. I can't anticipate that, but I always want to be open to that happening." With that caveat, over the next 5 to 10 years Levinson believes we will understand much more about protein function and understand more about metabolism and how proteins interact with other proteins. Out of that increased knowledge will come much faster access to and understanding about how to develop drugs that will either activate or inhibit a certain protein. It's not simply a matter of having more candidate proteins to work on, but learning more about how proteins function and how their function follows the structure of the protein.

"Today, if we have a gene sequence we can precisely infer the primary amino acid sequence of the protein it generates. And we kind of have an idea of how that primary sequence dictates the way the protein will fold. But we're not that good at it yet. Ten years from now, I think we'll be quite good at figuring out how a protein will fold. And from that knowledge we'll probably gain pretty good insights into what the function of the protein might be. And from the function comes the direction and the insights as to what to target for a drug process. I think that will make the whole industry much more efficient at developing drugs."

Levinson also thinks gene therapy will produce dramatic improvements in drug delivery. Today's ideal drug is a pill. If

ART LEVINSON ON WHY SCIENTISTS
NEED TO EDUCATE THE PUBLIC

We don't enter into the debate as to whether something should or should not happen, other than to say we want to be relatively unrestricted when it comes to scientific inquiry. About cloning, we would argue it wouldn't be good for society, it wouldn't be good for the industry, it wouldn't be good for us, Genentech, if it was defined in an extraordinarily narrow way. You could, for example, use the term cloning to refer to removing a cell from your body, drawing it in a test tube, and making two cells. I mean, that's cloning: one cell becomes two cells. If you describe it in an extremely narrow way and say, "This is bad," you could shut down the whole industry tomorrow. Because, that's what we do, as a tool to produce drugs.

Now, on the other extreme, if you define cloning as reproducing an entire human being, clearly there are all kinds of issues there. We don't even have to get into that debate because there's no reason for us to promote that position for our own purposes or for purposes of defending the industry, or even for promoting public health. We operate in an area that feels extremely safe to all of us. It doesn't seem to be contentious.

But If you don't work with the legislatures, and let them understand the words that they're using to describe various proposed laws and regulations, then you could get trapped by their ignorance. So we do work with people to make sure that they understand what the state of the industry is, what our state of knowledge is, and probably most importantly, what the implications might be of the words they use to describe A, B, C, D, and E. We do get involved in that kind of education and communication because weird ideas come up in a vacuum. To the extent that you can be clear with people, and educate them and enlighten them, that's much less threatening. They get a lot more security out of understanding something.

a drug is not orally available, you can take it in a shot. He imagines vectors emerging that will deliver a drug continuously from one injection. Forever. "One possible mechanism is getting a few cells in your body to act as internal factories for producing a particular desired protein." A hemophiliac, for example, needs to produce Factor VIII to correct the genetic deficiency that causes the condition. It's necessary for only a very small number of cells to produce Factor VIII to correct that genetic deficiency. "If you could develop a target vector that can introduce that gene into ten thousand cells in your body—which is nothing—and those cells take the gene and start expressing the protein, you could have cured your genetic disease. I think you're going to see that kind of breakthrough over the next 5 to 10 years."

Add Life for the Endurance Race: Ron Eastman, former CEO of Geron Corporation

Perhaps more than any other company in Silicon Valley, Geron Corporation captures the hope and imagination the general public has for the biotechnology industry. As practically every article on the company points out, Geron seems to have actually found what Ponce de Leon was looking for: the fountain of youth. It has found the clock that appears to control the life span of our bodies' cells, and it has found a way to rewind it. The possible results of this finding sound more magical than real: a way to detect and treat most cancers, and a way to treat and possibly eliminate a large number of age-related conditions ranging from wrinkled skin to hardened arteries. Geron's announced aim is to add more years of health to our life span; the public hopes it can also add more years of precious life.

Under Ronald W. Eastman, the company's CEO during its formative years in the 1990s, Geron's approach to vision has matched what lies between the present and its future goal. *[Note: When I met with Eastman in 1998 he was still CEO. In the summer of 1999, Geron's board of directors decided to name the company's head of R&D, a scientist with a medical background, as its new CEO. Eastman was to remain on the board and consult with the company on strategic planning.]* Geron is putting together a team for a long and incredibly arduous race in which the goal is clear and just reaching it may be victory enough for a lifetime. But the hostile and unpredictable environment the race must cover requires the team to break the course down into small chunks and to be alert for critical points when it might have to change course radically and possibly even choose a different goal. It faces problems in keeping alive and whole to realize its vision, not in lacking the imagination or intuition to see it clearly, and not in the inspiration or sense of direction it provides.

Geron *[as in gerontology]* is dedicated to providing therapies to treat age-related diseases. These therapies exploit the cellular mechanisms of aging which Geron is in the forefront of investigating: a part of our chromosomes called telomeres *[TEE lo meers]*, and a related enzyme called telomerase *[tuh LOM er aze]*.

Telomeres are a kind of tail on the end of our chromosomes that effectively act as a life span clock. The tails become shorter each time our cells divide. Eventually they're used up, which stops division and causes the cell to age and eventually die. Telomerase is a matching enzyme that does an extraordinary thing: it lengthens the telomere tail, thereby lengthening the number of times a cell can divide—which allows it to continue functioning in a normal, healthy, youthful way. In short, telomerase can make cells immortal. And Geron has found a way to do just that, at least in the laboratory: turn telomerase on or off, thereby turning on or off the aging process in our bodies' cells—indefinitely. Turning the clock off gives Geron a promising new tool to fight cancer, which produces cells that don't die. Rewinding the clock gives the company a tool to postpone or treat what happens to our bodies as we age, from wrinkled spotted skin to osteoporosis to atherosclerosis.

But Geron's discovery, and its vision for using it, isn't aimed at making people immortal—despite Ponce de Leon's and others' hopes. Tantalizing as that dream—or nightmare—may be, there is still no evidence that it's actually possible. Rather, Geron's intention is to "increase the human health span." Doing that will prove challenging—and rewarding—enough.

Geron, like the biotechnology industry in general, faces product development cycles that are longer and more complicated than Silicon Valley's high technology companies. And that fact of biotech life makes the business of a start-up biotech company rather unique and treacherous. The culture of venture capital puts great pressure on start-ups to either go public or seek a merger as quickly as is feasible, but certainly before the end of the typical ten-year fund. If a biotech company starts by focusing on a biological process in the body that's malfunctioning, and designs a product to correct it, 15 or 20 years may be required to bring that product to market—if it succeeds at all. Ten to 15 years seems to be the very shortest path from insight to product. Compare that to Yahoo!'s ability to roll out a new product practically overnight. Or even to the several years it may take Intel to come out with a new family of microprocessors.

In the best case, a new biotech company faces the daunting task of surviving the better part of 10 to 15 years as a public company without a product on the market. In the worst case, the biotech company faces the fate of most scientific experiments, which run their course but ultimately fail. Given the challenge Geron faces, Ron Eastman looks at a successful vision in much the same way he looks at therapies for aging: Both are concerned with managing a lifetime and the events that can change it.

■ THE EXPEDITION

Imagine that you're Ponce de Leon, in the early stage of a very long expedition through an unknown and dangerous swampland. You're looking for something you can see very clearly in your imagination, something you yearn for in every cell of your body: a liquid protein that can maintain youth and postpone or even eliminate death. You have a small but varied crew, most of them scientists and explorers who have the same goal you do and the same devotion to it. You have a fixed amount of resources supplied by the people who sponsored your expedition to this new world. Anything else you need must come from what you can make, or what you can trade for with the people you may find, although every time you trade you have to give up something you need. This is the image that captures Geron's vision and Eastman's approach to vision.

Before setting off you had done your best to select just the right crew, one that not only had the right set of skills but the right state of mind and spirit for the expedition. Everything will depend on the character of these people. And you made the best deal with your sponsors you could, getting the most resources at the best price you could command. But now it all comes down to what your team can do. You're on your own. You and your crew have built a platform raft to take you through the swamp. You tested the raft and built it carefully from the few trees and vines that had the necessary characteristics, so you feel as confident in it as you can. From other expeditions you've heard horror stories of similar rafts that either couldn't be built or that fell apart. The raft is the only solid thing you will have to stand on and rely on for the entire expedition, no matter how long it takes.

Several years into the expedition and with no end in sight, you still yearn for your goal, see it clearly in your imagination, and feel confident in your direction. Your raft has proven itself on a number of occasions, and your crew has even managed to enlarge it along the way after finding several new and appropriate trees. But you have a gnawing worry. On cold winter nights, you have to burn your cook fires all night long to keep warm, and fuel in the swamp is very difficult to find. You worry that before you reach your goal you'll have to start burning parts of the raft, maybe so much of it that you can't finish. And you worry that the swamp may suddenly change or that a terrible storm may come up and tear your raft apart, leaving all of you as food for the alligators.

To face these realities with the focus and clarity you need, you've adopted the strategy of making yearly plans with your crew. Maybe it's an odd consequence of the hope you have in what you're looking for, but you've found that concentrating on the indefinite length of your search makes it seem like the expedition itself is immortal, and you fear that could cause you to do something stupid or dangerous. So each year you decide together on what seems the most important thing to focus on, whether it's learning something new about this unknown wilderness and how to survive in it, or creating something new to make the expedition easier or faster. You've found that this way you can remain alert and better endure the rigors of the long expedition.

■ VISION MATRIX

When I asked Eastman to describe Geron's vision, he began by discussing the different time spans a vision may contemplate, and the unforeseen events that can occur during any period. For many of the CEOs I spoke with for this book, the appropriate time span was often tacitly built into their visions. In business, time spans are not so much dictated by vision as by the environment, especially markets and technology: either sources of capital demand a clear return within a given period of time, or technological and competitive cycles do. Perhaps because biotech inherently has cycles that differ from the norm in Silicon Valley, Eastman had contemplated the subject explicitly.

"As with so many things, there are various levels of vision. And regardless of level, there's an opportunity for that vision to change. Rapidly. Within any kind of time frame you want to set. So you really have a matrix of concepts

---

There are various levels of vision. And regardless of level, there's an opportunity for that vision to change.

---

here." One axis of the matrix is different levels of vision: The vision for what ought to be accomplished today and the vision for where the company should be at a certain point in the future. On the other axis are opportunity costs[1] and what Andy Grove calls "inflection points."[2] "If you do not recognize that there are huge opportunity costs along the way, and that they're a constant and a given, you will miss these inflection points. The world can change, and changes may invalidate your vision, or strengthen your vision, or alter it." And you've got to be prepared for all of those, at any time. At any level of vision.

■ LONG-TERM VISION

Given the matrix Eastman described, I asked him to tell me about Geron's long-term vision. The long-term vision, he explained, is really a product of Geron's founder, Mike West, who had always had an interest in aging. He saw scientific achievement in labs, primarily in this country, that seemed to signal the dawn of a real understanding of the biology of aging at the cellular level. As a medical student in his second year at Baylor, already possessing his Ph.D. in biology, West was working in the labs of people who are now Geron's collaborators. He generated some local interest at the time, which very quickly spilled over into the venture capital community, and the who's who in venture capital for biotechnology jumped on the bandwagon.

"Our vision is really Mike's vision. In one respect I am simply a bridge. My job is to build and maintain the bridge that gets us from Mike's vision to realizing it. And that vision

---

[1] In economics, an opportunity cost is the value of an alternative or opportunity which may have to be foregone in order to achieve a particular goal. Eastman used the term often in our conversation, many times in the related but inverse sense of an opportunity and therefore a cost that *should* be undertaken because of the value it will return.

[2] For Eastman, inflection points seem to have a similar meaning to opportunity costs: They are changes in the environment or opportunities which, if seized and pursued well, change the course of history—in this case for a company or an industry.

RON EASTMAN ON BIOTECH'S
VISION MATRIX

Are one or two different levels of vision in my matrix more important than the others? That's a very fair question, and if my answer isn't right and isn't practiced well, Geron will suffer. While I think it's important to have a good vision for the day, what you want to accomplish, and while I also think it's important to have a vision for the next three years, four years, I think—and I'm thinking out loud here, which is one of the benefits of our dialogue—the two most important levels of vision in our business are: What are you going to accomplish over the next six to twelve months? And, how is that consistent with what you want to accomplish over an extended period of time—say ten to twenty years? Kind of a mirror of the product development life cycle in our business.

Let me explain that by challenging the other levels of vision. What's wrong with the three- to five-year vision? Well, it's nice to have, and you ought to have thought about it. But many things can potentially happen over that time period that will dramatically affect which way you're ultimately traveling toward your long-term vision. If you spent a lot of time preparing that vision and a plan for realizing it, not only will you be terribly disappointed, but I think you will have a greater opportunity cost because you will miss some of those inflection points. Any shorter time frame, even if you do identify an inflection point, they're not going to be that material or significant.

Six to 12 months in our business: you're going to spend a lot of money, you're going to make a lot of decisions, and it's enough time to do something extremely important. Or extremely stupid. Which will have a material impact on whether you achieve that long-term vision. And you can look out that far in our industry and get, I don't know, what's the next notch below 20/20 vision? Whatever that is. So I would prioritize them that way—in our business.

is to treat age-related diseases using the knowledge we've gained about how mechanisms at the cellular level govern aging."

I was aware that Geron had recently announced some promising work on cancer, which is certainly a large field in itself, so to be clear I wanted to know how cancer fit within the focus on aging. There was, Eastman explained, a cycle: aging to cancer to aging. He told me Geron struggled early on with the question of how cancer fit with its mission, its vision. They could rationalize the issue away by saying that 85 percent of cancer patients are over the age of 55, or some such age. Cancer *is* an age-related disease. But children get cancer too. And the fact is, the problem with cancer cells is that they *don't* age—the opposite of most old-age diseases. Still, the biological mechanisms Geron and its collaborators had discovered apply equally to cancer and more traditional age-related diseases. "So, as good businesspeople we have built cancer into our vision and said, 'Look, the name of the game is products here. Let's use our common technology, and if cancer gets us to products first, let's go for it.'"

In the terms of the matrix Eastman had sketched, cancer was the first of the inflection points that Geron faced. "We had this scientific platform of understanding. We determined early on that applying it to cancer, whether it was therapeutics or diagnostics, was more fully validated and likely to lead to a product faster than it would on the aging side. So, just over the past four years, we have placed a huge bet on that and it's paying off extremely well."

Just recently, Geron had gone through another inflection point that Eastman described: Geron's discovery that by manipulating the molecular mechanisms its scientists focused on, which they learned about in cancer, they can make normal human cells divide—live longer, if you will. "That suggests we might be able to postpone various age-related diseases. Our work started with aging, which led us to cancer, which has brought us back to aging."

What brought Geron back to aging was, specifically, their discovery that cells can become immortal by "putting telomerase in or turning it on." With our skin, hair, bone, and eye cells, it appears there might be some benefit in our postponing aging, or slowing it down some.

Given all the age-old dreams of immortality in myths and literature, I wanted to know whether West's vision was to prolong human life or simply to help people remain healthier up to whatever point they die. That, Eastman explained, was and remains quite clear. And it is based largely on the science. The primary vision is to, as West would say, "add life to life." To increase the health span, not necessarily the life span. "There's no real valid evidence, in humans anyway, that the human life span can be extended beyond what appears to be a biological limit of around 120 years."

The vision is to add life to life.

Eastman told me the challenge for Geron is to keep people focused on the health span, not on whether there's an opportunity to extend life span. "We can't say it won't happen. And we shouldn't say that it will. It would be a distraction. And I suppose there is also the ethical issue of whether it's even justifiable—that's something we would have no interest in getting involved in unless it were a true goal of ours. It's not. I don't think too many would argue with the fact that treating a disease to improve comfort, productivity, and quality of life is a good end. And that is our end."

■ SHORT-TERM VISION

Besides a period of 10 to 20 years, the other time period Eastman had said was most relevant to Geron was 6 to 12 months. I asked him to describe that vision for the spring and summer of 1998.

He said Geron has to focus on what it takes to succeed in its business: capital and partnerships. He explained the necessity of leveraging the assets, knowledge, and capabilities of others because biotechnology is so difficult a business to compete in, so capital intensive, so knowledge-driven, that for one company to do it all is impossible. He believes the formation of alliances, usually with larger companies, is very critical—alliances with drug companies, but also with universities and the National Institutes of Health. "So, cash, partnerships, alliances. And patents. To be successful in this business, especially in the absence of products, you must have assets." One of those assets is knowledge and how you've protected it so *you* can exploit it and create value with it. Another is your people—the best in your business, motivated, driven and productive.

"And so our goals over the next year, if you look at those keys to success, include forming additional collaborations, partnerships primarily, with larger companies. Remember, we've just made this extremely important discovery, that we can make our normal cells divide longer. I don't think we fully appreciate the significance of this discovery."

He cited two areas of interest that make it significant. First, research on cells is being done around the world. Geron's discovery allows scientists to pursue their research perhaps a little more vigorously because the cells they're studying can be made to divide longer, live longer; that can prolong their experiments. Second, transplanted cells have a longer opportunity to be effective, for example in a bone marrow transplantation. The actual extraction of a cell for transplantation, and the growing of cells to put back in, dramatically ages those cells. "Turning on" telomerase or adding telomerase to those cells can give them extended life, or slow down the aging process so the transplanted cells will be more effective for a longer time.

"So these are very powerful applications. And then if we can figure out how to turn telomerase on in the body to potentially postpone osteoporosis, skin wrinkling, macular degeneration, and so on—conditions that appear to be clearly associated with just the fact that our cells age—that is very powerful."

If we can figure out how to turn telomerase
on in the body—that is very powerful.

I wanted to know how far Geron had gotten in proving these kinds of applications are really possible. He said Geron has proved that in the laboratory, in the dish, you can extend the life of those cells without in any way altering the behavior or the character or the structure of the cells.

That sounded positive, almost too good to be true, and I assumed the results also showed that the cells didn't become cancerous, since cancer cells also have telomerase. "Right. Which in many ways you'd predict, because telomerase is critical to our reproductive cells, yet those cells don't become cancerous any more than any other cells do. It's necessary in a lethal cancer to have telomerase turned on, but it's not sufficient. So with this new discovery we're now at a point like where we were in cancer three or four years ago of saying, 'Pharmaceutical world, we've got something important. To realize its potential and to satisfy some of your needs, let's work together.' And so we enter the phase of selling our programs to bring in cash and scientific expertise, and to accelerate our programs. That's one of the main things we're working on this year."

The company was also working on issuing one or more critical patents to ensure that all paths to telomerase and telomeres and their therapeutic applications come somehow through Geron, both in the United States and overseas, because their competitors are global. Patents are key for them.

"And people are extremely important to us. We're not a very old industry. In name, biotechnology is only a generation old, starting with the formation of Genentech. Securing key leadership to apply our technology to the development of products is also very important." So Geron had some specific goals on the kinds of people it wanted to hire in specific positions, mostly scientific researchers. And Eastman also mentioned a couple of opportunistic goals.

In comparing the long- and short-term visions I noticed that the long term could be stated very succinctly: Geron is about aging. The short term, while obviously practical and real, didn't seem to have the same focus, so I asked Eastman if he had any practical desire to be able to express the short term as succinctly. "Actually, when you look at it, our next year is one of implementation. Now you go back a year, take a look at last year's vision. Our vision for last year was to provide some scientific validation to who we are and what we're all about." Although they had some partnering and patent goals the previous year, they were much more heavily oriented toward scientific achievement, which meant cloning telomerase. That was accomplished faster than they anticipated, and then they were able to use that in turning on telomerase in normal cells. "So we found ourselves in a position we wouldn't have predicted we could or would be in for a much longer period of time. Hence, the inflection point." Had they not recognized that and capitalized on it, he noted, a huge opportunity would have been lost.

"This year, we're not as heavily weighted down by one or two critical scientific goals although we do have many of them. We're more heavily weighted down by implementation on the business side. The business of science."

■ HARSH ENVIRONMENT

The business of science for Geron, as for most start-up biotech companies, is a harsh environment that must somehow be endured over a long period of time. Vision gives them direction and inspiration to enter into this harsh environment, and it fortifies them with the discoveries and the resilience they will need to make the vision real. Geron's vision is about long healthy life, and realizing it is farther in the future than for a typical Silicon Valley company. In that context, I was interested in the fact that Geron's vision is focused on a problem, on something it wants to change, rather than on any particular product. I wanted to know more about why that is so, and how that kind of vision can sustain the company for the length of time required.

Eastman stressed that it's unrealistic for Geron to think about the creation of a product in the short term. "So then you have to say, 'Well, okay, we've got to survive, so we've got to sell something.' What are your products? Well, along the

---

We've got to survive, so we've got to sell something.

---

path to creating a therapeutic, which will be enormously beneficial to society and potentially return significant value to the shareholder, there are other products. Patents are products. Your science is a product. Selling to a large pharmaceutical company the potential of developing a product is a product."

So, the product Geron was selling in 1998 was the opportunity to align with the company in the pursuit of actual therapeutic and diagnostic products. Eastman said that in 1998 Geron would derive between 10 and 15 million dollars from those partnerships. People giving money to them to participate in Geron's longer term endeavor.

"I think today 5 percent of biotechnology companies have products, and 2 percent have profits. That's scary, of course. But you need to step back and say, 'Oh, I remember. The product development cycle is upwards of 15 to 20 years, and the industry is only a generation old. OK.'" Eastman went on to say that companies like Geron were now on the threshold, over the next 10 years or so, of demonstrating whether or not this industry is for real. He thinks it will be real. But the challenge is how to survive that first 5, 10, 15 years or more, especially as a public company, in the absence of significant product revenues. "It creates a tremendous challenge that we wouldn't have the opportunity to pursue if we didn't have patents. And if we didn't have the medical needs that we have."

Five percent of biotechnology companies have products, and 2 percent have profits.

According to Eastman, 50 percent of the diseases that we know about today have no real therapeutic solution. When you factor that together with a world population of some five billion people, that's a significant market opportunity. Many of those diseases are chronic and age related. "There's a huge market opportunity, a significant medical need, you have the protection of patents, and you have the potential to make a significant return to shareholders. So some are willing to take a significant risk, and put money into a long development cycle."

Eastman explained that the investment community that has followed biotechnology has matured dramatically and achieved a fairly good understanding of what the risks are over the past 5 to 10 years. They've had to, as the industry has grown up, matured, and demonstrated its strengths and its weaknesses.

As these investors in the biotech industry have matured, I wondered if Eastman found them pressing for something specific in place of product revenues. Had they determined that some other kind of result was the key to healthy progress? "To be honest, no," he replied. He said, "Geron has the portfolio of elements you'd want in a biotechnology company": a very broadly applicable scientific platform that appears to be fully validated in important therapeutic areas, and a solid intellectual property position.

According to Eastman, companies whose platforms have been invalidated should not be criticized. Someone once said to him, "The real art in biotechnology is this: you identify a biological mechanism and you pursue it single-mindedly to the end." If it fails at the end of the day, that's nevertheless what biotechnology is all about. The fact is, *most scientific experiments fail,* and you have to be able to live with that.

You identify a biological mechanism and you pursue it single-mindedly to the end.

From talking with venture capitalists and several biotech executives over the years, I had understood that it has always been harder for biotechnology to compete for investment dollars. I wanted to know if the situation had recently gotten worse.

Eastman thinks there's been an inflection point in the biotechnology industry that will make it much more difficult for the have-nots to raise the capital that's required in this very capital-intensive industry. It takes hundreds of millions of dollars and many many years to get a first significant revenue-gathering product on the market. The market is indicating that in the absence of products, or in the absence of a very clear and rapid pathway to a product, investors would just as soon take their money elsewhere, whether it's high-tech or bigger, more advanced biotechnology companies that have products already. When you can get a 30, 40, 50 percent return on Pfizer, why go after a biotech company that's years away from its first product? That's something Eastman worries about.

"There have been cycles where anybody with an idea—as long as they had a big name behind them and an important venture capitalist—could get funding and even take a company public. But just in the past year and a half, too many investors have decided they've lost too much money over too long a period of time, and too few have made a significant killing." A killing is almost necessary in such a high-risk industry. Eastman has found that analysts are leaving the industry, there are very few mutual funds focused on biotechnology, and there are very few big players. Even the investment banks available to take a company public are fewer in number, although that's partly because of consolidations. Raising capital will become an increasingly more difficult challenge. "So, you've got to have an awfully good vision for the long term, and you've got to be very good at executing your short-term vision to maintain interest and value and the opportunity to get financing."

You've got to have an awfully good vision for the long term, and be very good at executing your short-term vision to maintain interest and value.

Venture capitalists like Don Valentine have told me that most venture funds are set up to last only 10 years or so. That means the funds' investments have to pay off through an IPO or an acquisition within that 10-year period. If venture capitalists have to make their killing within 10 years, that automatically creates problems for biotechnology. It seemed as if Eastman was describing a built-in Catch-22 where the venture funding a biotech company needs to

RON EASTMAN ON BIOTECHNOLOGY
AND VENTURE CAPITAL

It is true first of all that biotechnology as an industry would not exist if it weren't for venture capital money. The great challenge, though, is that all biotech companies, or virtually all, ask the public marketplace to become venture capitalists. Many public investors are willing to do that. Unfortunately, very, very few, if any, public investors have the requisite venture capital mentality, the patience, and the long-term perspective that's required to deal with the risk and the time required in biotech. So, I would say there still is a gap. Thank God for the VCs, and thank God for the public marketplace. They've allowed biotech to form and these companies to get in shape. But yes, there's a gap here.

There's an investment strategy, an investor class that still hasn't been created that best suits the needs of companies like Geron. Companies that are still years from their first product, yet are perhaps a little beyond the venture capital stage. We're a live company. We're generating some revenues, although they're immaterial. We clearly have a pathway to products. And yet we're clearly asking our public investors to be VCs of a sort because of the risk that's still involved. I think financially the market will have to change a little bit.

begin its life ultimately pressures it to go public or be acquired before it's able to survive on its own.

Given a severe problem like this that threatens a biotech company's ability to realize its vision, I wanted to know if Eastman thought that solving the problem was therefore something he or the industry as a whole thought they had to take on. In talking with CEOs for this book, most emphasized in various ways that they didn't want to fight the environment. Part of the art of vision for many is helping to create changes the environment seems to want to make. For most, that means accepting the economic climate the way it is and economic institutions the way they are. In the case of biotechnology, where these economic practices cause problems, I wanted to know if there was something Eastman could or should do as a part of implementing his company's vision.

Eastman replied that some companies acquire products from other companies that are further along. Perhaps those products don't strategically fit with the originating company or fit more closely with what the acquiring company has and puts them closer to the marketplace with a revenue and profit stream. "The problem there is that the acquired product . . . I mean, obviously there's a reason why the other company's getting rid of it. Also, you still have a lot of risk unless the product's already on the market. And if it's already on the market, you're basically going to pay what the present value of future earnings is, unless you have a differential advantage. Very few biotechs do."

But looking for acquisitions can also be a distraction. "We have what we believe is one of the most powerful scientific platforms in the industry. What could possibly justify diverting our attention from realizing the value of that platform by getting involved with a product that we could realistically acquire from someone else?" So Geron has been rejecting the opportunities that come their way to acquire products that are further along in development. "We have an incredibly high standard for what we'd even be willing to consider. But that's one avenue—acquire later-stage products."

Another avenue is to leverage your asset base. Sell parts of it to bigger companies to generate cash and to bring in resources other than cash, especially scientific resources. The idea there is to speed up and fund your process along the way. The good news is, you form some very good collaborations. You do speed things up, you do fund them. But the bad news is you have to give away some of the family jewels. According to Eastman, that is probably the strategy most relied on for bridging the gap between science and products. "I think there will continue to be a place and a role for that, because the big companies don't have the innovative spirit, capability, or structure to foster innovation through research and the small companies don't have the resources. Also, the big companies, once they get rolling, have to feed their engine with new products at all stages of development. So, for many it's been a good relationship. I don't anticipate it changing as the preferred strategy."

Then, there's the final alternative—and that is to be acquired. Merge into a company that's more developed. "We tell ourselves that to manage to be bought is a foolish way to run your company because there's no assurance that somebody will be there to buy you. But if staying independent doesn't work, being bought may be the most valid way to maximize shareholder value over the long run." If you look at the biotech industry, Eastman says there are very few exceptions to the rule that at some point you will become part of a larger enterprise. Syntex has. Chiron has. Biogen hasn't been merged into, but they have sold much of their product base. Genentech sold more than 50 percent of their company to Roche. Amgen is a notable exception, as is Genzyme to a certain extent. "But you must recognize a merger as a potential end game, and a means for overcoming this big challenge."

As he outlined three possible avenues a company could take—acquire other companies' products, leverage its asset base, or be acquired—I began to wonder about the effects of these moves on the science these companies try to conduct. I wanted to know if Eastman saw any signs that these solutions to money problems inhibited the creativity of the science that makes biotechnology possible at all.

"It's difficult for me to point to the evidence of that. But if you focus on why people are at a place like Geron, they come here because there is a scientific effort they identify with and they want to be a part of." In his opinion, Geron's environment is more stimulating than either the academic world or a large pharmaceutical company. "At a place like Geron you are much like a family and you're figuring out how to grow together. It's yours. You've created it, you own it, you change

---

People come here because there is a scientific effort they identify with and want to be a part of.

with it or you change it." It's very hard for Eastman to imagine that the real movers and shakers, the people who really define the entity that is the biotech company, would feel as comfortable or be as productive—even if they stay—in a very different environment. And by definition, most of the big companies are very different.

"On the other hand, when most biotechnology companies get acquired they are already bigger companies. Chiron, when it was acquired, was thousands of employees. Same with Syntex. Same with Genentech. And they'd almost reached a level of maturity where they more resembled the big company culture than the Geron-type culture. So, as for the risk of losing some of the spirit and the creativity—whatever was going to be lost had pretty much been lost already."

Especially since acquisitions like these seem to be the expected norm in biotechnology, I wanted to know if Eastman thought these companies' visions had been lost along with their creativity. In his view the visions have been diluted and the realities of the marketplace have overwhelmed the companies. "You could venture to say, 'Look, if the vision was still in place and if it was a good vision to begin with, there should be no reason to be acquired.' Right? Well, that's not particularly valid because there are some prices at which even a strong company with a good vision would still be acquired and feel very good about it. Sometimes those prices are paid. Usually they're not."

He cited Chiron and Genentech as examples. In his view, Chiron had pretty much lost its way; the vision may still have been clear, but the execution had not been good. He's not sure there was a vision at the time Genentech was acquired, and execution had not been particularly good. Some loss of vision was a factor, and it's unlikely it became much clearer after acquisition, unless it became the vision of a subsidiary of a larger entity that dictated what the vision would be.

From Eastman's description of biotechnology's business environment, I got the distinct impression that it requires a very long and hard struggle, and in the end even the most successful companies will have been acquired or will have spent their intellectual assets in the attempt to stay alive.

■ PEOPLE

While Eastman was telling me about the difficult environment in which Geron had to survive, balanced with the benefits of being a small company, he had mentioned that Geron was like a family growing up together. And he contrasted the finite life span of a family with businesses' tendency to think of themselves as immortal. Now the family simile was taking on added meaning. It indicates something important about the attitude and the approach he takes to vision.

Eastman looks at a successful vision in much the same way as he looks at therapies for aging: Both have to do with managing a lifetime and the events that can change it. Searching for analogies that fit this serious purpose, he mentioned the family and raising children. What else do we have such great hopes and dreams for that we must work out over 20 or more years? And what other challenge do we have to muddle through the best we can, without any of the training we might wish for but could only describe in hindsight?

For Eastman, being a parent is the most important thing we do. As part of our parenting, we probably have a vision for our children, whether we've made it explicit or not. Our vision includes the many experiences like a college education that we may feel are necessary to prepare our children for life. But along the way we have to be ready to step back and ask whether our vision is really valid. Maybe our child is actually good at or interested in something else, not what we imagined. Maybe he or she doesn't really want to go to college. And so we have to be prepared to change our vision. And in any case, we eventually have to give up authority over the vision so our children can have their own. In families as in companies, you cannot really predict how long a vision will remain valid. And in companies as in families, a vision should be changeable but it should always aim with full honesty at what is most important—for the whole family, not for the one whose temporary job it is to be in charge.

This emphasis on what is best for the whole family—for the whole company—means more than just being willing to change a vision as the world and people change. It means people in the company should also participate in forming the vision, since the vision may ask them to change as well. Eastman believes people who can't accept necessary change should leave the company and free up space for somebody who would endorse it and would participate in it.

"We try to leverage our vision in terms of who's here. We don't try to sell people on it. You get it, you understand it, and you buy into it. Or you get it, you understand it, and you don't. It either attracts you to this place or it doesn't. We ask a lot of people, as most successful businesses do. Therefore, you want to make sure that there's some consistency in thought and purpose and values. And if there isn't, then it's not fair to you or your colleagues to pursue it. Life's too short and there are too many other things that you can do."

We don't try to sell people on it. You get it, or you don't.

If Geron's vision helps attract the right people to the company, it does so because it establishes a clear and inspiring direction for the company. But the clear direction also means that many other possible paths are not pursued, even those that feed off the same scientific platform. The company had debated going after cancer, and the debate could have gone the other way, especially if other products had already been further along in the development and approval process. Despite the positive ability of a vision to attract like-minded people, I wondered if it could also become a constraint to scientists who may want to pursue a promising line of research that seems to head away from aging. Does a vision also limit the freedom good scientists may want?

Eastman has found that fundamental research succeeds ultimately because there is a freedom to pursue different paths, yet businesses succeed because they take an idea, build on it, and create a product that's of value. So it's necessary to find a balance, and the balance within a company usually is more focus and less independence.

Many scientists measure their success through publications. For scientists in the business arena, this presents two

---

The balance within a company usually is more
focus and less independence.

---

problems. One, they're helping the competition. Two, it takes
time to write—time and effort that's not necessarily dedicated
to getting to a product. That creates a challenge for many of
Geron's scientific staff.

Like any problem, Geron deals with it first by getting it
out in the open. "One of our challenges strategically is going
from Geron University to Geron Pharmaceuticals. We're right
up front with folks about that." Second, they "layer on" a different kind of scientist, one with more industry experience,
"who can help us take the extraordinary scientific work we've
done and convert it into products." Finally, they reinforce,
whether by the incentive plan or by recognition within the
company, how much Geron values discoveries that enable
commercialization of products.

From that description, I got the impression that the scientists at Geron were being led to make concessions to business constraints. I wanted to know if Geron as a business had
also decided to make concessions to the scientific culture
and ego.

"Really they haven't been so much concessions as a
recognition that we *were* Geron University. And the way
Geron University gets credibility and funding and recognition *is* through its publications." Their publications, their
science, was the product, but now it's time to move on—the
product tomorrow has got to be drugs and cell therapeutics,
gene therapeutics. "So it's not so much that we made concessions. We knew who we were for that period of execution and
we had to operate that way. Now we're in a period of transition. We'll be more likely to keep trade secrets."

I understood Eastman's reasoning in trying to change
from Geron University to Geron Pharmaceuticals. Very
clearly the business environment puts increasing pressure
on a biotech start-up to do just that. But would that, in the
long run, for Geron's long-term vision, harm the scientific
platform the company is built on? After all, if all biotech

companies and all scientists made the same decision it would cut off the free flow of information that seems vital to the discoveries that eventually lead to drugs. Would a freer flow of information ultimately help everyone more?

"We need to recognize that for us to be successful over the long term, we must continue to build and worship our research capability. Our research strengths. Our competitive advantage in research. There's so much biology associated with telomeres and telomerase and cell aging and immortality that we can really place a long-term stake in the ground there. As long as we continue to reinforce that, depend on it, then I don't think we'll have a problem. If we walk away from that, and get exclusively focused on the products, eventually the well will run dry."

We must continue to build and worship
our research capability.

In addition to providing a sense of direction for a company, most of the CEOs I've talked to say that visions should also provide real inspiration for the people pursuing them. They define a larger purpose than just making a profit. I wanted to know if Eastman found that true at Geron as well. "Yes. I hear it especially from people who are interviewing here. At the end of the day, or at the end of a couple of days, they'll come back and they'll say, 'You know, it's very obvious that people here have a shared vision about why they're here and what it is they're trying to accomplish. And it's pretty damn exciting.'"

I noticed Eastman said "shared vision." Earlier he had said that the ideal was to have everyone in a company contribute to defining the vision, making it shared from the very beginning. But Geron's long-term vision was defined by Mike West when the company was founded. Despite that, Eastman was telling me that prospective employees perceived Geron's vision as shared, and that fact was important to them beyond the content of the vision itself. "Right. Regardless of who they talk to they hear the same vision. Each person might have a twist on how they interpret it and what parts of that vision are more exciting to them. But I do get encouraged by what I hear back from candidates who've talked to people at various levels in the organization."

If Geron has a shared vision it is not because the people there now all participated in defining it in the first place. I assumed that must have happened through the company's culture or the way Eastman and other executives communicated. I wanted to know how Geron maintains and communicates its vision to make it shared—and to keep it alive throughout the long race to making it real.

■ MAINTAINING AND COMMUNICATING A VISION

To develop its short-term vision, like most successful businesses Geron has an annual process of deciding and communicating what it wants to accomplish over the next period of time. Unlike many, it doesn't start with the numbers, with how much it has to spend. "We start with what we can get accomplished and what that buys us in the way of deliverables, announcements, discoveries. And then we ask what that's worth, and therefore what we're willing to pay for it. Then we kind of work both from the discovery end and from the financial end and reach a kind of compromise, if you will, as to what's affordable and what gets us to the next stage in the best way."

As for the longer term, Eastman said Geron doesn't do a lot to really challenge its thinking. "I'm not sure whether that's because it's clear to us, or whether it's because the timelines to realize the vision are so long, it would be foolish to rigorously challenge that long-term vision on an annual basis. Not a lot changes."

Since Geron doesn't spend a lot of time discussing and challenging its long-term vision, I wanted to know how it communicates it to the people there and to new employees. "We start with an employee manual [*Eastman took one from the table and opened it to the first page*] which has an introductory letter from me saying: 'You've joined a unique company committed to creating breakthrough solutions for diseases associated with aging. We're seeking to improve the human health span, enabling men and women to achieve greater comfort, enjoyment, and fulfillment as they age.'" The letter goes on to talk about Geron's four core values and stress that they will only pursue those opportunities that fall within their purpose and serve those values.

"And occasionally in our get-togethers as a group we'll remind ourselves of those. Probably not enough. And I suppose one of the things that drives it home for people is that we're constantly interviewing people to join our family, our team, and in the process of interviewing you have to explain who you are and what you're all about. And that kind of reinforces the message."

Eastman believes the most difficult way to deal with vision is in your everyday practice. Whether they know they're doing it or not, employees are constantly looking at every action that the CEO and other officers take as leaders in the company. Employees assess the consistency, the validity of your actions relative to the purpose and the values you've expressed. "The hardest thing to do is to maintain credibility and to convince the employees that you own the values, the purpose, the vision. That you practice them day after day after day. There is perhaps no greater demonstration and reinforcement than your day-to-day actions."

Eastman thinks actions are an excellent demonstration of vision. That may sound a little odd because an action is something that has been done, and a vision is something that projects forward. But action really is—or should be—a reflection of a vision. He used a simple visual to help show what he means.

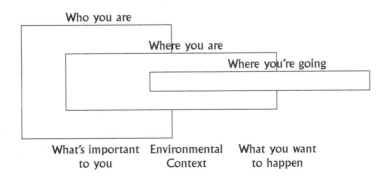

"You know, when you first think about vision, it's something going forward. To go forward you have to have a point of origin. And in fact the point of origin, whether it's you, me, the company, or some other entity, is extremely important. Because more than anything else, I think the vision is: who you really are. And so that's why the big box is labeled 'Who You Are,' it's where it all starts. Vision is also, I believe, a function of where you are—the environmental context of what's going on at the moment. And vision is obviously also this cellular component of where you're going—which is what most people think of when they think about vision. See how this projects backward: Where you're *going* is a function of who you *are*, and where you are is *also* a function of who you are. And so they're all interrelated."

Vision is who you really are.

Eastman thinks it's also important to remember that vision is not anticipating what's going to happen so that you can change who you are or where you are to prepare for it, although you may choose to do the latter as part of the exercise. It's really about what you want to happen. It's a self-fulfilling prophesy because if you want something to happen, you can invest aggressively in leveraging who you are and where you are to make it happen.

"So, this is how I think of vision. The smallest component is where you're going; the most important component is really who you are and what's important to you. What are your values? Going back to the discussion we had earlier, when you think about the vision for your family, what you really have to understand is what's important to the family. What are your values? What do you want to accomplish in life? What do you want to achieve before you die?"

In my experience people often don't really know who they are. And organizations know even less often. Eastman agrees that it's tough to figure out what your value system is, what your principles really are. "But you know, at the end of the day, what can be more important than who you are?

What else differentiates you from the next person—not just to be different, but to be complete?"

I wanted to know whether Geron had gone through some kind of exercise to define itself. "Yes," he said, they detailed their purpose and values and outlined how they would execute in a consistent fashion. "I think it's reflected in a large part of our culture, but not aggressively enough yet."

People don't open their employee manual and read the first page every day. But they will watch the actions of those around them: What is positively reinforced, what is negatively reinforced? "Our actions, I think, are largely very consistent. We aggressively challenge each other when our actions don't reflect what we want. We get on each other's case if we're stepping out of the bounds that we've set by our purpose and values."

We aggressively challenge each other when our actions
don't reflect our purpose and values.

■ THE ECO CHALLENGE

At about this point Eastman told me a story that seemed to capture much of his approach to vision. The Discovery Channel sponsors the Eco Challenge, an endurance event that takes place in a different country every year and traverses through a number of ecosystems. Teams of four or five, depending on the year, have to find their way through the 300-plus mile course and overcome challenges like hiking, kayaking, rafting, mountain biking, and mountain climbing and rappelling. They must do it as a team—all four or five have to finish. If one drops out the team is out.

The most recent Eco Challenge was in Australia. The experience is fun, but incredibly dangerous and very physically and mentally taxing. The winning teams do it in five or so days with perhaps a total of eight hours sleep over the entire five days, going some 330 miles. The cut-off time is ten days. Some teams don't make it in that; many drop out along the way, including teams as experienced as the Navy Seals. "So this is no walk in the park. It requires incredible teamwork. Why do the Navy Seals fall apart and not finish, while teams of rank amateurs you wouldn't think have either the physical or mental capability to do this, excel?"

The Eco Challenge has become an analogy for Eastman of what vision is all about. "I'm attracted to this. I've done an Ironman and a bunch of marathons, and I find endurance events interesting. They appeal to me. What is the vision associated with an Eco Challenge? For some it might be to win the race. For everyone, it is to finish the race."

What's the attraction in going with virtually no sleep for five to ten days, paddling down rivers with crocodiles, twisting an ankle, falling off a cliff, being stung by a cactus that can kill you, poisonous snakes, and just plain physical exhaustion? If people can get over that hurdle, and come to share a vision as a team, it's time to execute, from start to finish, keeping the team together, getting to a shared vision of each step along the way: How do we do the river? How do we do the cliff? How do we do the desert? How do we do the camel?

"So you've got to get people to share that vision, and you've got to keep them motivated all along the way, even though times can be incredibly tough." Interestingly, the teams that do best are those in which there's very little hierarchy. This is probably where the Seals fall apart—they're used to hierarchy. "Another key to success is that no one feels they have the capability to do this on their own. Everyone appreciates that they're very dependent on one another, and as such they need to be forthcoming about their strengths and especially about their weaknesses. You've got to be able to say, 'You know, I can't do it. I need help, let's get through this together.'" People who have difficulty with team decision making, with overcoming weaknesses and building on their strengths, don't succeed in the Eco Challenge. They don't succeed in maintaining the vision.

"So, what are some of the themes here? Well, you constantly have to help people appreciate why the vision is

---

You have to keep remembering who you really
are and not take things for granted.

---

important. Why it's worth having. What sets it apart. Otherwise you may just take it for granted that curing cancer or helping your mother-in-law live through another year and a half without the pain of osteoarthritis is important. You have to keep remembering who you really are and not take things for granted."

RON EASTMAN ON IMMORTALITY

One thing I struggle with about vision in a company, a business, is that . . . take a family. The unfortunate thing about families is that they end. The family has a finite life span. But companies, at least most of them, don't see things that way. The leaders, the companies, really don't envision themselves dying. They don't envision the race ending. They think about themselves as almost immortal even though most companies don't in fact last very long at all, far less than a human lifetime.

So I'm struggling with, maybe this notion of immortality is foolish. And maybe we really ought to think more like, "Well, okay. We have a ten-year vision and it's very inappropriate for us to think about a vision that goes any longer than that." And yet, if you go to the HP and the Merck model, it says come hell or high water the vision should be the same whether you live for 10 years, or 50, or 150. Obviously I've got to think this through some more but I think it might be better if we recognized a company has a finite existence.

We went through a major strategic planning exercise, about a year and a half ago. And I'm intent on going through another one, because we've opened up so many more doors of scientific pursuit, and at the same time our

RON EASTMAN ON
IMMORTALITY (Continued)

market environment has changed dramatically. How's it changed dramatically? Well, just sticking on the capital side for instance: There's more money out there. More people have made more money and want to invest that money. So the banks, the institutions, have more money to invest but they want their investments to be very liquid. Biotech companies in general, as is the case at Geron, are not big in terms of shares outstanding and market cap, and they're relatively illiquid. So that's a problem.

There are also fewer banks. They're consolidating. So you have fewer people to determine which biotech companies they want to finance and fewer analysts to follow and support these companies. You have 1,300 plus biotech companies, which is probably too many. It's kind of like . . . the vision that pops into my mind is, you know, sperm heading down the duct. Only the strongest will survive. There's a lot of luck in that, of course. Conditions have to be very good. And you know, I go back to my point: You decide what you want your future to look like, and if you have a pretty good idea you probably can do it. But it's getting a hell of a lot more difficult.

So, are companies going to go away, are they going to consolidate, are they going to just run out of money? It's daunting. Extremely daunting for us right now. At the same time that we have every reason to be more encouraged about our opportunity for long-term success, we're faced with this menacing threat of the short-term environment. There's always the alternative of saying, "Understanding the problem is 90 percent of being potentially successful at dealing with it." And you can understand the problem and decide you know it's challenging, but there's a wonderful opportunity here, and just go all out. And recognize that we might lose.

(continued)

RON EASTMAN ON
IMMORTALITY (Continued)

We might break an ankle, fall off a cliff, or somebody might beat us to the end. But you know, you get back to the race, you get back to life. They are finite. And as I said, I think CEOs and management teams rarely think in terms of a finite life span for their enterprises.

I think at least in part that's probably why we end up having these annual plans. So that our life span can be defined in chunks of time. If you're faced with a limited life span as a human, you're going to think a lot about what you want to accomplish during that period of time and what can be accomplished. As a result, you make some very specific choices along the way. In a company you have to force yourself to get that discipline with these annual plans, because otherwise we do think of our companies as immortal.

Now, what also brings biotech companies back to reality is the old survivability index. We know we're sitting here with cash to see us through two years. If nothing else happens—if we don't get any grants, get any partnerships, do any licensing deals—in two years we're out of business. Now, you know Merck doesn't think that way and Hewlett-Packard doesn't think that way. So, by definition we have a limited life span. And we govern accordingly. It affects our day-to-day performance and our long-term strategic thinking. But still, the concept for us isn't just to survive. We want to thrive. And thrive over an indefinite life span.

Learn How to Apply Technology: Gordon Moore, Founder and Chairman Emeritus of Intel

When Bill Hewlett and David Packard founded HP at the end of World War II, the business ecology of the San Francisco Bay Area began to favor new companies that formed around the faith they could find applications and customers for their technological expertise. Bob Noyce and Gordon Moore left Fairchild Semiconductor and founded Intel in 1968 on that same technology-fueled faith. They took this elemental force, which Hewlett-Packard had already shown could build and sustain an enterprise, and with it built products that put intelligence inside thousands of different products people use all over the world.

Intel—short for "integrated electronics"—first grew and prospered by producing silicon memories. But the Intel invention that transformed both it and the world is the microprocessor, the brain that controls the personal computer—and many thousands of other automatic or "smart" products. Microprocessors control the fuel systems that make cars go and the braking systems that make them stop. They control buildings from chicken coops to "smart" houses to high rises. They control common calculators and exotic scientific instruments. Microprocessors are manufactured first and later programmed to perform the variety of tasks they're given. They are a raw intelligence built at first with a very limited idea of who will finally use it or for what purpose; that will come later, through a very pragmatic learning process. The vision that has guided Intel works in a very similar way, as technical intelligence learning how to apply itself.

For all that he and his company have accomplished in the world, I found Gordon Moore a very modest and unassuming man. He is not one to readily call himself or his partner a visionary. Looking back at Intel 31 years after he founded it, he said, "I think it's interesting to contrast Intel now with the early Fairchild days. When we started out we really had no idea at all who was going to buy our products. We made a transistor. We found a guy to do marketing and sales, and he tracked down a customer with a particular application that looked like we could make a transistor to fit. They ordered our first 100 transistors. It was really a learning experience. We'd all come from research backgrounds, and had never been involved in a company that made and marketed successful products. Except for a technology vision of where we wanted to go, we really had nothing else. We didn't even know what we needed for our organization."

When we started out we really had no idea at all
who was going to buy our products.

In the learning process Gordon Moore and Intel went through, they started with technological goals, with competence and a belief they could build a company around it, and they succeeded. The process shows vision as action, vision as almost pure verb rather than noun. Intel didn't start with a picture of the future it wanted, but with faith in its tools and energy and ability to learn how to build its future.

■ THE STORY OF INTEL

When Bob Noyce and Gordon Moore founded Intel they saw an opportunity to change the leverage in the semiconductor industry. By 1968, the industry's technology was finally capable of making relatively complex products. The problem was, if you designed a complex product the application tended to be unique, maybe used by one customer. So a company couldn't amortize the cost of designing the product over very many pieces, which ruined the economics of producing it. As a result, the industry was making a lot of simple circuits. The packaging and testing was often a lot more expensive than the piece of silicon itself, which created a competitive advantage for companies with large assembly plants in Southeast Asia. According to Moore, "We saw in semiconductor memory a chance to make something quite complex that was used in all digital systems, so we could amortize the cost of the design."

The problem was, the closest thing to a semiconductor memory that existed commercially at the time cost a couple of dollars per bit, and the entrenched technology, which was magnetic cores, cost a penny or two per bit. So Intel would have to create a 100- to 200-fold decrease in costs in order to be competitive with the existing technology. "And that is what we set off to do," said Moore. "Memory was a function used in all digital systems. Magnetic cores was an acceptable technology. But it wasn't going to get any cheaper or much faster. Semiconductors at least would be faster, and because of the way the technology has developed, it eventually became a lot cheaper. We were trying to change the technology."

Magnetic cores were not very applicable in small memories, so that gave Intel an initial market opportunity. Magnetic cores had a lot of circuitry around their edges. That meant you had to have a big array of cores before the cost could come down, because the cost of the driving and sensing circuitry was so high. A billion bits or more was required before core memory was practical. There were applications for much smaller memories in instrumentation and various other devices that needed to record a small amount of data. Many of these applications wouldn't be considered computer applications 30 years later. Intel's first two products were these small memories. One was a 64-bit memory, the other was a 256-bit memory.

The 256-bit memory was relatively slow. The 64-bit memory was high speed, used for so-called scratch pad memories in bigger computers where you wanted something that worked rapidly but wouldn't save the data long term. It was an application that customers would pay more per memory bit for because it was faster than a memory core, therefore speeding up the whole computer system. "Those were the stepping stones that got us going. Our ultimate goal was to tackle the main memory. It was at least our third memory product before we had something that was remotely competitive. That was the first dynamic random access memory or DRAM chip. But our basic idea was to try to find complex circuits we could build in large volume."

Our basic idea was to try to find complex circuits
we could build in large volume.

Memory was the first example in that class of high volume, complex circuits. Soon after Intel got its memory business going it thought calculators could be another member of that class. After all, calculators sold in large volume. That's how Intel got tied up with Busicom, the Japanese calculator company for whom they developed the microprocessor. "We thought we had a better way of solving their problem. We couldn't have done it the way they wanted, we were way too small. I think they wanted 12 or 13 different complex circuits, and our engineering team couldn't begin to do that. One of our guys, Ted Hoff, saw that by using a general purpose computer architecture you could do all 13 of these. And he saw that it was possible to make a chip with such an architecture that would be about as complex as the memory chips we were making." The time had come. They hired Federico Faggin to run the team to make it.

In the early 1970s, Moore and Intel saw the microprocessor as a complex circuit they could build in large volume, not as the seminal product it was to become. The semiconductor industry had gone in the direction of making simple circuits in large volume. Intel was looking at something different that gave a start-up company an opportunity, an advantage. According to Moore, they saw that by going to complex circuits Intel could put the leverage of the business back into the processing of the silicon rather than the packaging and testing. It was an opportunity to take the industry in a different direction. "We started out with three technological directions that were different from what the industry was doing at the time. Basically, we were technologists who thought doing the technology was kind of fun. One of those technologies, the silicon gate, turned out to be just right. I've referred to it as our Goldilocks Strategy."

We were technologists who thought doing
the technology was kind of fun.

Intel was able to quietly develop and use its silicon gate technology virtually alone because the established companies were too busy with their own technologies. They didn't pay much attention to what Intel was doing until it became obvious that Intel was becoming successful. "Start-ups don't show up on the radar screen of a big company very early. You've got to develop some real momentum before they see you. It was probably five years before they recognized we were here, and it took them a couple more years to get going. It was seven years before there were other silicon gate products on the market—other than one."

In those days big customers especially wouldn't use your product unless you had multiple sources, so Intel had to set up a second source for the DRAM it developed. That was a

GORDON MOORE ON THE GOLDILOCKS STRATEGY

We picked three technologies. One was too hard, one was too easy, and one was just right. The one that was just right was silicon gate MOS, which has been the mainstream of our business ever since. The one that was too hard was multiple chip packaging, putting several different chips all together in essentially a memory chip, in one package. We're just getting to the point in 1999 where we can do that successfully. You have to be able to test them. To make it economically feasible you have to be able to find out which one is bad and take it off and put a new one on, and those things turned out to be a lot more difficult than we thought they were going to be. The one that was too easy was a variation on the transistor technology being used at the time. It was so straightforward that once we did it the established people were able to copy it right away, so we didn't maintain an advantage there very long. But in the technology that was just right, when we had all our energy focused on it we were able to solve the couple of technical problems that came up and it was something like seven years before we had any direct competition. That gave us a long time to get started.

Canadian company called MIL—Microelectronics International Limited. For a while the second source worked very well. "And then they tried to change things a bit and lost control of their process and just kind of disappeared off the face of the earth."

➤ From Memories to Microprocessors

Intel succeeded with its idea of making complex circuits in large volume. That was still the source of most of its business 30 years later. But its focus changed dramatically. For nearly

17 years, Intel concentrated on making memories, but that was gradually becoming a commodity business. "Finally in 1985 we were looking at the next card in the DRAM business. We had developed the next-generation product and the process for making it, and we were looking at having to build two plants at something like $400 million in order to get enough market share to be significant." Nobody was making any money in the business and it wasn't clear when anybody would again. Intel decided it didn't make any sense and pulled the plug on DRAMs to refocus all its technology development on the microprocessor, which at that time was really taking off. That was some 14 years after the microprocessor was first invented.

As Intel shifted to concentrate on microprocessors it managed to gain several advantages it hadn't had earlier in the memory business. One of the most significant advantages came from a major change it was able to make in its sales contracts. Unlike the days when it had to set up MIL as a second source, Intel no longer had to give the design and the technology of its products to a competitor in order to get customers. According to Moore, they decided to try to change the industry practice. In the generation of chips introduced in the early 1980s, which included the 80286, Intel responded to customers' stated need by broadly giving away second source licenses to the 286—to AMD, Fujitsu, and Siemens. One in the United States, one in Japan, one in Europe. "The demand customers told us they wanted us to meet was three times what we could build. It turned out they used one-third of what they said they were going to, so we had put all these competitors in business and the market didn't develop. We just gave away the profits on a whole generation. We felt our customers had really done us dirt on that one."

We felt our customers had really done us dirt on that one.

When they came out with the 386 they weren't committed to giving it away to anyone. "AMD would have had an opportunity, but they fell down on their part of the bargain. So when we started talking about that I said, 'Let's try it without a second source.' We had a different kind of customer base then, a lot of PC manufacturers, not a few big ones who were driving the whole thing. We also had all this software out there, and our new chips were compatible with the old software. So we said, 'Okay, if we can't make everything people will need they'll be short a few processors.' We tried to do it that way and it succeeded." The device was generally well received and they've kept doing that ever since.

Earlier, when Intel was building up its microprocessor business, it found itself back in a similar position to the one Moore and Noyce had been in when they made their first transistor and later when they made their first memories. Who would buy a microprocessor, and what would they use it for? At least there had been a definable market for transistors and memories, even if Fairchild and later Intel weren't sure who their customers would be. Hard as it may be for most people to remember, for a long time the market for microprocessors wasn't very clear at all. The microprocessor mostly went into applications that hadn't existed before, but it went into a lot of them. "From the very beginning we got a whole bunch of design wins for screwy things. I remember one guy automated his chicken house with one of the early microprocessors. They went into controlling instruments. Blood analyzers. A marijuana sniffer. Things like that. We didn't know where we were going to end up."

One guy automated his chicken house with
one of the early microprocessors.

In 1979, Intel had a major program called Design Wins for finding an application that would cause somebody to commit to using a microprocessor for something. It usually takes a few months or a few years to develop one. Their goal, Moore explained, was 2,000 design wins for the current family of microprocessors, and they actually got about 3,000. "These were all different applications. One of those was the IBM PC—it was just one of 3,000. But any win at IBM was significant, because they tended to use quite a bit of whatever they used. We had no idea it was going to change the nature of the company. We didn't even know exactly what it was."

We had no idea it was going to change the
nature of the company.

When Intel's salesmen dealt with IBM they sat in a conference room; a blanket was drawn across the middle of the room. The IBM people would ask the salesmen questions and they would answer, but they couldn't see what the people were doing on the other side. "IBM really kept that under a blanket."

In a less forceful effort, Intel had been trying to find applications for the microprocessor all along, even before the Design Wins program. It started doing that from the initial 4004—as soon as it got the rights back from Busicom. Busicom had paid for the design, so it had the rights to the product. The company came to Intel a few months after the microprocessor was ready and asked for a lower price. Intel said it would have to have more volume, so it negotiated the rights to sell the microprocessor for other, noncalculator applications. Then, about six months later, Busicom was near bankruptcy and Intel was able to buy back the complete rights for the price of the initial design—$68,000, according to Moore's memory. If events had turned out differently, Busicom might still own the rights to the original microprocessor. And Intel would have had to start over designing a new and different one—if it thought the effort was worthwhile.

As an important part of its efforts to find and encourage applications, Intel developed and sold what at the time it called "development systems," which were complete computer systems including hardware and software for people developing and debugging applications. These systems became a significant business alongside memories. For many years it was a bigger business for Intel than the microprocessors themselves. These systems would later be known as engineering design stations—the products of the multibillion dollar Computer Aided Engineering and later the Electronic

Design Automation industry. Just as Intel helped spawn the semiconductor equipment business, it helped spawn the EDA business as well.

By the late 1970s, Motorola was starting to have a significant impact on the microprocessor business. It had a 16-bit microprocessor on the market before Intel did. That was when Intel put on its push to get all the design wins it could for its own 16-bit chip. Competition from Motorola made Intel increase its sales effort. The PC was still not on the radar screen. "We weren't focusing on any particular segment of the business. We were just trying to get these things spread around. We must have had a couple thousand salesmen in the field by then. They were all out pushing it. We had developed the products and now it was a sales and marketing job." Bill Davidow, who later became a venture capitalist, ran the operation.

➤ Other Applications

While nearly everyone on earth knows about the PC, many fewer are aware of the other 2,999 applications—by now many more than that—that came from Intel's marketing push and from the efforts of other microprocessor suppliers like Motorola. According to Moore, "There's a huge number of other applications. Your automobile is jammed full of them. All your major appliances. They still go in all these broad applications. It's just that instead of being $200 processors most of the others are $10 processors. They're much less sophisticated and they don't have the ability to take advantage of the doubling of computer power every couple of years. You can't use a lot more computational power in your automatic braking system. In numbers of units, these applications far exceed the number that go into PCs. Even PCs have several of those other chips in them. The printer will have its own microprocessor in it, all the major peripherals will. They're just spread all over the place. That's still a very large market with big impact, it just doesn't get the press. We never got Intel Inside stamped on a Mercedes."

Moore had been looking at the brochure for the new Mercedes. It had all kinds of new options. You could get a little radar in front that will follow the car ahead at whatever distance you want, presumably up to an inch. "It's got GPS systems. It's an electronic car. A couple years ago the Mercedes 500 had 50 microprocessors in it. That new one must have added a couple dozen at least. We make a lot more of those smaller microprocessors than the ones that go into PCs. But our market share is not very large. Motorola's a lot bigger in that market than we are. Philips makes a lot of them. Japanese companies make a lot of them. Billions of units go into these applications every year."

Intel doesn't pursue these embedded applications as much as PCs because they're much less profitable. For example, Intel worked closely with Ford for many years and has supplied most of its microprocessors. But Moore has found that "they're more interested in driving the cost down and we're more interested in increasing functionality. You get back to where we were when Intel was first set up and the chip gets less and less valuable and the assembly becomes more valuable. We continue making quite a few of those. It's about a billion dollar business for us. PCs are many times that."

They're more interested in driving the cost down and we're more interested in increasing functionality.

The PC came as a pleasant surprise to Intel. It wasn't in a picture of the future Intel saw and worked to create. It was, however, an opportunity Intel found that fit within its original technology vision of developing complex circuits it could sell in large volume. Like Tim Koogle and Yahoo!, the approach to vision that Moore and Intel demonstrate is not foresight. It is instead a deep insight into a technology it develops coupled with a pragmatic effort to see and learn and build on the lessons that come from putting the technology into other peoples' hands. In this approach, vision provides a compass heading and a unique capability as the company plunges into unknown territory with the intent of exploring and surviving in it.

■ LESSONS LEARNED

As Intel has built on its technical vision and learned how to apply it in commercially successful products, a number of lessons have emerged that seem firmly planted in the company's culture. Many of these lessons apply to the semiconductor industry as a whole and to other high-tech businesses. The first one goes back to the foundation on which Intel has built its business.

➤ Build It and They Will Use It

Moore explained that Intel's starting point was technology. "And our product thrust has principally been driven by technology rather than the market or economics. That's the way it's been in this business as long as I've been in it. People didn't know they wanted a microprocessor until somebody came around and said, 'Look what this thing can do.' And they said, 'That's neat. I can use one.' Then you have to adjust to what people want after that, and keep coming up with what they want. But it starts from the technology. Really new products always do. You can't go out and do a market survey on a product that doesn't exist. You don't get any useful information at all."

> You can't go out and do a market survey
> on a product that doesn't exist.

Making something new before you know there's a market for it takes some courage in a market economy. It also takes faith and at least some idea for how the product will be used. When Ted Hoff saw Intel could do the Japanese calculators with a general-purpose architecture, he also saw that it could accomplish a lot of other control functions. "I remember him talking specifically about traffic light controls and elevator controls when he was convincing us it was a good idea. It didn't take much convincing. So we had one customer that had an application we hoped was going to go. We saw other things you could do with it. It seemed like a good investment of our people. But I guess we've done those things mostly on faith. If I go back one company earlier to Fairchild, we started out to make a silicon transistor. We didn't have any idea who was going to buy it, but people were buying transistors. Silicon made better transistors than germanium did, so we naively thought if we made a transistor maybe somebody would buy it. Much to our surprise they did. I guess it's just something that worked in this industry. It worked for us."

I guess we've done things mostly on faith.

Making something new has been more than the starting point for Intel. That's also what it does when faced with hard times. The industry thrives on change—it's the only thing that's constant. Moore believes in a slow economic period the worst thing to do is cut back spending. "Because the old products are never the ones you get well on. It's always a completely new generation of products. You have to spend to develop products across the economic dip or you're dead. That's something that we just know by having been through enough of those by now. It's not the gut reaction of a guy who's just gotten out of business school. But it tends to be after you've lived in this business. You have to invest in new products—even more so in economic downturns. It's the only way you're going to get well."

➤ Reach, and Be Willing to Fail

While pursuing its vision, Intel has been able to gain an edge where its technology produces something that proves useful and economically successful—and difficult for others to copy. Finding that edge requires trial and error, sometimes going too far and sometimes not far enough, as exemplified in Intel's Goldilocks Strategy. That means you have to be willing to fail.

"We've blown a few of our projects. The third idea we had for one of those complex chips we could sell in large volume was the electronic watch. I still wear mine. We were the first ones into the liquid crystal watch business." It got to the point where the little push pins on the side cost more than the silicon chip. "The economics just went the wrong way." Within two years a competitor took the watch from the best way to tell time to the cheapest way to tell time. Intel folded its tent.

"We have other experiences like that. We've taken a couple of very aggressive shots at new computer architectures. For one particular idea we said, 'OK, we have one chance to do it right. Let's start all over.' We took a very far-reaching step using all of the most modern everything the computer scientists had come up with." They ended up with a chip, Moore explained, that was a big step in the wrong direction because it went back to the old model of the computer industry—a vertical solution to the problem instead of many companies doing horizontal solutions. Further, he said, in order to get the functionality they wanted, they sacrificed performance. "By the time we got done with it, it was so slow that our regular microprocessors would beat it on standard applications. I don't feel bad about that. We took a shot. I always say if everything works you're not shooting far enough. You have to try things, and they're not cheap. As a start-up, if you try them and they don't work you're dead. When you get bigger you can afford a sprinkling of failures. Part of the process is being willing to fail. It's a learning process."

I always say if everything works you're not shooting far enough.

➤ Narrow the Focus, Widen the Input

As Intel has gotten larger and the microprocessor has become more successful, it no longer spends the same energy going out to find new uses for it. It did not institutionalize the Design Wins program that found 3,000 new uses for the microprocessor. As a bigger and more mature company, Intel tends to let new applications come to it. Moore believes the sales force is probably smaller now because the customer base in the PC business is relatively limited now; it's a lot easier to serve them. Intel turned a lot of its smaller customers over to its industrial distributors. When you do that you gain economies, but you lose direct contact. He's not sure that was the right decision, but it allowed Intel to focus where business was strongest.

Historically, customers had a very small input into Intel's products. That has changed. "When we do a new microprocessor now we go around to the 20 top customers and we go through in gory detail what we want to add, what they think is appropriate, and discuss the differences." Intel finally decides and makes the compromise. They've accepted as much of their customers' input as they can to be sure they understand what the customers want to do. One key difference now is that Intel's customers have gotten much more sophisticated in understanding their markets. "That has not always been the case. Before, they couldn't have given us that kind of input. We couldn't have gone to Ford in the early days and said, 'What kind of a microprocessor would you like to control the braking system?' They probably hadn't even thought about it. So we were inclined to make something and go to them and say, 'With this, if you sense the acceleration, you can do that.' They could program it, and then they learned to use these things and became sophisticated." Moore explained that a lot of industries have been dragged into electronics by having to design control systems using microprocessors. In the time Intel has been dealing with Ford they've gone from almost no knowledge in this area to being very sophisticated about controlling engines and all the rest of the parameters in the car electronically.

"Our customers teach us. We work together and we each bring a part of the solution. It's a collaborative effort with some of our customers now. But when you're dealing with a large number you can't be that close to many of them unless you're a lot bigger than we are."

➤ Drive Quantities Up, Prices Down

Intel backed away from the memory and liquid crystal watch businesses when they became commodities without sufficient profit or leverage. The problem was in the profit, not the commodity. "We tend to make commodities out of a lot of our products. Our technology enables us to make things in large quantity very cheaply. We have to get the quantity curve up in order to get the cost down. So we tend to drive in the direction of commoditizing everything we touch."

We tend to make commodities out of a lot of our products.

Much of "commoditizing" depends on manufacturing. Wafers are processed in batches. "The more of them we do the better we get at it, so the process continually gets polished as we run it. We do that pretty well. The number of chips in one of those batches is huge now." Moore explained that Intel typically runs 25 wafers per batch, and a given eight inch wafer may have 200 potential microprocessors on it. For the smaller chips there are a lot more than that. "So 200 times 25 is 5,000 in a batch, and we're running a lot of batches."

Intel had to make some significant process breakthroughs to get to this point. It was all new technology in the beginning; they had to learn to get that into manufacturing. Moore cited several examples. In the 1970s, the company took an aggressive leap into using projection lithography in the manufacturing area; that hadn't been used before and gave Intel a big leg up for quite a while. Then, at the end of the 1970s and into the 1980s, the Japanese entered the arena and everything about their manufacturing seemed better—not only better than Intel but better than the U.S. industry. "Where we could get information and they used the same equipment we did, theirs worked 95 percent of the time, ours worked 80 percent of the time. They got 200 wafers an hour through, we got 100 wafers an hour. They were better than we were in everything that related to manufacturing."

Concerned, the industry got together and set up SEMAT-ECH, an industry-government partnership that's been useful. But more important, Moore told me, Intel mounted programs internally to improve its own manufacturing. "Since that time we've made huge improvements in what we can do. Now if we do these comparisons we're as good as anybody. In fact, I don't think anybody in the world can match us. We keep up an intense effort in making progress. Making these chips is an extremely complicated process. That's the end of it I grew up in. I can't believe how good a job we do today."

We keep up an intense effort in making progress.

➤ **Watch Productivity and Be Tenacious**

Historically, the semiconductor industry has been cyclical. Intel itself experienced two bad downturns, the first one in 1974 around the time of the oil crisis and the worldwide recession that followed. "We had to get rid of one-third of our workforce. That's very tough to do. Fortunately, that came after a very good time. We were ridiculously profitable up through mid-1974. We were making 40 percent-plus pre-tax margins, and that went down to around 20 percent." The company was mostly making memories then. The microprocessor business was developing, but, basically, three memory chips were driving Intel at that time.

In 1984, a decade later, another problem arose—the projected volume didn't materialize for the 286. The industry had been on a two-year, grow-as-fast-as-you-can plan. "When the volume didn't develop we just fell off a cliff. Memory prices plummeted. I think in 1985 the U.S. industry collectively lost a billion dollars and the Japanese lost two billion, mostly on

DRAMs. We actually went into a loss position in 1986." Moore said Intel would have been hit hard in 1985 except for a contract with IBM that required IBM to take the product in 1985. That, however, just postponed the inevitable. Once again, Intel laid off a third of its workforce. "Very traumatic," he said, "but there was just no demand for our product."

Intel was very careful how fast it grew after that. It also pushed productivity. "We started looking at sales per employee, for example, as a strong indicator of how we were doing. If that wasn't going up it was time to slow headcount growth down. But I don't know if there are any general lessons. Every one of these cycles is different. They're not predictable. If they were you could avoid them." The industry hit another down cycle at the end of the 1990s, driven by overcapacity, particularly in DRAMs. "Fortunately, with our product line, we were pretty well insulated from it. We still have a main memory product line called flash memory, where we're market leaders. Fortunately, we had other things that did quite nicely."

We started looking at sales per employee as a
strong indicator of how we were doing.

The market for main memory chips hasn't been Intel's focus since the mid-1980s. But even though it reduced its dependence on memory then, Intel didn't abandon the market entirely. The reason for this reflects one more of the lessons learned from pursuing its technology vision: tenacity. "We got into memories first. It's a product that goes nicely with some of the microprocessor applications. The BIOS chip in most computers today is a flash memory. We've got 30 percent market share or something like that. If we pulled out, I don't know who'd pick up the slack." And businesses are cyclical, Moore explained. "If you get out of them every time there's a down cycle you run out of things to go into eventually. In fact, the easiest time to grow market share is often during one of these recessions. But you may not enjoy the process."

The easiest time to grow market share is often during one of these recessions. But you may not enjoy the process.

➤ Use Elasticity to Build Markets

Intel has consistently developed new technology for complex circuits it can manufacture and sell in large volume. It has consistently built products before it knows who will buy them and just what they will use them for, confident a market will exist and the company will learn how to serve it. It has consistently followed the same compass heading and used the same competencies to survive and prosper in new territory it has helped create as much as discover. When asked, the modest Moore is reluctant to call this vision. "Maybe it's pragmatism. One thing the industry discovered fairly early is that most of the markets we deal in are quite elastic. The net result is, the immediate reaction when the market slows down is to lower the price. That nearly always drives the elasticity and we come out the other side with a much bigger market. It's really led to some unique dynamics. That's one of the reasons we try to gain efficiencies and bring prices down. Elasticity has almost become an article of faith. I don't know if it's as true as it used to be, but for decades if you could get the price down low enough people would find more applications."

■ GOLDILOCKS

Imagine a very clean, well-lit room that looks something like a large kitchen, one that could produce huge quantities of food. There are special ovens for heating and cooking, special washing machines for cleaning, and special tools for making intricate designs in whatever is being cooked here. Presiding over this kitchen is a woman with golden hair, though you can barely see it since she and everyone working with her are wearing white suits and white hoods with masks. Her most striking feature therefore becomes her eyes, which gleam with passion as she goes about her work. Whatever she's making, whatever it may be good for, you can see she loves the making of it. You can tell from her eyes that she wanted to work in this kitchen and found something to make that people wanted so she could stay there. This is the image that captures Gordon Moore's approach to vision at Intel.

The kitchen doesn't produce food that anything likes to eat, but silicon chips that machines like to have wired inside them to make them feel smarter. You can tell machines like the chips by the way they light up and are eager to communicate with each other and the people around them. By now, many machines must be using these chips because the kitchen is busy producing as many batches of them as it can. On the walls of the kitchen you see three pictures from earlier days, when the woman with golden hair was just getting started, that show it wasn't always like this.

In the first picture you can see her trying out the results of three different recipes. She had to get the recipe just right, hard enough so other people couldn't easily copy it but easy enough that she could still make something that worked. Evidently one recipe was too easy because next to it were copies of what looked like transistor radios made by other brands you recognize. Another recipe must have been too hard because the packaging was there but nothing was inside. But one recipe must have worked just right, because she's holding up a gleaming piece of silicon and smiling with satisfaction.

The second picture shows the golden-haired woman at a contest, offering her silicon chips to thousands of different machines to see how they liked them and what they would do with them. There were cars and calculators and instruments of all kinds, even buildings. Once more, she was looking for what was just right, a fit with a machine doing something difficult enough that she could make her chips too complex for other people to copy easily, but not so difficult or unique that not many machines would be needed. The picture seems to have been taken while the contest was still underway, because the winner—a personal computer that was just part of the crowd of contestants—is indicated by a small sticker pasted on it outside of the picture.

The third picture shows the golden-haired woman at a cash register, being paid for her silicon chips. Like the recipe, the price had to be just right. From the contest she'd learned that the lower the price she asked the more contestants would enter and the more business she would have. But from working in her kitchen she also remembered that once the price became too low she couldn't afford to make her chips, and in any case they became cheaper than the packages they went in, meaning the packagers had more control over the final product than she did. To her, the chips she loves to make are what have to count, not their packages. Although you can barely make it out, the register seems to show $200.

As you focus again on the golden-haired woman at work you can appreciate all the things she had to learn to stay in the kitchen she loves. She's clearly pleased that people and machines like what she makes, but she hasn't left the kitchen long to watch them enjoy the results of her work. In her eyes you can see that what pleases her most is making her chips and learning how to make them better.

Chapter

11

Stick with It Honestly: Arthur Rock, Arthur Rock & Company

The histories of the venture capital industry and Silicon Valley are so intertwined that neither might exist without the other. One of the men who brought the two together and helped establish the relationships through which each learned to grow and make use of the other is Arthur Rock. When Rock and his partner Tommy Davis formed Davis & Rock in the San Francisco Bay Area in 1961 it was one of the first professional venture capital firms anywhere, after General Georges Doriot and American Research & Development in Boston, and it was the first of many to follow in Silicon Valley. Rock was probably the first person to apply the term "venture capital" to the new form of investing he and his partner were inventing. And he helped found and develop the companies that pioneered the semiconductor and personal computer industries: Fairchild Semiconductor, Intel, and Apple Computer.

Semi-retired and looking back at this 40-year history in 1999, Rock's view of what start-ups with a new idea must do to succeed can be reduced to a few simple-sounding prescriptions: "Be open-ended and don't set any limits. Get some good people with a good idea and run with it. Learn one step at a time." The prescriptions aren't so hard to understand, just hard to execute. Vision helps. Without vision they are mere managerial slogans. With vision they prescribe an active learning process through which new companies and new industries can lead the way into new territory. "The difference between a leader and a manager," says Rock, "is vision."

The difference between a leader and a manager is vision.

■ FROM VENTURE CAPITAL TO ANGELS

In 1957, while still working for a Wall Street investment banking firm, Hayden Stone & Co., Art Rock helped the so-called Traitorous Eight leave Shockley Semiconductor Laboratories and form Fairchild Semiconductor, which became the forefather of virtually all semiconductor companies in Silicon Valley. The idea that technically talented men like these could start their own separate company was considered so new and risky that Rock couldn't find enough backing for them. So he convinced Sherman Fairchild, an inventor who had started Fairchild Camera and Instrument, to back them with the $1.5 million they needed. After that, Rock kept coming to California looking for still more opportunities, and he soon left his Wall Street job to form the partnership with Tommy Davis.

Of the $5 million they had in their first fund, Davis & Rock only managed to invest some $3 million. As much as anything else that was because they didn't have time to invest more. They believed in spending time with the companies they'd invested in, getting involved to a degree that 40 years later would be impossible. Venture capital funds have grown too large and partnerships have too many investments to give the attention Davis & Rock believed in. But from this $3 million they earned the kind of return that attracted the attention of many others to this new kind of investing: Davis & Rock returned some $90 million to their limited partners. Two of their major successes were Teledyne and Scientific Data Systems (SDS).

With these successes already establishing his reputation, Rock made his most famous investments. He helped Bob Noyce and Gordon Moore leave Fairchild Semiconductor and found Intel in 1968. Later, Mike Markkula, an ex-Intel executive, convinced Rock to help Steve Jobs and Steve Wozniak found Apple Computer in 1977. These two companies and their technologies helped change the world. But since then the world has changed again.

For one thing, the Internet has replaced semiconductors and personal computers as the dominant technology. According to Rock, "The Internet is the big driver of technology today. The last big invention was around 1950 when Bardeen, Brattain, and Shockley invented the transistor. Really, there's been no invention since then." All the developments and all the smaller inventions are the result of the semiconductor. Even the breakthroughs in biology and biotechnology would not have been possible without the semiconductor and personal computers. The advances made in medical instruments are the result of the semiconductor. "It seemed to me in the late 1980s we were pushing the limits of that invention. It was becoming just mundane development."

In the mid-1990s, Goldman Sachs, the underwriter of Microsoft, downgraded Microsoft's stock because Microsoft had no Internet strategy. "I can't tell you that was the cause, but immediately thereafter Gates began his famous tirade about changing and becoming an Internet company. At that point I realized there was a new invention for the next 50 years. The Internet will drive new developments the way semiconductors did. It's a 50-year proposition."

The Internet will drive new developments
the way semiconductors did.

Pushed in part by the Internet, the pace and size of the venture capital business have increased enormously since it began in the 1960s, which in turn has led to fundamental changes in its way of doing business. According to Rock, a different pace emerged in the 1990s compared to when he was in the business. Venture capital firms have much more money and they have to invest it. When a deal comes along they believe if they don't make the investment somebody else soon will, so they go ahead. There will be more mistakes made this way, but there will also be more money made because prices are so high. "Venture capital firms are not going to make so many mistakes that they're going to lose money. They'll probably make more money than I ever made. Today if you go into every deal that comes into your shop you'll be way ahead. Just on the odds. I don't know how long that will last, but it's been that way for the past few years."

The change in the pace of investing means venture capitalists and the management teams they work with have to change the way they think about their work. "You just don't have time to investigate all the things we used to. Things move so fast and the payoffs are so big that people have to use more intuition and imagination than thorough rational analysis of the situation. It's like basketball. Forty years ago people shot two-handed and from a set position—and it was a very studied shot. You can't do that today. The game moves too fast. Even if you wanted to move in a more analytical way in venture capital you don't have time because you've got so much money to invest."

People have to use more intuition and imagination than rational analysis.

All these changes are profound enough that in less than 40 years venture capital as Rock helped invent it no longer exists. Time didn't so much pass it by as squeeze it out. He thinks of many venture capital firms now as portfolio companies rather than venture capital firms. They have so many partners, so much money to invest, and so many deals to do, they can't spend time with their companies. "They don't have time to study anything or do things the way I used to because they'll lose it. There are very few real start-ups being done. Venture capital firms have got to put too much money to work. It's caused a new industry called angel investing. The angels are what venture capitalists used to be. I do a little bit of that now."

Angels are what venture capitalists used to be.

Rock emphasizes that one of the tradeoffs from so much money being put into venture capital is that time has become scarce. "I used to go down to Intel every week in the early days to sit in on staff meetings. I'd go to Los Angeles a couple times a month and sit in on SDS and Teledyne staff meetings. Regular staff meetings. I was there to observe and participate. I was always interested in how the business was going, whether it was a viable business, whether what they were doing was going to break the company. Money was hard to come by in those days. Greater losses didn't mean greater investment."

While venture capitalists have less time to devote to the companies they add to their portfolios, they sometimes compound the loss by not taking the time to make sure these companies have solid leadership. "In the past when people have come in with a business proposal they would have a leader. I try to evaluate whether that person is really capable of *being* a leader. That's changed some in the last few years as the Internet has evolved. Because venture capitalists feel they have to move so fast on so many deals, some of them have their own executive recruiting people. But they still can't find enough CEOs. They're even starting companies without CEOs, without leaders. They go out and find a CEO, or they go ahead and develop products and then merge with somebody." Things are moving too fast, Rock explained, to let leaders develop like they did at Fairchild or Intel. A lack of CEO talent contributes to mergers. Venture capitalists can't hire people to run companies. Instead, they merge them with companies that do have the talent.

■ FINDING LEADERS

Instead of gathering a portfolio of companies to invest in, Rock's approach is to find good people and invest both his time and his money with them. Venture capital may have evolved to where it can no longer work that way, but by doing things his way Rock learned some valuable lessons about people, and about vision, that still apply—especially if you want to build an organization that will last and benefit the society around it.

Many Silicon Valley companies don't survive their founders to become enduring enterprises. For every Hewlett-Packard there are many more Daisys that bloom briefly and then fade. Intel has survived and prospered at least in part because of the leaders who developed there, from Bob Noyce to Gordon Moore to Andy Grove. According to Rock, the basic approach they all took was the same, but people have to develop at their own pace. When the Traitorous Eight started Fairchild Semiconductor, none of them thought they knew how to run a company. They hired someone to do it, and yet there were at least two natural leaders in that eight—Bob Noyce and Gordon Moore. "Bob developed his leadership ability a little quicker than Gordon, but they both had it, and both were excellent at running the company. I didn't know who had it, but I knew someone would come up with something. These were extremely bright, intellectually honest people who wanted to get something done and to work together."

The way Rock found out who was capable of being a leader at Intel is the same way he finds out who can lead in the other companies he's involved with. He spends time with them and talks with them. "You've got to figure out whether the entrepreneurs have the qualities you're looking for." Do they have a fire in their belly? Do they want to succeed at all costs? These are some of the qualities he looks for.

You've got to figure out whether the entrepreneurs
have the qualities you're looking for.

ART ROCK ON ATTITUDE
AND INVOLVEMENT

The prevalent attitude today is "I've got all this money to invest and I'll go into your deal if you'll go into mine. If you've got this deal and want to partner we'll go in, otherwise don't bother us." This is driven by the enormity of the funds and the few people managing them: ten partners, seven partners, a dozen partners. If you figure out how much time each partner has per investment you'll find it's maybe a half an hour a week. I tend to be that way now too because I just don't have the energy to do what I once did. But that isn't the way to do it.

You need to attend staff meetings and really be involved. Hopefully, you've seen the problems before so you can add something; companies continually run into the same problems. That's part of why I don't have the energy to do it anymore—I get bored. I've heard them all, or at least most of them: We can't get sales, we can't hire good people, this guy's going to leave, how do we account for revenue, we're not going to make our profits this quarter so what do we do about it?

All I can ever do is ask questions, I can't give directions. If lack of sales is the main problem of the company, how much time is the CEO spending trying to get sales? I was recently in a meeting of a company having a sales problem and the CEO just wouldn't go out and make calls. Bob Noyce went out and made a lot of calls for Intel.

He talks with them, spending a lot of time with them over many sessions. "The first session everyone's on their best behavior. If they're even half-way intelligent they all come in and make a good impression the first time. But over time do they say the same things? How do they approach things? You try to see how their minds work. You see a lot of people who eventually will say, 'I want to make a lot of money.' Well, that isn't a good way to start a company. Those guys get thrown out the door the first time I hear that statement. Or, 'This guy did it and I'm better than he is so I can do it.' A better way to start a company is with the idea that you're going to make some products that are beneficial and you really want to build an organization. Build something, not just make a lot of money. You're going to hire a lot of people, advance the economy, make life easier for people."

◼ INTELLECTUAL HONESTY

One of the qualities Rock mentioned he'd seen in Bob Noyce and Gordon Moore is intellectual honesty. That turns out to be perhaps the single most important quality he looks for, the one he believes is most valuable to people who want to build something new that will benefit society and last.

"The two main qualities I look for are a lot of drive and intellectual honesty. Intellectual honesty means seeing things as they are instead of as you want them. It means there's no wishful thinking. You really can't do any wishful thinking. You can't say, 'This is going to turn out all right' when you don't know it, or that someone isn't fooling you when you don't know it."

The two main qualities I look for are a lot
of drive and intellectual honesty.

Rock told me he once was associated with a company that was going to make a new kind of computer. The CEO had been vice president of a large computer company. He knew all about the computer business. He had a vice president of software and a vice president of hardware. The hardware was going along very smoothly. The vice president of software said the software was going along smoothly. So the CEO set up his factory and got a salesforce and was taking orders. He was out on a sales call when the vice president of software called and said, "I've got to tell you. We're going to be a year late." "This CEO had *wanted* to believe his vice president. He knew better. He just wanted to believe."

Rock's point is that you can't let what you want to believe get in the way of what you know. If you've got people working for you that you like, are you going to trust them more than someone you don't like? Or someone you don't have a relationship with? Intellectual honesty applies to what you can really do with the people you work with. It's easy to believe in intellectual honesty, or at least say you do, but it's hard to practice it. "You have to have good people. You can't instill this honesty from the outside."

You can't let what you want to believe get
in the way of what you know.

According to Rock, people who make things work have intellectual honesty. They separate the chaff from the wheat. "There are so many paths you can go down, somebody's got to figure out which one has the best odds of working. Someone's got to say, 'Our resources are limited, we're not going to do everything, now let's do this and do it right.'"

In my own experience, intellectual honesty is very difficult to find in daily business practice. The competition for power, flattery, ego, greed, fear, politics—all kinds of things get in the way. According to Rock, it all comes down to good people who are intellectually honest themselves and demand it of others. He won't stand for any politics. He believes intellectual honesty is extremely rare and considers himself lucky to have been associated with a few of those people who have it.

Rock has also been associated with people who don't—or didn't—have and work with the intellectual honesty he believes is so essential. "Apple was purely political. That's an overstatement, but there was a lot of politics involved in who was going to do what for whom. 'If you back me on this I'll back you on this other thing.' It wasn't a good atmosphere." That atmosphere, in Rock's view, didn't come from Steve Wozniak; Steve Jobs promulgated it. "I don't know whether he does that today. I doubt he does. I think he's probably learned how to go about things. He was very young. But that was certainly part of the problem when he left, one he created. Companies usually take on the personality of their CEO. That's why it's so important to find people who are intellectually honest. The politics at Apple just didn't work. The board saw and recognized the problem and knew we had to get rid of Steve Jobs. We tried to talk to him but it didn't make any difference. He thought he was right."

Rock said he himself doesn't know how to change a company that's fallen into the trap of running on politics, but it looks as though Apple has done that since Jobs came back. "I haven't had any contact with Steve at all since he left Apple the first time, but just as an observer I'd say the company is run a lot differently in 1999 than it was 10 years ago."

Rock believes that every company he has been involved with shows either a positive or negative effect depending on whether the leaders have intellectual honesty. He cites Intel as a positive example. "Andy Grove and Gordon Moore aren't going to stand for any shenanigans. It's a little more confrontational over at Intel than I've seen at other places. But it's done with honesty. People know where they stand; they get everything out in the open and figure out what they're going to do." Throughout his 40 years in business, Rock has found that intellectual honesty is a constant: Companies that have been successful have it and those that haven't worked out so well do not. "That hasn't changed. What has changed is there's a lot of money around to start companies that wouldn't have gotten started under normal circumstances. Can you imagine someone in the 1980s or 1970s saying, 'We made money in the last quarter, but it was a mistake, and we'll never do it again'? And the stock goes up ten points? You can't imagine that. There's just so much money around in 1999."

➤ No Limits

Intellectual honesty about the way things really are may sound like a prescription for doing nothing new or daring.

Not so. You need honesty most when you're trying to do something new and make it work. You need it to be clear about what you don't know so you can find out. You need it because you don't know the answers you need and you don't want to fill in the void with wishful thinking. You need it so you won't limit your thinking and so you can see something new when it appears.

"It's important not to set limits. To be completely open-ended. You get some good people and a good idea and you run with it. You don't say, 'We can only go this far.' Or, 'Gee, this is only good for this.'" Rock recalled that the only use people thought about for the first semiconductor device was in hearing aids. General Transistor, the first independent semiconductor company, founded in 1954 or 1955, made devices for hearing aids. People didn't think of computers at the early stages. "If you went to a transistor company and asked what the market is for hearing aids, you'd limit yourself. You can't limit yourself."

It's important not to set limits. You get some good people and a good idea and you run with it.

It may sound surprising, but Rock beleives you can't think in terms of what the market is even if you have the right people running an organization. He reminded me that IBM turned down UNIVAC and Eckert-Mauchly. IBM thought all the uses for computers were known and saturated. "I'm sure Tom Watson Jr. says that was one of their big mistakes. In World War I, a well-known scientist went to the War Department and offered their services; the Secretary of War at the time said, 'We have a scientist.' One scientist was all the War Department thought it needed. Those are mistakes people make because they limit their thinking. You've got to think, 'Gee, this is a wonderful device, and something good is going to happen.'"

The drive Rock looks for is to do something that benefits people, even if you don't know exactly how. "We had no idea what semiconductors were going to amount to. Anybody who says they did is crazy. Yet we had the feeling that the device would be very, very important. You'd look at vacuum tubes and say those things are big and create a lot of heat and they fail frequently. You just said to yourself, 'Maybe eventually there will be something to these semiconductor devices.'"

■ ONE STEP AT A TIME

Looking to benefit people and not limiting yourself does not mean you should take on the world and try to change everything at once. Building something that hasn't been built before is a learning process. "You have to take small steps. If bringing a vision to reality was based on foresight instead of a learning process it would be easy. I wrote an article for *Harvard Business Review* a couple of years ago that said strategy is easy, it's tactics that are very difficult. Many people have a lot of strategies, but only good people can execute them. It takes a step-by-step approach, and the ability to execute." Everybody who comes into his office, Rock explained, has a strategy, but most of the strategies don't work because people don't know how to execute. Good people can change strategies if something's not working. "You do need a spark of imagination and faith in yourself and what you're doing."

If bringing a vision to reality was based on foresight instead of a learning process it would be easy.

The counsel to move ahead one step at a time, to have faith in what you're doing, speaks to another issue vital to a start-up's success—and to venture capital's success: not being afraid to fail. According to Rock, the absence of fear of failure distinguishes Silicon Valley and the American economy from most others. It's entirely different abroad, primarily for two reasons: One, failure is not a stigma here. You can go on a second and a third time, whereas in other countries one mistake signals the end. Two, there's a developed market for IPOs of small companies in the United States. That's just developing in a small way in England and Germany, "and that's about it. That's just started." Why has it taken them so long? They're older societies, more traditional. The traditions in the United States aren't that old. It comes back to the benefit of having no limits. "The downside is that we have a lot of failures, but that's part of the process. Then too, companies can reach their limits. Intel has tried more than once to take the path that leads directly to the consumer and has failed. They keep on trying, but they keep on failing. They're not geared up for that. But the most important advice I have for anyone trying to make a vision real is this: You've just got to stick with it."

The most important advice I have for anyone trying
to make a vision real is to stick with it.

Conclusion

Taken altogether, the major visions of Silicon Valley create a mosaic of a world that offers people everywhere more of what vision itself is finally all about: the power to make ideas real. More powerful microprocessors and neural network computers will allow people to interact with and direct all kinds of machines to do their minds' bidding, through speech and touch and emotion. Computer software will allow almost anyone, not just engineers, to imagine and test and even produce many of the fun or useful products they want in their lives, and it will provide creative tools to enlarge the capacity to communicate ideas with artistry and power. The Internet will cut out more and more of the mass market intermediaries that stand between people and ideas and products, giving all of us greater choices and more power as consumers, and more ability to research, define, and create just exactly what we want for ourselves in our own lives. Biotechnology will not only let us read our biological horoscopes but enlist our own and others' DNA to maintain or restore our health and life span.

> Vision is finally about the power to make ideas real.

At least one of the common elements in the visions of Silicon Valley is just this push to put more creative power in the hands of individual people, whether in their work or play. With this power, more and more people in their working and private lives can share the opportunity that Silicon Valley CEOs have: to dream a vision and turn it into reality. As this creative power becomes more widely available, vision moves out of the rarified realm of top leaders to allow all kinds of people to design their own lives. Vision becomes a more vital opportunity for us all. Which means we need to understand what vision is, what it does, what it's made of, where it comes from, and what it takes to turn one into reality. Whether we're the leader of a billion people or simply of ourselves, we need vision to know how to make a world we truly want to live in.

■ WHAT IS VISION?

Vision is both an activity and the product of that activity. Its secret seems to lie in the lively interaction and reverberation between the two. Beginning with the activity: *To vision or to envision is to sense a different and better possibility for some part of the world that's significant to you, and to feel both inspired and guided in the work necessary to make that possibility real.* People often link this sense metaphorically and sometimes literally to seeing—but also to hearing, touching, smelling, tasting, or a feeling in one's gut. Visioning is feeling. More fundamentally, to vision is to intuit and to imagine something new, whether it's a product, an organization, or a way of life. (The word *envision* is so strongly linked to forming a picture in our minds that it suggests overly narrow limits for both intuition and imagination, so I have usually tried to avoid it.) To inspire and provide a sense of direction, this intuition and imagination must arouse and command the visionary's will, and must be aligned with his or her basic values and beliefs. And although people sometimes equate visioning with foreseeing the future, it is instead connected to a keen feeling for and insight into the present, the world as it is, and a feeling for how the forces in this world can be guided to create something new and better.

Vision is to intuit and imagine something new.

The product of visioning is then a specific image or intuition of a different and better world. It is an image present in people's minds, an intuition alive in their souls, not a frozen picture or a plaque on a wall that may at best only represent the vision or remind people of it. A vision needs the activity of visioning to remain alive and present, to constantly recreate and improve it. In that way a vision is like an oral story. Especially in its early stages, it seems to exist only in the minds of people who hear about it, and it survives only if it is told and retold. Each retelling is not an exact copy but a slightly different version, depending on the experiences of the storyteller, the needs of the audience, and the changes in the world the vision describes and interacts with. If you want your vision to be alive to inspire and direct beyond your own work, you've got to constantly tell the story out loud and hope other people will tell it as well, even if they forget you were the original author. Costello speaks of this as giving your vision away.

If you want your vision to be alive , you've got to constantly tell the story out loud.

But what *is* the world or object that is imagined and intuited? In the beginning a vision is not concrete, yet at some point it seems to become more and different from something merely imagined and intuited. Faggin speaks of a vision as being a new species, alive and interacting with the environment. Costello speaks of the way a simulated, visionary world at some point hangs together with its own integrity, much like a model in physics. People who work with vision speak of it as having its own existence and validity independent of their thinking even if nothing in the material world resembles it yet.

To use slightly different terms, as the activity of visioning paints a picture of the world and continues to refresh it, a vision seems to take on an existence similar to the circles and squares and other objects in geometry. These objects aren't the same as the pictures we form in our mind's eye— some, like four-dimensional space, can't be pictured at all— nor are they the same as the figures we draw on paper and whiteboards to represent them. Not mere concepts but not real objects either, they are ideal objects that we can study *and have knowledge of.* Visioning produces ideas with their own existence and integrity, and in turn these ideas and knowledge of them enable people to produce the real objects or conditions that correspond to them.

■ PATTERNS AMONG VISIONS

In addition to the fundamental capability of turning ideas into reality, other patterns emerge from the visionary activity in Silicon Valley. One seems to be the result of the interaction between visioning and vision: Visions come to resemble the activity that produces them. Different visions do not seem to be produced by exactly the same process, but by different processes that match them. This isn't like saying car factories produce cars. It's more like saying a car factory works like a car does. If you look at how the product of one of Silicon Valley's visions works, you may see that the visionary process behind it works in a similar way:

➤ Costello's model of the vision process—simulating, selling, then executing a vision—resembles the functions of the CAD/CAM systems his vision is aimed at producing. CAD/CAM systems are used to design and analyze, communicate and sell, and finally produce the products engineers work on.

Visions come to resemble the activity that produces them.

➤ Koogle's description of the way Yahoo!'s navigational guide grows resembles his description of the way Yahoo's vision grows: through paying very close attention to what people consume on the Web and offering them more, in what amounts to controlled experiments in natural selection.

➤ Eastman and Geron's vision is focused on helping people survive with their health into old age, and Eastman's approach to vision is focused on surviving the long and challenging course to bring approved drugs to market.

➤ Colligan's vision was to help creative people put together and produce whatever they could imagine, and for him visions are the creative products of leaders who, like artists, imagine them and then work to make them real.

➤ Faggin describes the critical moment in creating a vision as recognizing new patterns, and the neural network computers he works on now make use of the fundamental computing power of pattern recognition.

The resemblances are much more extensive than the preceding descriptions, and the same pattern appears more or less strongly in most if not all of the visions presented in this book. The pattern appears strongest among the people who have thought most about vision and how they use it in their work. After I began noticing this resemblance in others I noticed it between my own approach to vision and the content of my vision of a knowledge economy. I see vision as a way of knowing what you're doing when you're trying to do something new, and I see this competence as critical for building and living in a knowledge society. If this resemblance is the result of some kind of disease, I've got it, too.

The pattern seems too striking to be a mere fluke, although I'm not sure what it means or what causes it. At first I was tempted to dismiss it with an easy psychological explanation, something like the power of metaphors or our acquired points of view to color and shape almost anything we think about or do. Even if there's some truth in an explanation like that it finishes the subject in a dead end of relativism. A more interesting and useful explanation may lie in the ways we produce new knowledge and use it to make new products. Making a vision real means creating and then using a picture of a different world to, in effect, help create itself. As you continually repaint the picture of the world you want—to articulate and sell it, for example—you begin to paint in a way that resembles the workings of that world, as if the production of the idea had to mirror the production of the real thing. The grammar of production seems to require agreement between your vision and your visioning.

Making a vision real means creating and then using a picture of a different world to, in effect, help create itself.

However the resemblance comes about, there may be some practical consequences worth considering. One may be a caution to take care in choosing a vision: The vision you choose may eventually shape your mind and your way of working, for good or ill. Work to create a better world and your mind may come to work the way this better world works. Work to create something worse or uglier and your mind may come to resemble that. A similar caution applies to choosing a way of visioning: Your way of thinking and working may not only limit but determine and define what you're able to envision. It has often been said that thinking something truly new is difficult and rare, and this may be one reason why. To think something different you have to think in a different pattern, a different way—although any new pattern you're able to adopt would still determine what you could envision with it. In any case, if your vision and approach to vision don't resemble each other you may not have thought about them enough.

This pattern of resemblance may also help explain the numerous and differing definitions of vision among people who work with it. You would expect the definitions to vary because the visions and vision processes vary. Most people are talking about and primarily familiar with their own species of vision. By their nature visions tend to be so all-consuming that if you're working on your own you don't have much time or incentive to look at others. But in looking, some things vary greatly among visions, and some stay rather constant.

■ KEY PARAMETERS

Time is the medium of vision. It is the dimension that vision, like thought, requires and moves in: Without time it would be impossible to distinguish one vision—or one thought—from another, and it would be impossible to tell whether a vision was progressing toward being realized. Choosing the right moment in time to work on a vision, the right length of time to make it real, and the right rhythm to review progress and modify a vision are all central to the practical art of vision. The environment that each vision works in and the technology it works with seem to dictate the appropriate time frame and rhythm more than anything else. And you have to be aware that, like it or not, time limits the focus and scope of the visions that can be made real in the business world.

Time is the medium of vision.

Within limits tolerated by the world of business, visions vary greatly both in how far they look into the future and in how often they're subjected to review. For practically all Silicon Valley companies time seemed to have speeded up in the 1990s. (As Rock pointed out, that has made lengthy analysis impractical and so has put a premium on intuition and imagination.) If time horizons didn't become shorter, review cycles did. Doerr says Kleiner Perkins' vision looks about three years into the future, and that they now review it every six months—formerly they reviewed it once a year. That's probably a good average for the Valley at the end of the 1990s. On the longer side, Eastman says Geron's vision looks 15 to 20 years into the future, and that while the long-term vision tends to stay rather constant they derive new operating plans on a yearly cycle. On the shorter side, Koogle talks about Yahoo!'s long-term vision being rather constant, but the more important short-term vision is reviewed and changed almost daily.

Visions also vary in how detailed or "granular" they are. For some CEOs, making a vision real means making it more detailed and extensive. Koogle sees vision that way. In contrast, Levinson's vision of science has very little detail. The detail comes in plans that are designed to implement the vision.

Other ways in which visions vary in Silicon Valley seem to be more a matter of personality and values than anything inherent in the visions or the industries they're part of. Most CEOs tend to see visioning as a top down process, where they and perhaps several of their key lieutenants take the responsibility to create and communicate a vision to their employees and the outside world. But even when the process is top down, many CEOs want individual employees to develop their own visions to fill in the part they're responsible for, making sure they fit with but also extend the overall vision for the company. Other CEOs see the different parts of their organizations as being responsible simply for executing their assigned part of the operating plans derived from a vision. The vision itself provides an integrating and motivating framework. The difference between asking employees to have vision or merely to have a plan is the difference between what inspires and guides their work: their own intuition and imagination or a translation of someone else's.

The difference between asking employees to have vision or merely to have a plan is the difference between what inspires and guides their work.

More rarely in Silicon Valley, CEOs favor a more democratic, even bottom up process for developing visions. This approach seems more common in new start-up or smaller companies than in larger and more established ones, but it has some great advantages. As one CEO said to me, "If people participate in developing a vision you don't have to sell them on it. They buy into it automatically because they

---

If people participate in developing a
vision you don't have to sell them on it.

---

created it." Whatever approach companies take, virtually all
the CEOs seem to agree that the more widely shared a vision
is the more effective and powerful it will be.

■ CONSTANTS

Ultimately, whether CEOs adopt a top-down approach to vision or a more democratic one, most acknowledge that visions are more collective than individual. As Doerr says,
individuals don't accomplish great things, teams and groups
of people do. If you look carefully at real examples, more than
one individual creates a vision, even though, as Faggin says,
we often want to anoint a lone hero. And if a vision is to grow
and succeed many more people must not only adopt it but
add to it. Costello talks about how much larger and better a vision becomes in the process of communicating and selling
it—other people add the force of their own imagination and
intuition.

Another constant is that, almost by definition, visions require taking risks, although even in Silicon Valley they're
limited ones. Visions require you to get to the knife's edge of
what is possible, as Faggin says—but not past it. For Koogle,
that means extending a vision carefully, step by step. The
CEOs in this book don't mind an occasional failure in reaching too far with their visions. Moore says if you don't fail
from time to time it's a sign you aren't reaching far enough.
Being too conservative in reaching for the edge of possibility
can put you out of the game of vision and high-tech competition entirely. But still these CEOs strive to be on time, not
ahead of their time, in terms of what they can produce and
what markets will accept.

Finding the knife's edge comes back to intuition and
imagination more than market studies or anything rational

and certain. Moore among other CEOs reminds us that you can't get any useful information from a market survey on a product that doesn't exist yet. You have to make it first and then let people figure out what they can do with it. As he says, maybe it takes faith as much as vision. To some degree you are moving into unknown territory; the trick is determining how far you can go. As part of getting a feel for just how far he can go, Costello talks about working to get alignment with the forces in the world that can help his vision, and finding ways to counter those forces that will oppose him. Like the other CEOs he prefers to work *with* these forces, not against them. They want to change the world in ways it's ready to accept even if it doesn't know it yet. Working with vision requires both a sense for the world as it is and for how it *could be* just over the horizon.

Vision requires a sense for the world as it is
and *could be* just over the horizon.

While Silicon Valley visions try to reach no further than the edge of the possible, most—but not all—also aim to serve a larger purpose of some kind, whether spiritual, humanitarian, or social. This aspect of a vision must be firmly grounded in values and intentions actually held, otherwise the vision comes across as cynical manipulation aimed at motivating employees or building a positive public image. If people come to doubt this part of a vision, they will likely come to doubt the whole of it almost immediately. Mere words convey this real purpose less than the consistency in day to day actions Eastman talks about. Perhaps because of this, most of the CEOs I've spoken with are reticent to talk too much about their larger purposes, although they acknowledge these are important to them and to their companies. They'd rather let people judge their sincerity over time. Those who don't really have a larger purpose don't pretend—and are better off not to.

A larger purpose is precisely the source of the inspirational energy many Silicon Valley CEOs want in a vision.

The inspiration comes from building not just a new world, but a *better* one, not only better for the visionary company but for its customers and more. This is part of the altruism I see behind the most powerful visions. It's what leads Costello to give away his vision and what causes it to gain even more power when he does. If just one person or one company holds a vision its power is inherently limited. The more people who feel the vision is their own, the more powerful it becomes.

Colligan believes that merely making money is not the main motivation of most employees—they're hungry to serve a larger purpose. I agree. As business life has required more and more time from Silicon Valley workers, as they have less and less time to devote to family, community, and spiritual life, they have no place else to fulfill a desire to be a part of something more important than themselves except in business. Business vision can be a double-edged sword: It helps provide people with a sense they're part of something larger and hence leads them to willingly devote more time to it; but in doing so it can also increase their separation from the other parts of their lives that are more appropriate for providing this fulfillment. It is no accident that so many of Silicon Valley's business leaders are single or divorced. Better balance would come not so much from diminishing business vision as from enlarging the full and balanced set of visions that make life worth living for people.

Better balance would come from enlarging the
set of visions that make life worth living.

Vision is too powerful and useful to be limited to business alone. It seems to be rather new there and I want to help it grow and spread. But business should not be the only subject of vision. The purposes and concerns of even the best businesses and the combined business system are far narrower than the full range of human and social concerns. We also need vision for ourselves, our families, our communities, and perhaps even our global village.

■ VISION IS A PROCESS

Although the actual processes responsible for producing each of Silicon Valley's visions differ and tend to resemble the visions they produce, a more general process does emerge when they're combined into a kind of superset. This amalgamated "arc of vision," as Faggin calls it, makes up a basic vision process that can guide and offer suggestions to people and companies who want to review or develop their own visions.

➤ Creation

The first step, creating the vision, is the most private and personal. Even if the vision comes from a group, it is usually a small group in which each individual has to dig deeply into his or her own soul. You have to put yourself and your thoughts on the edge between chaos and order that Faggin talks about.

Putting yourself on this edge usually includes putting yourself in a smaller, somewhat isolated environment from the larger organization and the larger world. It helps greatly if the larger environment is stimulating and provides at least most of the resources you need. People living here recognize that Silicon Valley provides such an environment: Several great universities are doing leading-edge basic research, there is direct access to numerous venture capitalists in the business of supporting entrepreneurs, and large numbers of technical innovators feed off and stimulate each other to do even more than they could if isolated. Even the Mediterranean climate and a great city like San Francisco seem to help. The whole environment makes for a complex ecology of innovation that works and that isn't easy to duplicate elsewhere. But even here visions are created in relative if temporary isolation.

In this isolation, the critical activity seems to be a dialogue between reason and intellect on the one hand and imagination and intuition on the other. Reason and intellect

> The critical activity seems to be a dialogue
> between reason and intellect on the one hand and
> imagination and intuition on the other.

may define the original problem that needs to be solved. But the main source of the vision, the "aha" Faggin speaks about, seems to come from intuition and imagination. Then the dialogue continues. Intuition and imagination have to be felt and explored, then tested, extended, and educated by reason and intellect. What intuition suggests may be at odds with what is reasonable and logical, and so the two sides need to be brought out, each one listening to and drawing out the other in turn. In this process, the intuited and imagined vision either becomes stronger, filled out, and supported by reason and testing or it dies because it just doesn't make enough sense. You have to accept that.

The content of this creation phase is obviously different for each different vision. But for any given practitioner the dialogue that produces it seems to develop a personal pattern. For Costello it is a simulation. For Clark it is figuring out and feeling the next logical step some part of the world will take. Furthermore, many visionaries seem to focus more on the change they want to make or the benefit they want to bring to the world, rather than on the means that will enable them to do that. They focus on the *what* more than the *how*, even if in the end figuring out and executing the how takes up more of their time and resources. This indirection seems important to vision. The answer comes from focusing on the question more than a rush to possible answers.

For Faggin, who rightly emphasizes the novelty necessary in a vision, to answer a vision's question is to recognize a new pattern. The new pattern helps explain something and helps you do something new. Finding it means you've learned something useful. For Levinson, these answers are discoveries about the way a given biological process works. If the questions are profound enough the answers unlock still more answers to many other questions—and to practical products not foreseen or foreseeable when the process began.

➤ Articulation

Articulation begins almost at the moment a vision is created, as reason and intellect engage with the products of intuition and imagination, and it is the bridge to all the later steps. If you can't express your vision you won't get very far in the internal dialogue that creates it, and you certainly won't get very far in gathering allies and making your vision real. But just as Moses relied on Aaron, it often seems to happen that the individuals who create a vision aren't necessarily the ones best able to articulate it. This is often where a CEO comes in. Even if CEOs don't create their company's vision, it is vital that they articulate it well.

The constant act of articulation seems more important than any single product of it. Different audiences will need different messages in different media. A technical or scientific vision generally requires a written account because that forces you to be precise and writing is the medium expected by the technical and scientific community. Visions may also be expressed in pictures, in poems, or any form that works to communicate with the people you need to communicate with. But the basic form is dialogue, and for that oral communication is especially important. No matter how well you express your vision in whatever form, your audience will have questions if you are really engaging them, and you will need to answer them if you want to communicate and improve your vision and see it grow. Even in the technical and scientific community, published papers receive written commentary, and many are presented orally at conferences and in seminars. Oral communication, not written vision statements, is the key to communicating a vision.

> The basic form is dialogue, and for that, oral
> communication is especially important.

➤ Mobilization

Besides improving it, the purpose of communicating your vision is of course to create a movement around it, to gather allies to help you and to let the outside world know what you see. Your vision will dictate who you need to communicate with to build an organization, find partners, and attract customers. As with the creation phase, this selling phase seems to work best if you focus on the change you want to make, on the better world, rather than on the means to that end which your company may offer. You will certainly need to talk about your product or service; if you are selling a vision as well as a product, though, you can open a more useful channel of communication with potential customers and partners by focusing together on the better world you want to create rather than simply pushing your company or your product. This is not the same thing as solution selling: You aren't just trying to find out your customer's problem so you can more effectively sell your product. You're engaging in a dialogue about a different world that will benefit you both and others as well, a world you want to help create together with your customer. You may need to sell a product, but you want to give your vision away freely.

This selling seems to work best if you focus on the change you want to make rather than on the means to that end.

As Costello points out, if you've done your homework and are truly inspired by and understand your vision, you will naturally have a passion for it, and that passion sells. So let it show. You'll make mistakes and not everyone will like your vision, but if your passion is genuine and you pay attention to and learn from the feedback you get, you will be moving and you'll have a chance to form a movement. If you don't have that passion, you may not really have a vision, and other people probably won't believe you do.

It is vital in creating this movement to keep your communication real. This isn't a public relations campaign. You are trying to communicate something you deeply believe and you want others to believe and feel as you do. You want to communicate soul to soul, not use tricks. The tricks of persuasion and advertising do work on people, and you've got to deal with them and maybe even utilize them, too. But eventually, to create a movement around your vision you have to have people intuiting and imagining their version of the picture you see, you have to get them to understand that your idea holds together and makes sense and improves the world. Otherwise your message may at best offer a few moments of excitement and then be replaced by the next and latest exciting thing.

In creating a movement around your vision you're keeping it alive and helping it expand. You aren't forcing it on the world or conning the world into accepting it, but creating an environment where it can take hold and grow. The important thing is to keep talking about it, acting in a way that's consistent with it, and work on offering the proof that people need to fully believe the vision's real.

➤ Realization

After creating, articulating, and selling your vision to gather people around it, the final critical phase is execution. Doing all the previous steps well should mean you have a group of inspired people with a similar goal and sense of direction. Your vision is felt and imagined, and has even become a model, an idea that hangs together and seems to explain the part of the world you're working on. Now it has to be made real and concrete.

When I ask CEOs what execution requires I often hear references to what the preceding phases have produced: It requires conviction, an absolute commitment to persevere through obstacles and disappointments. That should serve as a reminder that the activity of visioning is not a one-time event; the process is not a series of steps you take once and are finished with. You have to keep going back to the beginning and do more simulation as you learn more about the direction you need to take, and imagine and feel the vision again for the energy and sense of purpose it gives you. And you have to keep talking and listening to people.

The actual work and techniques required to execute a vision appear on the outside to be no different from what leaders have long known about completing any set of tasks. Koogle talks about the importance of simply listing the things that are most important to do today, doing those, then relisting priorities and doing those, and so on. Doerr talks about the process he learned at Intel where the strategy, each objective, and finally each individual's work plan are written down, using only one piece of paper for each. Then both results and the continued relevance of the results are reviewed regularly, once a quarter being a good rhythm. To find the difference vision makes you have to look more closely.

Vision modulates the work of execution in a number of ways. It supplies the needed energy and commitment, and to the extent the vision is shared it focuses that energy on the same goal, without the many hidden agendas that otherwise have the power to divert and dissipate the energies of organizations. It focuses that energy better on the truly important tasks and makes it easier to identify and ignore the unimportant tasks, as Costello says. It allows people to come together more easily and work as teams. And it allows you to react faster because you're not waiting for someone else to analyze the situation and present you with a plan. As Costello says, at least in high-tech industries you're riding a big wave. If you're not working from the educated instinct you've developed through your vision you're not likely to survive on the wave for long.

Executing a vision requires the in-the-moment awareness of your environment and where you're headed that Costello's image of riding a big wave and Koogle's image of Darwinian natural selection evoke. You have the feeling that your very life is at stake, and yet you are able to keep focused on what you need to do and what is happening around you that you can take advantage of. At the same time that your vision gives you an acute awareness of the moment it also keeps you oriented toward your long-term goal. You can be opportunistic about unforeseen events that further your goals and are in alignment with your values while avoiding those that divert you.

The execution phase is a dangerous time for a vision. Using its power means choosing to let the vision lead, letting the best ideas win, as Doerr says, rather than ego and other competing forces. If people in an organization see that this isn't happening, despite what leaders may say, the vision loses and other forces take over. People start jockeying for power or focusing primarily on the money they're making. The same vision statement may appear in marketing materials, the same plan may be presented to the board of directors, but real vision is gone. Employees know it. Customers soon know it. As Eastman says, you have to be aware that everything you say and do reflects your values and your vision.

One of the important milestones in executing a vision is often a proof that the idea actually works. Faggin talks about how he had to prove to Intel that the microprocessor he'd built could actually and easily do more than drive a calculator. In the biotechnology and pharmaceutical world, scientific theories and models have to be proved in clinical trials. Whatever you have to do or build to provide this proof may not be a finished and marketable product, and it may be far from the final change you want to make in the world. But it takes your vision over the critical threshold from idea to reality. Faggin even says at this point it's no longer a vision—it's real. Now it's something even people who don't share your vision can see and believe and benefit from. In business, as Colligan says and most people know, it's results that count.

■ VISION IS KNOWING

Visions are wonderfully powerful in a very personal way to the people who live by them. They do tend to create feelings of tension because of the difference between the world as it is and as you want it to be. And they tend to create still more discomfort during the long work required to change conditions or people who may not be eager to change at first. But they also give you the positive energy and progressively the know-how to make these changes anyway. They provide a certain feeling of getting to the core of the problem or opportunity behind the change you want to make, a feeling for the leverage of basic knowledge about how a particular part of the world works. Levinson speaks about this when he describes his preference for science over the brute force of random trial and error. Costello talks about the explanatory power a vision has. This isn't external knowledge that comes at you like instructions or a recipe in a book, but internal knowledge that is felt as intuition and ultimately as a reasoned proof. And still it is knowledge about something not quite yet present or perceivable. Clark, for example, describes a feeling for the next logical step the world will likely take — but hasn't yet.

This feeling of knowing doesn't arrive full-blown and all at once, but it grows as the vision is created, communicated, and realized. To vision is also to learn. There are indeed moments of sudden understanding, Faggin's "aha!" after he's worked on and lived with a problem for some time. That is the spark of life in a vision. As it grows and inflames you, you learn and so your sense of knowing grows as well. Your intuition and imagination have to be educated, as Faggin says, or they can lead you to make critical mistakes. Partly that's a matter of using your rational mind to make sure the vision is logical and complete and fits the data you have. Costello calls this simulation. But, as many of these men pointed out, at some point a vision seems to become an organic, living thing in its own right. So partly you also learn by paying attention to the wholeness and integrity of the vision itself, and to the interaction between it and its environment. Koogle says you learn through watching and guiding the evolution of your vision.

To vision is to learn.

Besides the sheer pleasure in it, this feeling of knowing is what guides and directs you in the work to make your vision real. The growing feeling of competence leads also to a growing feeling of confidence, as Koogle points out. It's a feeling not so much of being able to do anything you want, but more a feeling of being able to control yourself and your future in the midst of a dangerous world that's far more powerful than you are. The knowledge you gain with vision is not really about belief or confidence in your belief. As important as they are, conviction and confidence seem to be secondary to a growing, learning competence and to the integrity and growth of the idea of a vision. You need to develop a sense for it as an organic, living thing, perhaps as an infant you need to protect and nurture, but one with its own life force and logic as well. Koogle speaks of a sense of "organic uptake" to describe this life force and the ability to grow in an environment. Costello speaks of a vision as being on rails at a certain point, once it's in alignment with critical forces in the environment and has gained momentum. Although you may feel intimately connected to a vision, you also need a certain detachment to get a sense of its inherent logic and life force.

You need a certain detachment to sense its
inherent logic and life force.

The life force people sense in a vision seems to be connected to the quality of creativity they feel in working to realize one. They talk more like parents than architects. Perhaps this creative parenthood is also partly responsible for the deep feelings of honesty, authenticity, and integrity that an effective vision calls for. Some people refer to these as the values that must accompany a vision. To have the power to inspire and guide you a vision has to be in alignment with what you honestly want to do and who you are. Eastman speaks of this as being the largest part of vision and its real source. Rock says that intellectual honesty is one of the distinguishing characteristics of a leader with vision and perhaps the most important ingredient in a successful organization. Values seem to be similar to and inseparable from vision. Like vision, they are something intangible you want to create and constantly move toward more than something you've accomplished. In the real world these values aren't so easy to achieve or maintain. They

> A vision has to be in alignment with what you
> honestly want to do and who you are.

require constant effort, constant learning, and commitment—
all the things visions require.

■ VISIONS ARE USEFUL

If visions were only good for what they helped people feel
and know they might not be so important. But what they
make people feel and what they empower and embolden
them to do turns out to be extremely useful. As Koogle says,
CEOs in business have to be practical. If vision weren't practical, CEOs would not waste much time talking about them
or working on them. As intangible as visions may be, as hard
to bottle up and present to a business school class, they are
also an extraordinarily powerful way to build the kind of
company or organization that can create a new industry and
change the world.

As with other forms of knowledge, it's hard to quantify vision or its effects with standard business measuring tools—
the more so since visions by their nature tend to create
discontinuities, to change the rules of business. But the problem is more in our measuring than our knowing. Leaders
who work with vision understand its power and aren't much
bothered that someone hasn't found a way to count it. They
work on the same practical faith that led Moore and his colleagues to pursue the microprocessor despite the fact they
couldn't quantify a market for it, the same practical faith that
has Levinson letting science find Genentech's new products
despite the fact that by their nature scientific experiments are
highly uncertain. Rock says this uncertainty is always present
when people are trying to build new enterprises. Still, for
those who need reassurance, people who work with visions do
mention practical side effects. Among the more tangible benefits reported to me by CEOs are these:

➤ Improved overall productivity, perhaps from more inspired and self-motivated employees, perhaps from greater self-direction and less required oversight.

➤ Strategic focus, mostly because people have a much clearer idea of what they need to do and therefore also a much clearer idea of what is a waste of time and effort.

➤ Faster response to opportunities and threats, probably from acting on a lively sense of intuition as opposed to an overly analytical and bureaucratic study.

➤ Greater survivability, in part from commitment to a vision, in part from the sense that only new products and new ideas will help pull a company through hard times.

➤ Stronger ability to attract and keep the right employees, and the right customers, mostly through the self-selection that occurs when people see a vision and either find they resonate with it or don't.

➤ Ability to attract needed capital faster and at a better price, largely due to the energy of a team working to realize a vision and their ability to explain and show real passion for their work.

➤ Better sales focus on the right customers with the right offering, and better ability to get their attention.

Despite these and no doubt other indicators of the usefulness and value of vision to an organization, they still don't get to the heart of the matter. Vision is useful in the way knowledge is useful. It permits you to do something you otherwise could not do at all or could only do by accident. Vision, like other forms of knowledge, is the necessary ingredient that transforms labor from mere energy to work that accomplishes something. Knowledge is what enables labor to transform raw materials into a finished product. Vision is a form of knowledge that enables us to transform materials into brand *new* products. The usefulness of vision is its ability to create a different and better world. A cost benefit analysis wouldn't know what to look for or measure, often

---

Vision is a form of knowledge that enables us to transform
materials into brand *new* products.

---

even after that new world comes into existence. Recall
Moore's story: the personal computer was only one of 3,000
different applications Intel identified for the microprocessor it had built, and until the PC took off no one could have
predicted that it would be any more important than the
other 2,999.

■ VISION NEEDS CARE

As powerful as vision is, it is also subtle and easily destroyed
or lost. As the venture capitalists all say, visions depend on
good people. If the actions of people who champion a vision
aren't in harmony with the vision—or worse, if they contra-
dict or violate it—the people around them tend to become
cynical not only about the champion but about the vision.
The image and intuition that make up a vision can quickly
lose their positive power and become forces that depress, de-
moralize, and disperse the energies of people.

In real economic life in real companies vision has to
compete with other forces in energizing and guiding work.
Sometimes those forces are also positive, but very often they
aren't. Greed, fear, and the desire for personal power also
motivate people and guide their actions, despite what they
may say or how they may want to appear. Even individuals
like Clark with an apparent talent for vision may choose to
subordinate their vision to other desires and ways of guiding
themselves. The mere presence of vision doesn't mean it is
truly in power. People have to choose to put it in power and
keep it there. The values and skills of a company's founders
appear to be critical in establishing a pattern for
vision—for good or bad. If they take vision seriously it's easier for succeeding generations to take it seriously. If they
don't, it's very hard to create a legacy later on.

■ VISION IS A SKILL

Perhaps it goes back to old myths that tell stories of heroic men and women being given visions by the gods. Perhaps it's tied to the structural fact of life that in hierarchical businesses there are few positions for leaders and many for followers. And perhaps it has to do with the subtlety of intuition and imagination. Whatever the source, there seems to be a tendency to think that vision is an uncommon gift or a special faculty that certain rare individuals possess. Although as with most activities some people may be better at it than others, visioning is a skill that is available to virtually anyone—and one that even the most talented must practice and work at. Like other skills, vision can be learned and developed.

Visioning is a skill available to virtually anyone.

Experience in the part of the world you want to change is probably helpful, especially for the hard work of making a vision real. Sometimes, as Koogle says, less experience can help you do things that veterans would say is impossible. Still, the kind of vision that can lead a business seems to require some seasoning, like the experience Koogle acquired at Motorola, or even the relatively brief experience Clark had before he left teaching at Stanford.

Given some experience and the right environment, almost anyone can develop the skill to work with vision. It takes desire, focus, and effort—and many times the un-learning of conflicting skills and habits. In Silicon Valley, as in many places, businesses are often run more like a private army than a visionary movement. Many people learn how power—the power of money and the power attached to your position in the company—either rules outright or trumps other forces in day-to-day business. Besides creating environments that aren't conducive to vision—or to healthy human relationships—the raw rule of power also tends to create bad habits that conflict with or negate skill in vision. The intuition and imagination and ideas of vision can't be purchased with money or ordered into being. Costello says that in a knowledge business vision must be the bond that attracts people and keeps them together. He says you can't just tell knowledge workers what to do; you need to work to see that they're infected with and contribute to the same vision the company is working on.

■ DIALOGUE FEEDS VISION

Through all the phases of creating a vision and making it real there is one activity, one skill that seems be the most important engine to the whole process: dialogue. A dialogue between your intuition and imagination on the one hand and your intellect and reason on the other creates and articulates your vision. A dialogue between you and the people you want to share your vision with improves and enlarges your vision. A continuing dialogue among you and your employees and customers gives you the commitment and focus to execute the vision. In general, a dialogue between your idea and the world is what makes your vision real. From beginning to end, dialogue is the engine that moves a vision forward.

Dialogue is the engine that moves a vision forward.

From Plato some 2,000 years ago to the twentieth-century physicist David Bohm, dialogue has been presented and advocated as an effective way to develop shared and examined ideas in a group of people. Much of our conscious thinking is an interior dialogue among different voices in our heads. Some ancient forms of meditation focus on quieting this dialogue, others on observing or directing it toward certain desired ends. So the idea and the experience of dialogue aren't new. However, many of us don't seem to be very aware of it or good at it. If there's one skill that people who want to work with vision need to develop, it's skill in honest and probing dialogue.

Much of my own idea and method of dialogue has come from my reading of Plato and my experience using it in teaching and consulting. A dialogue is a conversation between people about something meaningful to them that they want to understand together. It isn't a debate in which the tools of rhetoric are used to persuade the public and to demolish an opponent. Debates have their places and uses, but as someone who has participated in debate I don't much like what I become as a debater and I don't think debates are very good at producing better or shared ideas. The parody of debates that proliferated in 1990s television programs like the McLaughlin Group demonstrate the problem: People simply tend to take ever more hardened positions and to look for ever more clever ways to pique an opponent. They create heat but very little light. Debate won't produce a vision, much less a shared one.

Nor is a dialogue simply an ordinary discussion. Devotees of David Bohm's approach to dialogue like Peter Senge and some of his colleagues have made a kind of etymological argument against discussions, suggesting that the word's Latin root-meaning of breaking something up still haunts discussions and makes them divisive. However that may be, most discussions I've experienced don't have the atmosphere, focus, rigor, structure, or intent that a vision dialogue calls for.

The kind of Socratic dialogue I have in mind is a rather one-sided conversation in that for an extended period of time a questioner and an answerer both keep to those roles. The idea is for the questioner to suspend his or her own beliefs, unlike in a debate, and focus on drawing out the ideas and thinking of the answerer, step by step so that everyone present understands every part of the argument or story as the dialogue goes along. The questioner needs to be respectful of the answers in this process, as long as they're sincere and honest, and in fact this respect tends to encourage the answerer to be so. The respect is not just for the person but for the ideas, and for the likelihood that the answerer, like most of us, really knows more than he or she realizes. Whether in an internal meditation or in a dialogue between people, this process can pull from people ideas they didn't know they had until they articulate them.

After ideas have been developed for a while the questioner and answerer may shift to a more critical mode and together start examining whether these ideas are logical and fit with experience. They may look for the unspoken assumptions behind the ideas, or for their implications. But in any case the focus is on testing and improving the ideas, not scoring points for or against the answerer. The intent is to find and build on good ideas, whoever may be their source and whatever direction they may take. If a given dialogue doesn't end up producing a sound or at least a better idea, it may still end up helping people discard bad ideas or recognize their ignorance about something they thought they knew.

Dialogues tend to be about big issues and issues that truly matter to people, otherwise they don't seem to work. They demand intellectual honesty and a sincere effort to get at and try to understand issues. And they tend to go on either to exhaustion or until people feel they understand the issue better. Modern worklife may not offer the leisure or unstructured time to let this happen in one continuous event, but if a dialogue can be continued over a period of time long enough to allow for reflection but short enough that the process stays alive, it can still be very effective.

An on-going dialogue helps to develop and maintain the intellectual honesty that Rock talks about, and it helps you figure out how to make the step-by-step progress he and Koogle advocate. It helps develop awareness, understanding, and confidence in what you're doing. And it can help you avoid the dark side of vision, such as an excessive preoccupation with one goal that doesn't allow room for pursuing a full or balanced set of human and social goals.

■ THE IMAGE OF VISION

Imagine a valley that curls and widens out like a cornucopia as its mouth opens wide toward an ocean bay. Hidden below the valley floor and below the low mountains that mark its sides are fault lines that periodically bring earthquakes to shake and threaten the cornucopia and remind all who live there that nature is more powerful than anything they can build. Between quakes many people forget that lesson, but master builders know it is the truth that underlies the valley and all that goes on there. The best ones seem to have their own sensors to detect the earth's rhythms. They have a sense of where and when the earth can move and they strive to work in harmony with it. And in fact this same sensitivity seems to reach into other forces in their environment, whether in the natural or the social worlds they work in.

There's a huge new bridge under construction, supervised by one of the master builders attuned to the natural and social forces in the valley. As you look at the bridge you notice several things that strike you as odd. The most immediate one is that this isn't like any bridge you've ever seen before. Most of it seems to be made of bright shimmering light rather than anything material, and instead of spanning over the bay as you'd expected, it arches up and out of the valley like a huge rainbow, reaching out just beyond the horizon, as if connecting today to tomorrow. As you focus in on where construction is going on, where the light seems to be hardening into something more substantial, you see a group of people who are using the arch of light to guide their work. The light sparkles around them and not only illuminates what they're doing but actually seems to electrify them with its energy. Moving among these working people you can see the master builder, distinguishable primarily by the brighter gleam in his eyes and the assurance with which he moves.

As you watch him work, something else strikes you as odd. Where you come from builders work from blueprints and plans and they consult them often. Sometimes the architect who figured out and drew up the plans comes on site to confer with the builders. But this master builder is obviously his own architect, and instead of working from a set plan he is experimenting and learning and deciding just what to do as he builds the bridge. He usually places himself at the very furthest edge of the bridge's construction, guiding and paying attention to the experiments he is conducting as he goes along to decide what engineering, materials, and construction techniques he'll use. From the way his body is relaxed you see he isn't afraid to fall: He isn't stiff and frozen like you imagine you would be, but fluid and self-correcting like a tightrope walker. Several apprentices follow him around, trying to absorb his methods and learning as best they can, although sometimes they seem almost overcome by vertigo when they get close to the edge.

Among the features you notice are four huge pillars that grow out of and support the bridge. Each looks distinctly different from the other, evidently the result of different experiments and different needs, but all of them look something like huge totem poles with figures either carved or built into them. The first one has what looks like a sandstone base which gives way to a round, shining, mirror-smooth section, which higher up becomes etched with tiny lines that resemble a huge city street map; at the very top it is crowned with a structure that looks rather like a human brain with a light shining from it up into the heavens. This pillar reminds you of the microprocessors and neural network computers that have come from the valley cornucopia.

The second pillar seems to rest on the soft mud of the bay. Whatever is on the inside, the outside of the pillar starts out looking like huge punch-cards at the bottom, which give way higher up to paper printouts with endless strings of ones and zeroes, which give way to huge computer monitors showing some kind of stylized, coded language, which in turn give way to what looks like a hologram of people talking and dancing together. This pillar reminds you of the computers and computer software that have come out of the valley.

The third pillar, further out on the bridge, seems to rest in the wetlands surrounding the bay, teeming with life. It is made of two vertical pieces that twist in a spiral as they rise, with many horizontal connections that altogether make it look like a spiral ladder. It's too far away to make out the details clearly, but it looks as if the pillar is under continuous construction, as if engineers are experimenting to find just what they want. They seem to be splicing different materials into various vertical segments of the pillar, then watching what happens, and then trying new combinations of materials. This pillar recalls the biotechnology that has come from the valley.

Finally, the fourth pillar seems to be growing as you watch it, a huge mass of interconnected wires, wriggling and moving like live snakes. The ends of the countless wires send out flashes of lightning that temporarily connect to countless unseen points both in the valley and over every point on the circular horizon. This pillar reminds you of the Internet that has so recently come from and energized the valley.

Seeing these pillars and watching the master builder, you begin to detect a pattern in the cycles of work. When the builder wants to add a new feature or structure he goes to the very edge between light and material where he wants to put it, sometimes alone, sometimes with a few assistants. As they talk among themselves, they usually get to a point where they suddenly become more animated. Light seems almost to spark from them. Then they talk and talk more, and as they do the light where the new feature will go seems to take on more definition and character, more detail. Then they bring more of the workers over to show them what they've got and this whole group talks some more and begins building various pieces of the feature. Although they keep talking from time to time, all the workers seem to know what they're doing without much guidance from the master builder. And each seems to know what the others are doing, too. Sometimes what they start to build falls down when they test it, or they tear it down and try something different. But with remarkable speed, the bridge grows. From a distance, it seems almost to extend itself as the bright light turns into richly detailed and solid material.

This bridge rising out of a cornucopia-shaped valley is the image that captures Silicon Valley's vision and its way of working with vision. As the venture capitalists say, it all depends on good people. It depends in particular on their ideas and their energy. Vision, starting as intuition and imagination, born out of an intention to do something beneficial, and in tune with the direction the world can take, is grounded in and grows out of intellectually honest dialogue. As the dialogue continues, intuition and imagination become more coherent, tested, and substantial ideas with their own integrity, their own living reality. Now the vision has an ability to guide people and inflame them with a deep desire to do whatever it takes to make the ideas real. Finally, the continuing honest dialogue, the learning, and the hard work—much hard work— bring the ideas all the way to reality. These aren't ideas that foresee the future. They're ideas that make it.

Index